MW01094329

The Substance of the Faith

The Substance of the Faith

Luther's Doctrinal Theology for Today

Dennis Bielfeldt, Mickey L. Mattox,
and Paul R. Hinlicky

Edited and Introduced by Paul R. Hinlicky

Fortress Press
Minneapolis

THE SUBSTANCE OF THE FAITH
Luther's Doctrinal Theology for Today

Scripture quotations are from the New Revised Standard Version Bible © 1989 Division of Christian Education of the National Council of the Churches of Christ in the United States of America. Used by permission. All rights reserved.

Excerpts from *Luther as Nominalist*, by Graham White (Helsinki: Lutheran-Agricola Society, 1994). Reprinted by permission of the publisher. "From Faith to the Text and Back Again" by M. Mattox, from *Pro Ecclesia*, 15/3, Summer 2006. Used by permission. "Sancta Sara, Mater Ecclesiae" by M. Mattox, from *Pro Ecclesia*, 10/3, Fall 2001. Used by permission. Excerpts from, "Studies in Medieval and Reformation Thought" in the chapter titled, "Sancta Domina-Luther's Catholic Exegesis of Sarah" in *Defender of the Most Holy Matriarchs* by Mickey Leland Mattox (Boston: Brill, 2003), pp. 128-38. Used by permission.

Cover design: Christa Rubsam
Book design: PerfecType, Nashville

Library of Congress Cataloging-in-Publication Data
Bielfeldt, Dennis D.
The substance of the faith : Luther's doctrinal theology for today /
Dennis Bielfeldt, Mickey L. Mattox, Paul R. Hinlicky ; edited and
introduced by Paul R. Hinlicky.
    p. cm.
Includes bibliographical references and index.
ISBN 978-0-8006-6253-0 (alk. paper)
1. Luther, Martin, 1483-1546. I. Mattox, Mickey Leland, 1956- II.
Hinlicky, Paul R. III. Title.
BR333.3.B54 2008
230'.41—dc22   2007044770

The paper used in this publication meets the minimum requirements of American National Standard for Information Sciences—Permanence of Paper for Printed Library Materials, ANSI Z329.48-1984.

Manufactured in the U.S.A.

12 11 10 09 08   1 2 3 4 5 6 7 8 9 10

CONTENTS

ABBREVIATIONS

ANF   Ante-Nicene Fathers

BC   *The Book of Concord: The Confessions of the Evangelical Lutheran Church*

BSLK   *Die Bekenntnisschriften der evangelisch-lutherischen Kirche*

CCSL   Corpus Christianorum: Series latina. Turnhout, 1953–.

CGAP   City of God against the Pagans

CHLMP *The Cambridge History of Later Medieval Philosophy*

CSEL   Corpus scriptorum ecclesiasticorum latinorum

ET   English translation

JDDJ   "Joint Declaration on the Doctrine of Justification"

LC   Large Catechism

LW   *Luther's Works*

NPNF1 Nicene and Post-Nicene Fathers, Series 1

NPNF2 Nicene and Post-Nicene Fathers, Series 2

PG   Patrologia graeca [= Patrologiae cursus completus: Series graeca]. Edited by J.-P. Migne. 162 vols. Paris, 1857–1886.

PL   Patrologia latina [= Patrologiae cursus completus: Series latina]. Edited by J.-P. Migne. 217 vols. Paris, 1844–1864.

SC   Small Catechism

ST   *Studia theologica*

TR   Tischreden (Table Talks)

WA   Martin Luther, Kritische Gesamtausgabe (= "Weimar" edition)

WADB Weimar Ausgabe–Deutsche Bibel

WATR Weimar Ausgabe–Tischreden

Introduction

Paul R. Hinlicky

This book is intended for those vitally concerned with theology in the tradition of Martin Luther: professional theologians but also pastors, seminarians, and the educated laity (not only of today's nominally Lutheran denominations). It is about a little-known turn in thought by the mature Luther to the academic theology of the "disputation" to analyze and better understand the ecumenical dogmas concerning the Trinity and the person of Christ. Luther so turns, to be sure, in light of the Reformer's renewal of Augustine's theology of grace, Paul's doctrine of faith, and years of labor in the Scriptures according to the new "grammatical method." We the authors believe that recent scholarship exploring this genre puts the evolution of early Lutheran theology in a more favorable light than it had seemed to the dominant post-Kantian and existentialist interpretations of the nineteenth and twentieth centuries. We think that renewal of this kind of argumentative procedure could speak to the needs of the church today for the delicate task of sustaining both faithfulness and openness in postmodernity, especially if certain dangers in Luther's approach (particularly his resort to apocalyptic invective to "demonize" theological opponents) can be isolated and rejected in the process. Our book, then, is meant as an appeal to renew classical doctrinal theology in the tradition of Luther.

Developed in the Christian West during the Middle Ages, the disputation was an academic exercise aimed at clarifying Christian truth. During the years that Luther served as dean of the Faculty of Theology at Wittenberg University (1533–1546), disputations were used for the examination of candidates for the doctor's degree. The disputation consisted in a series of theses or doctrinal propositions composed by Luther or other senior faculty members at Wittenberg University for the examination. The gathered faculty would debate these theses with the candidate, who had to defend them to the faculty's collective satisfaction. New scholarship is uncovering a wealth of material here that illuminates many traditional perplexities of Luther's theological legacy. Paradox and dualism give way to clarity and tension. Within the confessional boundaries that had emerged in the churches of the Reformation thereafter, the genre of the disputation permitted and indeed encouraged the exploration of difficult problems, deepening insight into the coherence of theological truth while demanding logical clarity and conceptual consequence.

The origins of this book may be traced to the Tenth International Congress for Luther Research. Held in Copenhagen in July 2002, its theme was "The Theology of the Old Luther," acknowledging this important dimension of the Reformer's thought that has been ignored, if not actively devalued. The results of the various contributions, all valuable in their own way, and the lively discussion of them in plenary sessions were inconclusive. For some, the old Luther was by far a wiser and sadder man who yet remained consistent in his thought with the widely admired insights of his early "evangelical breakthrough." For others, the old Luther was "a man in contradiction" who, by his intolerant tirades lashing out against all enemies, betrayed his best insights. Some, including we three scholars here, came away thinking that the Congress had not penetrated to the real questions and possibilities of the late Luther's theology. Admirers and critics alike of the old Luther held up Luther's "breakthrough," it seemed, as if it were some timeless standard by which to judge everything else. The approach is problematic enough in terms of assessing the evolution in the early Luther's work; it is even more so with respect to the ongoing developments in thought of this battle-weary veteran. As William R. Russell cogently argued in his 1999 exposition of the 1537 Schmalkald Articles: "It is possible, and in many ways preferable, to interpret Luther's basic theological program from its end point. . . . Here is where we can see precisely what Luther thought the Reformation was all about."[1]

---

[1]William R. Russell, *The Schmalkald Articles: Luther's Theological Testament* (Minneapolis: Fortress Press, 1999), 115.

In spite of nuanced and sometimes quite fruitful applications of the "evangelical breakthrough" approach to understanding Luther—for example, the subtle and engaging work of Oswald Bayer[2]—we find that the approach itself tends to be ahistorical and theologically a blind alley. It denies to Luther's theology the right to be a work in progress, to develop and even to make a midcourse correction in the light of experience. It denies us the right to ask theological questions about manifestly dubious writings not only of the old Luther but also of the young Luther (for instance, the public judgment, following his excommunication, that the pope is the Antichrist). Importantly, it blinds us to the interesting initiative the elder dean Martin Luther took with the reintroduction at Wittenberg of the medieval "disputation," and thus his recourse to a theological procedure that—not to put too fine a point on it—represents a return in theology to scholastic method and classical dogmatic content. Luther returned to scholastic analysis of dogma, as mentioned above, after years of intense research in the Scriptures with the new "grammatical" method. This combination made for sophisticated and innovative theological work, though it remains little known and poorly understood. This book is about making that theology of the old Luther better known and useful for our theological work today. To facilitate the reader's understanding and to make Luther's work in this genre better known, we have added an appendix containing newly translated and annotated disputations by Luther that were previously unavailable in English.

A certain, still influential understanding of the Reformation slogan *sola scriptura*, however, threatens to close off this path from the outset. As we shall see in the following chapters, Luther holds Scripture and ecumenical dogma together to form a hermeneutical whole—pace the influential thesis of Gerhard Ebeling reducing

---

[2]Bayer impressively argued that the *Sitz im Leben* of the "evangelical breakthrough" was the confessional, where nothing less than assured faith could still the doubting conscience. This approach had the merit of locating the "breakthrough" in a public practice of the church rather than in the private depths of Luther's anxiety-ridden soul. This allowed Bayer to go on and develop theology in the tradition of Luther for today. Of course, his approach inevitably retains the systematic bias in favor of the "young Luther." It is crime against scholarship that Bayer's weighty Luther studies are still not translated into English. Mark C. Mattes and Jeffery Silcock, I understand, are translating Bayer's 1994 volume in the *Handbuch Systematicscher Theologie* for publication under the working title *Theology the Lutheran Way*.

theology in Luther's tradition to the *epaphax* of a historical event and its hermeneutical appropriation for contemporary proclamation.[3]

Mickey Mattox's opening chapter sorts out some of the questions at stake here, showing how the mature Luther moves confidently enough from exegetical labors to doctrinal theology and back again in a context that is formed by the faith of the church through the ages and across cultures. According to Mattox, Luther was an accomplished teacher of the Bible who worked hard in the classroom to model exegesis that was ever vigilant for the interplay of law and gospel, particularly in the narratives of the Old Testament "saints." At the same time, Luther also taught his students to apply the church's "rule of faith" to the interpretation of texts. The "substance" of Holy Scripture, that is, the faith as a whole that it promotes, provides the key to unlock the authentic meaning of its words. The words serve the content, and not vice versa. From a modern perspective, we might be tempted to label this a hermeneutical "strategy." But the self-conscious artifice (*eisegesis*) suggested by that term betrays it immediately as foreign to Luther's thought. As the study of his Large Catechism instantly reveals, Luther believed that Scripture as a whole teaches faith in the triune God. Employing faith in the triune God as a light to illumine the biblical text in turn does not impose on the text something foreign to it but instead reads the text in view of what it truly is. In addition, Mattox will show, Luther used his classroom work in biblical exposition to school his students in the rudiments of catholic trinitarianism, easily moving from a discussion of the text to the explanation of classical trinitarian formulas. In short, by means of biblical exposition, Luther taught his students much of what he had learned in his own training in scholastic theology.

The return of the "old Luther" to the logical tools of scholasticism to parse classical dogmatic content began no later than the mid-career eucharistic controversies of the 1520s. Luther distinguished then between the faith that believes—his celebrated *fiducia*, justifying faith from the heart—and the faith that is believed. Henceforth he gave ever-increasing attention to the latter.

---

[3]See Gerhard Ebeling's programmatic, post–World War II essay "The Significance of the Critical Historical Method," in *Word and Faith*, trans. J. W. Leitch (Philadelphia: Fortress Press, 1960), 17–61. Our effort may be read as the endeavor to overturn this program for theology in the tradition of Luther point by point.

First, what one should believe, that is, the *objectum fidei*, that is, the work or thing in which one believes or to which one is to adhere. Secondly, the faith itself, or the use which one should properly make of that in which he believes. The first lives outside the heart and is presented to our eyes externally, namely, the sacrament itself, concerning which we believe that Christ's body and blood are truly present in the bread and wine. The second is internal, within the heart, and cannot be externalized. It consists in the attitude which the heart should have toward the external sacrament. . . . Up to now I have not preached very much about the first part, but have treated only the second, which is also the best part. But because the first part is now being assailed by man, and the preachers, even those who are considered the best, are splitting up into factions over the matter . . . the times demand that I say something on this subject also.[4]

Luther here expressly permits himself to develop theologically. What is at stake in this professed development?

In her important study published a few years before the Tenth Congress, Christine Helmer pointed out that at least since the time of Ritschl, German scholarship has sought *das Novum* in Luther, therewith construing the Old as "the 'unchanging and monolithic' block of 'metaphysical theology,'" that us "the specifically medieval shape of theology from which Luther, in the eyes of his interpreters, is distanced."[5] In other words, everything in the above citation designated as *objectum fidei* would be regarded as old stuff, from which Luther's insights for today need to be liberated. We shall see, however, that this old stuff is exactly what the mature Luther will call the "new language" of the Spirit. On the basis of her extended discussion of modern Luther research, Helmer therefore drew a highly salient conclusion against this research bias: "Luther's anti-speculative bent against a specific determination of the hidden God cannot be confused with the thematization of the immanent Trinity as a theological task of reason in obedience to faith. In fact, Luther preached regularly on the immanent Trinity,

---

[4]See LW 36:335; WA 19:482.25–483.19.

[5]Christine Helmer, *The Trinity and Martin Luther: A Study on the Relationship Between Genre, Language and the Trinity in Luther's Works (1523–1546)* (Mainz: Verlag Philipp von Zabern, 1999), 8. "The Reformation turn towards a *Glaubenslehre*, prompted by Luther's discovery of faith as trust in God's justifying activity, represented a break with the 'Summe tradirter Lehren' or the 'Lehre der Concilien' or the 'unfehlbare[n] Lehre' that von Harnack associated with the spirit of Greek speculation" (9).

and his disputations document lively exchanges concerning this locus in great detail."[6]

Helmer's study is among the most stimulating English-language monographs to have appeared on Luther in the last quarter century. She argues the controversial but crucial thesis that the important experience of the hiddenness of God for Luther is a moment that occurs *within*, and not *over against*, the scriptural narrative of trinitarian advent—indeed, it occurs at its center, in the cross of the Son. This confrontation of God with God means, in turn, that the classic theological problems of trinitarianism cannot but emerge for Luther, just as the late disputations demonstrate. One cannot think to get Luther right and have in mind a unitarian God the Father (or, today, Mother), with Jesus as the perfectly God-conscious, or perfectly God-forsaken, human model of existential faith (and the Holy Spirit as Fifth Wheel or, perhaps, Independent Operator).

With the criticism of Helmer and others[7] of the dominant paradigm of Luther scholarship percolating through the ranks in the years since the Tenth Congress, the immediate origin of this volume can be found at the North American Luther Forum, held at Luther Seminary, St. Paul, in April 2006. There I presented some of my work from the 2002 Congress on Luther's 1540 *Disputatio de divinitate et humanitate Christi* to a working group that included Dennis Bielfeldt and Mickey Mattox.[8] Lively discussion led to the discovery that we shared a contemporary theological interest in the late Luther—given certain critical qualifications, especially in regard to Luther's anti-Judaism and demonological invective. Present at the conference, Augsburg Fortress chief executive officer Beth Lewis asked me about a book coming from the proceedings, which led in turn to the proposal for this project of three linked studies by the aforementioned scholars with me serving also as editor.

Linked as is our work, careful readers may still detect subtle differences in approach and subsequently in interpretation among us.

---

[6]Ibid., 22–23.

[7]Many (e.g., Graham White, Bruce Marshall, and Risto Saarinen) are discussed in the chapters that follow. Worthy of note is also the scathing work of James M. Stayer, *Martin Luther, German Saviour: German Evangelical Theological Factions and the Interpretation of Luther, 1917–1933* (Montreal: McGill-Queen's University Press, 2000).

[8]Now published in *Creator est creatura: Luthers Christologie als Lehre von der Idiomenkommunikation*, ed. O. Bayer and Benjamin Gleede (Berlin: Walter de Gruyter, 2007), 139–85.

We have in fact worked hard to discipline ourselves to write in ways that build on one another's contributions. We have learned during our collaboration that what differences exist between us may as often be a function of the disciplinary tradition or philosophical apparatus with which we work. But theology of the kind we recommend here may employ a variety of philosophical resources[9] and needs a number of disciplinary foci, so long as it remains clear that theology is that peculiar function of the church that also stands at some prophetic and apostolic distance from the church, not to mention the society. A lonely place! Theology is not the consciousness of the contemporary religious community, let alone the *Volk,* but is addressed to the church, calling it to faithfulness by the word of God, "testing the spirits to see whether they are of God." On this manifestly "Lutheran" idea of a teaching theology's homelessness in the world, we wholeheartedly concur. Our aim is that this volume coherently recommends the theology of the old Luther as something contemporaneous and helpful for an exhausted Euro-American Christianity that has lost its way.

That is not our opinion alone. In that influential post–World War II essay that set another direction for theology in Luther's tradition than the one we are recommending, Ebeling nonetheless acknowledged something similar. He sketched the sad picture of "modern Protestantism" in contrast to Roman Catholicism: "countless splits in all directions, progressive dissolution not only of its unity but also of its dogmatic substance, such infection by modern thought as apparently leads to internal sepsis, and where the attempt is made to defend or revitalize the old, the unseasonable, the distinctive and indispensable, there we find a defensive attitude towards the outside opponent that savours of anxiety, grimness or despair."[10] In our present effort at retrieval, we certainly hope to have avoided grim anxiety and hopelessness! This the reader of course must judge.

Ebeling, in any case, was willing to acknowledge as a fact Protestant dissolution and argue nevertheless that there is no alternative to playing

---

[9]In Bruce Marshall's words: "If analytic philosophy (or any other discipline) makes claims which are incompatible with central Christian beliefs, then so much the worse for analytic philosophy." Bruce D. Marshall, *Trinity and Truth* (Cambridge: Cambridge University Press, 2000), 13. Marshall argues both that rival philosophies could be compatible with Christian belief and that beliefs incompatible with Christian belief might have better argumentative support. His own work's engagement with analytic philosophy "aims not to provide a philosophical basis for Christian beliefs."

[10]Ebeling, "Significance of the Critical Historical Method," 50.

out the hand, since the only alternative would be return to Mother Church, sacramentalism, metaphysics, and sundry other forms of flight from historical existence. Today, however, the picture Ebeling sketched holds equally across the historic confessional divide. As the unmitigated antithesis Ebeling posited between Protestantism and Catholicism holds less and less today, his attempt to save the theology of the nineteenth century from "neoorthodoxy" by means of an anti-Catholic smear finds increasingly less traction. Historically, Ebeling's equally forthright acknowledgment of the tendentiousness of his "stylized" portrait of Luther's theology—the "situation in detail is essentially more complicated[; t]he relation to Catholicism is not exhausted by the plain, antithetical statements"[11]—provides a solid clue where to look today for a new orientation, now that Ebeling's hand has played itself out.

The reader should expect from the following a programmatic statement, a summons to a task, the vision for a research project welcoming readers aboard—far, then, from a worked-out system but, at best, a new beginning. In the nature of the case, many arguments are indicated but left hanging because our purpose is to identify problems and issues in calling theology in the tradition of Luther to a new task in a new direction that differs from what has predominated since midcentury. Certainly we the authors are not of one mind on any number of "hot button" issues before the church and theology today. But we are united in thinking that the late Luther's logically rigorous turn in method to trinitarianism is something significant for the confused and troubled Christianity of today's Euro-American world. Consequently, there *is* a definite plan to what we present.

As already mentioned, Mattox argues the important thesis in the opening chapter that for Luther we miss the theological meaning of the words of Scripture, however well understood historically and critically, if we do not use the Spirit's key, the content, the matter (which is Christ), to unlock them. Similarly, Bielfeldt argues in chapter 2 that Luther was "catholic" in his trinitarian thought in being a *semantic realist* with respect to the trinitarian assertions. Simply put, Luther believes that theological statements possess *truth-conditions*. That means that the way that God *is* determines the truth or falsity of statements about God. However, Luther also recognizes that the ordinary language of philosophy—a language that is completely legitimate for

---

[11]Ibid., 37.

the earthly realm—must signify in a new way when dealing with the incomprehensible things of the heavenly realm. Bielfeldt suggests that the "new meaning" that arises in the "new language" (*nova lingua*) of theology makes use of older semantic elements from the tradition of Augustine no longer present in the *via moderna* tradition. This new language of theology is used by Luther to state the incomprehensible three-in-one constitution of the Trinity, for example, that the one simple divine essence nonetheless generates. The incomprehensibility of the Trinity means, for Luther, that the processional and relational accounts of divine personhood are equally useful for stating trinitarian truths. In a tradition that privileged the relational account, this means that Luther's own thinking looks more processional. Finally, Bielfeldt suggests that the use by Luther of both accounts connects quite nicely with the theological equivalency of Eastern and Western views on the Trinity generally. That would be no small contribution to contemporary, ecumenical trinitarian theology.

Building on these more historically oriented probes into the old Luther's theology, I attempt in chapter 3 a contemporary proposal about the nature of theology as *critical dogmatics* stemming from Luther's intriguing discussions of theology as "new language"—a notion in Luther's thought that appears already with the eucharistic controversies.[12] I argue that theology in the tradition of Luther ought to take up his thought of the new language of the Spirit, understood in classically trinitarian rather than idealist or existentialist fashion. I require, however, that this retrieval be a critical one, which identifies and refuses Luther's resort to demonizing invective of theological opponents in favor of the hermeneutics of charity and the ecumenical ideal of achieving disagreement. At the same time, I find it necessary not to abandon the figure of the devil but, rather, to refigure it by resort to the gospel narrative as the hermeneutical basis for dogmatic theology today. The unholy spirit is exposed as the one who denies that Christ has come in the flesh, who attacks the new covenant made in His person by His work—not the one who fails to understand this or understands it poorly. It is the willful separation of what God has joined together, and this only, that contradicts the God Who wills and works in Christ the reconciliation of the world (also, then, of the heterodox and believers of other perspectives).

---

[12]LW 37:252ff.

Finally, a word about our policy on inclusive language. In conformity with the theology we recommend in this book, we have adopted the *Lutheran Forum guidelines* as follows:

> Pronouns create confusion and mistakes in English-language letters nowadays, so we have to set an editorial policy about their use. If we are referring to hypothetical individuals, we find the most felicitous solution to be alternation between "he" and "she," since "s/he" is cumbersome and "one" can be a bit too formal and "they" usually is followed by grammatical errors. (And when we talk about multiple members of the human race, we use terms like "humanity" and "people" rather than "men," since "men" sounds like "many males" rather than "many persons.") When we speak of God and find it necessary to employ a pronoun, we use "He" (also "Him" and "His") with the capital *H*. This is for two reasons. First, because Scripture authorizes the use of the masculine pronoun while clarifying that God is neither male nor masculine. Secondly, because the lower-case "he" used in the same casual fashion as for human males can in fact be misleading about the non-maleness and non-masculinity of God. The person of Jesus Christ may be referred to with a lower-case "he," however, since he was truly human at the same time He was truly God. For consistency's sake, relative and second-person pronouns used of God will be capitalized as well (e.g., "You" and "Who"). We generally do not like endless repetition of the word "God," as in "God Godself saved God's people," as it implies a kind of robotic impersonality alongside the syntactical awkwardness. . . . "She" as a referent to God has no canonical basis, and to our minds only encourages the erroneous notion that God is sexual or perhaps hermaphroditic, which neither mitigates the problem of the "He" nor finds scriptural warrant.[13]

We recognize that this has not been the standard policy on inclusive language at Fortress Press and thus appreciate the respect shown for the authors' consciences in accepting this alternative approach to inclusive language. We alone are responsible for it.

---

[13] "Editorial and Confessional Standards," *Lutheran Forum* Web site, available at http://www.lutheranforum.org/folder.2007-08-22.9250967752/editorial-and-confessional-standards (accessed October 9, 2007).

CHAPTER ONE

Luther's Interpretation of Scripture
Biblical Understanding in Trinitarian Shape

Mickey L. Mattox

Saint Jerome reports that he was moved to translate the Bible anew from Hebrew into Latin by the sneering reproach of the enemies of Christ, the Jews, to the effect that Christians did not have the correct Bible in the version then in use throughout Christendom. . . . And in our day, too, so many are busying themselves with translating that history may repeat itself and there may be so many Bibles in the course of time and so many wiseacres who claim a mastery of the Hebrew tongue that there will be no end to it. . . . If I were offered free choice either to have St. Augustine's and the dear fathers', that is, the apostles', understanding of Scripture, together with the handicap that St. Augustine occasionally lacks the correct Hebrew letters and words—as the Jews sneeringly accuse him, or to have the Jews' correct letters and

*words—which they, in fact, do not have everywhere—but
minus St. Augustine's and the fathers' understanding, that is,
with the Jews' interpretation, it can be easily imagined which
of the two I would choose. . . . In brief, if we do not apply
all diligence to interpret the Hebrew Bible, wherever that is
feasible, in the direction of the New Testament, in opposition to the interpretation of the rabbis, it would be better to
keep the old translation (which, after all, retains, thanks to
the New Testament, most of the good elements) than to have
so many translations just because a few passages presumably
have a different reading or are still not understood.*

OLD MAN MARTIN LUTHER,
"TREATISE ON THE LAST WORDS OF DAVID," 1543[1]

Knowledge of the triune God, on Martin Luther's account, is
what Holy Scripture gives. At the same time, knowledge of the triune God is the means by which alone one reads and understands the
Scriptures aright. To put the matter just a bit differently: Scripture
teaches faith in the triune God, and faith in the triune God, itself a
gift of the Spirit of God given in the sacrament of baptism, is the
essential prerequisite for understanding what Scripture teaches. The
Spirit of God, Who unites believers to Christ and thus opens the way
to the fatherly heart of God, has inspired the text and its writer; just
so, and still today, the same Spirit illumines the text to the faithful
reader.

Luther's understanding of the process of discerning divinely
intended meaning in the biblical text sounds circular, and it is. To
be sure, the hard work involved in study and reflection on the biblical text presumes the use of human rationality. Without hesitation
or excuse, Luther dedicates the full powers of all his divinely given
faculties to that work. At the same time, however, he is not particularly troubled by the recognition that human reason runs within a
course set and defined for it by God. God is behind us and before
us in Luther's understanding, and if we know ourselves as creatures
of God's making and God Himself as the Creator Who has brought
us forth from nothing, then it stands, yes, to reason that God is
both the beginning and the end of the process of authentic Christian

[1]LW 15:266–70; WA 54:29–31.

scriptural interpretation. The circle in which the reader of the Bible finds herself, in other words, is not a philosophically vicious one in which human reason pointlessly chases its own tail, but a relational one within which the baptized Christian is known by God and thus knows God. God is ever the initiator in Luther's theology, so the Christian search for the truth about God given in Scripture begins with the very knowledge of God with which it should end, and there is little evidence to suggest that Luther was uncomfortable with that fact. Hard as ever the exegete can and must work, authentic spiritual understanding remains a gift of God from beginning to end.[2] As the only true God is a trinity of Persons in one undivided divine substance, moreover, the gift of scriptural understanding bears a distinctive trinitarian shape.

If the above summarizes accurately the existential situation of the Christian reader as Luther understood it, then one would expect to see it reflected in his exegetical practice. One would expect Luther to put his formidable interpretive energies into a distinctive kind of exegesis, one that reflects both the theological circularity of the Christian's relationship with God and the gift character of authentic knowledge of God. This chapter is dedicated to showing that this is indeed the case. To achieve that goal, several examples of Luther's exposition will be put on display below, all of them from the Old Testament. As professor of Bible (*Doctor in Biblia*), Luther lectured almost exclusively on the Old Testament after 1522. The Hebrew Scriptures provided challenges aplenty for the Christian reader, as they had since the time of the early church. As shall be shown in this chapter, Luther both followed the trinitarian readings of the Old Testament that had been developed by patristic and medieval writers, and pioneered new ways of reading texts he thought had been overlooked by the church fathers. In other words, he put trinitarian faith to work in concert with his knowledge of the Hebrew language in order to buttress and extend the Christian reading of the text.

---

[2]Following some recent work on Luther's understanding of ethics, it seems that exegesis is probably a special case of the so-called "opus theologicum," that is, a *theologically* good work that has God the Holy Spirit as both its instrumental and its final cause. Luther admits that some good works are indeed good before God, but he refuses to grant that they are produced, even instrumentally, by human agency. On this topic, see Risto Saarinen, "Ethics in Luther's Theology," in *Moral Philosophy on the Threshold of Modernity* (Dordrecht, Germany: Springer, 2005); Reijo Työrinoja, "Opus Theologicum: Luther and Medieval Theories of Action," *Neue Zeitschrift für Systematische Theologie und Religionsphilosopie* 44 (2002): 119–53.

The point of reviewing these episodes in Luther's Old Testament interpretation is not merely to say something historically true about Martin Luther, although accurate historical description is certainly a laudable goal. Instead, the point is to open up space for readers to meet Luther as a biblical expositor, to listen in on his exegetical work with ears attuned to its difference, its historical distance and otherness from what one might expect, say, in a modern course on scriptural exegesis. This difference and distance, the otherness we find in Luther's reading of Scripture, has the potential to help readers better understand the suppositions on which they rely in their own reading of the text and, insofar as it does so, to help make possible faithful postcritical readings of Scripture. For all who value the heritage of Martin Luther, it can also help make clear what it would mean to read the Scriptures in his tradition and after his example. As will be shown below, the doctrine of the Trinity—or, better, living faith in the God Who is Father, Son, and Holy Spirit—stands at the very heart of this tradition and example.

1. Luther as an Interpreter of the Bible
Luther's Biblicism: Christocentric and Trinitarian

Luther's work on the Bible has always, and rightly, attracted attention. Scriptural interpretation was at the center of the indulgences controversy that broke out in 1517 and led eventually to the Reformation. More important, Scripture provided the authority to which Luther appealed against the authority of the pope and the Roman curia, and it soon became the basis for Protestant theology, a position that was eventually codified in the so-called *Schriftprinzip* (Scripture principle) under the formula of *sola Scriptura* (Scripture alone).[3] Luther devoted himself tirelessly to the exposition and, a bit later, to the translation of the Bible, and his efforts were recorded and published with great enthusiasm by a cadre of admiring students. The Lutheran theological tradition, however, was established not on the basis of Luther's exegetical writings but on that of Scripture and the Lutheran Confessions (including several of Luther's own works). To be sure, Luther's non-Confessional writings, including his sermons and biblical commentaries, were received with respect, but the extent

---

[3]For a brief review, see Walter Sparn, "Schriftprinzip," in *Lexikon für Theologie und Kirche*, ed. Walter Kasper, 3rd ed., vol. 9 (Freiburg, Germany: Herder & Herder, 1993–2000); 266–268.ß.

to which even the earliest generations of Lutheran biblical exegetes were indebted to the actual exegesis of Martin Luther is unclear.[4] Indeed, one could argue plausibly that Luther's actual work as an exegete has had more influence in the last one hundred years than at any other time in the past, including Luther's own lifetime. For one thing, thanks to the production of the modern, critical "Weimar edition" of his work, scholars now have a definitive source for examining Luther's exegesis. Even more important, researchers of every conceivable theological stripe and from many different ecclesial traditions have found Luther an engaging and stimulating conversation partner. Theological arguments and crises of various sorts—the Luther Renaissance, debates over scriptural authority and inerrancy, the interests of neoorthodox theology, ecumenical theology, canon criticism, and, more recently, the "new perspective" on Paul, just to name a few—have driven researchers back repeatedly to Luther to see what help he can provide for the task of interpretation today. The results of these efforts have been impressive, and they have given us the standard vocabulary by which Luther's greatness as an exegete is typically expressed and understood.

Scholars have long recognized that Christ stands at the center of Luther's reading of the Bible, and not a few works have explored the shape and content of Luther's christocentric biblicism. It is widely agreed that Luther is an important figure in a centuries-long movement that began in the Middle Ages, one that increasingly emphasized the primacy of the literal sense of Scripture rather than the allegorical one. The Scriptures in their literal sense are, in Luther's memorable phrase, the "swaddling clothes" in which the Christ has been laid. This same Christ himself provides the hermeneutical key to Scripture as a whole, a conviction Luther himself memorably epitomized in the formula "whatever promotes Christ" (*was Christum treibet*).[5] Scripture is central, moreover, to Luther's understanding

[4]For an examination of Luther's influence on sixteenth-century Lutheran exegesis of Genesis, see Mickey L. Mattox, *"Defender of the Most Holy Matriarchs": Martin Luther's Interpretation of the Women of Genesis in the Enarrationes in Genesin, 1535–1545* (Leiden: Brill, 2003), ch. 6. Cf. Robert Kolb, "Sixteenth-Century Lutheran Commentary on Genesis and the Genesis Commentary of Martin Luther," in *Théorie et pratique de l'exégèse*, ed. Irena Backus (Genève: Librairie Droz, 1990), 243–58. Mattox argues that Luther influences Lutheran expositors but that they back away from his more daring exegetical claims. Kolb finds relatively little influence.
[5]Vorrhede auff die Episteln Sanct Jacobi unnd Judas, 1522. WADB 7.384. Cf. LW 35:396.

of what we today might call "spirituality"; the Christian life finds its dynamic center in a cyclical process of prayer (*oratio*), of meditation on the "sacred page" of Holy Scripture (*meditatio*), and of the temptation that drives one back to prayer (*tentatio*) and thus back to Scripture, back to temptation, and so on. The reader must ever distinguish, moreover, between the law, the word of God that meets the sinner as insuperable demand, and the gospel, the word of God that heralds the unmerited gift of salvation given solely on account of Christ.[6] Ideas like these have long been part of the everyday conversation about the theology of Martin Luther, and they have shaped and informed exegesis wherever Luther's work and heritage are valued, particularly within the confines of the churches that eventually identified themselves as Lutheran.

Of course, Luther's exegetical christocentrism has always been related to the doctrine of justification. Indeed, modern scholars have not infrequently taken justification as the first truth in Luther's system, or at least as the first truth in systems of theology that would be faithful to Luther. Justification is, as a broad consensus in Luther research would have it, the "article by which the church stands or falls" (*articulus stantis et cadentis ecclesiae*).[7] Not a few have taken the notion that justification is the first truth in Luther's theology in a foundational sense, that is, as if the doctrine of justification itself is the first in a coherent system of truths, the foundation on which the system of theology is established. Chapters 2 and 3 will help show what is right and helpful as well as what is not right and sometimes, indeed, quite unhelpful about this way of understanding Luther. Suffice it for the moment to say that it sadly underestimates the centrality of the trinitarian faith in Luther's theology as a whole.

One sees that centrality clearly, for example, in the bold statement

---

[6]For Luther and the Bible, see Jaroslav Pelikan, *Luther the Expositor: Introduction to the Reformer's Exegetical Writings* (St. Louis: Concordia, 1959); David C. Steinmetz, *Luther in Context*, 2nd ed. (Grand Rapids: Baker Academic, 2002); A. Skevington Wood, *Captive to the Word: Martin Luther, Doctor of Sacred Scripture* (Devon, U.K.: Paternoster, 1969); Scott H. Hendrix, "Luther against the Background of the History of Biblical Interpretation," *Interpretation* 37 (1983): 229–39. For an overview of Luther's theological approach to Scripture, one may consult Mickey L. Mattox, "Martin Luther," in *Christian Theologies of Scripture: A Comparative Introduction*, ed. Justin S. Holcomb (New York: New York University Press, 2006), 94–113.

[7]For the origins of this phrase in developing Protestant theology, see Theodor Mahlmann, "Zur Geschichte der Formel 'Articulus Stantis Et Cadentis Ecclesiae,'" *Lutherische Theologie und Kirche* 17, no. 4 (1993): 187–94.

of faith with which Luther concluded his "Confession Concerning Christ's Supper" (1528), written near the end of his long contention for the real presence of Christ in the sacrament of the Lord's Supper against the Swiss Reformers Ulrich Zwingli and Johannes Oecolampad. Following the pattern of the catholic creeds, Luther gave solemn witness to a personal faith that was emphatically trinitarian.[8] This is not at all to say that Luther offered an abstruse confession of his faith, as if "trinitarian" referred to, say, a peculiarly complex mathematical formula about oneness and threeness. To the contrary, he gave an imminently practical account of the faith in which he was prepared to live and die, which, as he understood it, was the church's own faith, centered in the ecclesial experience of God's self-giving through Word and Sacrament. The self-communication of God as Father, Son, and Spirit—the trinitarian self-giving—stands at the very center of the Christian faith, and thus also of Luther's faith:

> These are the three persons and one God, who has given himself to us all wholly and completely, with all that he is and has. The Father gives himself to us, with heaven and earth and all the creatures, in order that they may serve us and benefit us. But this gift has become obscured and useless through Adam's fall. Therefore the Son himself subsequently gave himself and bestowed all his works, sufferings, wisdom, and righteousness, and reconciled us to the Father, in order that restored to life and righteousness, we might also know and have the Father and his gifts. But because this grace would benefit no one if it remained so profoundly hidden and could not come to us, the Holy Spirit comes and gives himself to us also, wholly and completely. He teaches us to understand this deed of Christ which has been manifested to us, helps us receive and preserve it, use it to our advantage and impart it to others, increase and extend it. He does this both inwardly and outwardly—inwardly by means of faith and other spiritual gifts, outwardly through the gospel, baptism, and the sacrament of the altar, through which as through three means or methods he comes to us and inculcates the sufferings of Christ for the benefit of our salvation.[9]

---

[8] The same could well be said of the Schmalkald Articles, written by Luther in 1536. William R. Russell points out the "testamentary" character of this document, that is, its function as a statement of the faith in which Luther was prepared to die. Russell also draws attention to Luther's staunch assertion of trinitarian and christological orthodoxy, in explicit agreement with the Church of Rome. See Russell, *Luther's Theological Testament: The Schmalkald Articles* (Minneapolis: Fortress Press, 1995).
[9] LW 37:366.

This tripersonal God "who has given himself to us all wholly and completely" is the God to whom Luther clings in living faith. Any account of Luther's faith that marginalizes the trinitarian faith even slightly both misunderstands what faith meant to Luther and at the same time wrongly distances Luther from the Western Catholic tradition. Luther's narrative understanding of the trinitarian God, received in baptism and embodied in the catholic creeds, functions as the "rule of faith" (*regula fidei*) that informs his reading of Scripture. The God Who saves is the Holy Trinity confessed in the Apostles' Creed, and ipso facto the narratives of divine salvation and self-revelation found in Holy Scripture are witnesses to the work and to the reality of the triune God.

The trinitarian understanding of God that informs Luther's exegetical practice can be made even clearer by a brief look at his Large Catechism, particularly his exposition of the Apostles' Creed.[10] The creed, Luther writes, "teaches us *to know God* wholly and completely."[11] Indeed, the creedal identification of the triune God is *in toto* gospel, a word of grace that tells us who God is and what God has done for us. As the first article of the creed indicates, by faith the Christian sees the creation for what it is, that is, as a display of the paternal benevolence of God the Father. By faith the Christian recognizes that all she receives with respect to earthly blessings— "good government, peace, and security"—proceeds from the love of God. By faith, in short, the believer knows God as Creator, which means, conversely, to know the self as creature, as one whose limits have been determined by God.[12] The recognition that God alone is the Creator also brings to an end every form of autonomous human self-assertion over against God. For Luther, as Althaus reminds us, God creates out of nothing and "even out of its opposite."[13] God as God has the power not only to call the creation into being out

---

[10]I cite the original German of the LC from *Die Bekenntnisschriften der evangelisch-lutherischen Kirche*, 6th ed. (Göttingen: Vandenhoeck & Ruprecht, 1967) (hereafter abbreviated BSLK). ET in *The Book of Concord: The Confessions of the Evangelical Lutheran Church*, ed. Robert Kolb and Timothy J. Wengert (Minneapolis: Fortress Press, 2000) (hereafter abbreviated BC).

[11]BSLK, 646: ". . . ihn ganz und gar erkennen lehret." Cf. BC, 431. Emphasis mine.

[12]BSLK, 648; BC, 433: "Thus we learn from this article that none of us has life— or anything else that has been mentioned here or can be mentioned—from ourselves, nor can we by ourselves preserve any of them, however small and unimportant."

[13]Paul Althaus, *The Theology of Martin Luther* (Philadelphia: Fortress Press, 1966), 34.

of nothing but also to create sons of God out of the nothing, so to speak, of sinful humanity. God creates humankind *ex nihilo*, in other words, no less in redemption than in creation. Luther's insistence that in both of these arenas we let the Creator God *be* God stands as the negation of every form of idolatry, including the idolatry of a righteousness based on human works. To know God as Father is to know "pure love and goodness," that is, the unmerited grace by which He makes provision for every aspect of human life, in this life and in the life to come. In the rich goodness of the created order, moreover, the Christian perceives God's "fatherly heart [*väterlich Herz*] and his boundless love toward us."[14] Thus, "our hearts will be warmed and kindled with gratitude to God and a desire to use all these blessings to his glory and praise. . . . For here we see how the Father has given himself to us."[15]

As Peters notes, Luther's point here is precisely that in the Son and through the Holy Spirit, the Father not only discloses but also gives Himself to us as a gift.[16] *Knowing* the God and Father revealed and confessed in the creed therefore means much more than merely intellectually apprehending that there is a benevolent Creator by means of the created order. However we may choose to label the divine-human contact Luther speaks of here—be it *knowledge, participation, grasp*, or some other term—it is clear that he understands it as *real*. By faith, the believer really lays hold of the God Who really gives Himself in the means of grace.

In his surprisingly concise treatment of the second article, Luther says that to know God the Son is "to get to know the second person of the Godhead [*die andere person der Gottheit*]," the "true Son of God" who has become "Lord" through his victory over sin, the devil, death, and evil.[17] The Son "has bought us back from the devil to God, from death to life, from sin to righteousness."[18] The significance of Christology in the context of Luther's broader trinitarian theological

---

[14]BSLK, 650; BC, 433.

[15]BSLK, 650. I have altered the translation slightly from what one finds at BC, 433.

[16]See Albrecht Peters, "Verborgener Gott—Dreieiniger Gott: Beobachtungen und überlegungen zum Gottesverständnis Martin Luthers," in *Martin Luther, "Reformator und Vater im Glauben,"* ed. Peter Manns (Wiesbaden: Franz Steiner Verlag, 1985), 74–105; here 83.

[17]BSLK, 651; BC, 434.

[18]BSLK, 652; BC, 434. As Oberman insists, the interpreter of Luther must remain ever mindful that, for Luther, the Christian's struggle for faith takes place not primarily in the "Protestant citadel" of the conscience but in the titanic and very

reflection is of course greater than might be inferred on the basis of the short exposition found here. As Simo Peura has observed, the starting place for Luther's trinitarian theology is the work and person of the Redeemer. Directing the reader's attention to Luther's 1538 treatise tellingly entitled "The Three Symbols of the Christian Faith," Peura remarks that the knowledge of God for Luther is grounded first, last, and always in the humanity of Christ. This is not, however, to say that God the Father or God the Holy Spirit is not to be known, as if either could somehow be rendered superfluous by Luther's christocentrism. To the contrary, it is the Son who in his incarnate humanity opens the way to knowing God—Father, Son, and Spirit—in a saving way.[19]

Strikingly, the bulk of Luther's exposition of the Apostle's Creed is directed to the third article: "Sanctification" (*die Heiligung*). The ministry of the Holy Spirit is the starting point of Christian faith and life, for the Spirit brings the Christian to Christ and through Christ reveals the love of the Father. Moreover, the work of the Spirit is the ground and origin of the church into which the Christian has been called and gathered.[20] The Holy Spirit effects the *communio sanctorum* by leading sinners to Christ and by offering and applying to them the benefits of the redeeming work of the Son. In a certain sense, then, sanctification means for Luther simply being incorporated into Christ, our righteousness. But that incorporation is itself impossible without the ministry of the Spirit in the church. No Spirit, no church, no Christ, and, therefore, no salvation. Thus, one could as well say for Luther as for St. Cyprian, *extra ecclesiam nulla salus*.[21] The church is "the mother that begets and bears every Christian through the Word."[22]

Luther's pneumatology here also has an eschatological orientation, for it is the Spirit who will raise the faithful and bring them to eternal life. With this end in view, the Spirit works in the present to

much this-worldly battle between God and the devil. Heiko A. Oberman, *Luther: Man between God and the Devil* (New Haven: Yale University Press, 1989), 155.

[19]Simo Peura, "Das Sich-Geben Gottes: Die Trinitätslehre als integrales Problem der Theologie Martin Luthers," in *Luther und die trinitarische Tradition: Ökumenische und philosophische Perspektiven* (Erlangen: Martin-Luther-Verlag, 1994), 131–46.

[20]On the Spirit's work in calling and gathering the church in Luther's catechesis, one may consult Jared Wicks, S.J., "Holy Spirit—Church—Sanctification: Insights from Luther's Instructions on the Faith," in *Pro Ecclesia* 2 (1993): 150–72.

[21]BSLK, 658; BC, 438.
[22]BSLK, 655; BC, 436.

make the faithful "pure saints under one Head, Christ,"[23] and the Spirit does so by applying the gospel in all its aspects. What makes the church indispensable for salvation, then, is precisely the Spirit's presence, for it is within the church that the Spirit unites believers "in one faith, mind and understanding."[24] For Luther, in short, the knowledge of God certainly means, as Philip Melanchthon had already famously put it,[25] to know God's benefits, both the paternal ones revealed in God's activity in creation as well as the unmerited divine favor that is given to believers through faith alone in Christ alone. But to *know* God either as benevolent Father or as redeeming Son requires that one be brought ever and again into the holy Christian church by the ministry of the Spirit, "him who daily brings us into this community through the Word, and imparts, increases, and strengthens faith through the same Word and the forgiveness of sins."[26]

In Luther's understanding, the ministry of the Spirit also leans eschatologically forward, not in such a way as to negate God's work of either creation or redemption, but instead to bring those works to their completion and fulfillment. The works of God in creation, redemption, and sanctification are thus directed alike toward an ultimate fulfillment in which each has reached its final end. "For creation is now behind us, and redemption has also taken place, but the Holy Spirit continues his work without ceasing until the Last Day."[27] As the Spirit reveals the grace and favor of the Son, so also the Son brings us to the Father, Who reveals to us the "most profound depths of his fatherly heart, his sheer, unutterable love."[28] Viewed from the standpoint of Christian experience, then, the knowledge of God given in the symbol proceeds in the Spirit, through the Son, and to the Father. Here living faith in fact lays hold of God, for "in the Creed you have the entire essence, will, and work of God."[29]

[23]BSLK, 657; BC, 437.
[24]Ibid.
[25]The phrase is found in the first edition of his *Loci Communes Theologici*. ET in *Melanchthon and Bucer*, ed. Wilhelm Pauck (Philadelphia: Westminster, 1969), 21.
[26]BSLK, 660; BC, 439.
[27]BSLK, 659–60; BC, 439.
[28]BSLK, 660; BC, 439. The German text reads: "Den da hat er selbs offenbaret und aufgetan den tiefsten Abgrund seines väterlichen Herzens und eitel unaussprechlicher Liebe in allen dreien Artikeln."
[29]BSLK, 660; BC, 439. German: "Siehe, da hast Du das ganze göttliche Wesen, Willen und Werk."

This brief look at Luther's exposition of the Apostles' Creed shows that the trinitarian faith of Catholic tradition is much more central to Luther's teaching than some have suggested. Indeed, if the "chief article" (*Hauptartikel*) of justification means justification *by grace through faith alone*, then faith itself means much more than simply giving one's "assent to the promise of God, in which forgiveness of sins and justification are bestowed freely on account of Christ."[30] For Luther, faith in God as given to the Christian through the means of grace consists of nothing less than *knowledge* of the God Who is—and very much of God *as* God is: Father, Son, Holy Spirit. Readers of Luther's biblical commentaries or sermons will do well to attend with care to the robustly trinitarian conception of salvation that informs his exegesis and, by doing so, will gain a better understanding of the faith for which he contended with such energy and courage. Before we consider Luther's trinitarian reading of Scripture, however, it will be helpful to review in brief his thorough acquaintance with the Bible and with the critical tools available in his day for the task of biblical exegesis. Luther worked very much at the methodological forefront of sixteenth-century theology. Chapters 2 and 3 will demonstrate that he also used the best tools available both for articulating his trinitarian theology and for developing his understanding of the "new language of the Holy Spirit" that transcends all such language. The same can certainly be said for his work on the Bible.

Luther and the Bible: Critical Tools, Original Languages

From his childhood in a pious Christian family to his university days in Erfurt, for the two decades during which he wore the habit of an Augustinian friar, and on through his many years as dedicated priest, *Hausvater*, and professor of Bible in the German frontier town of Wittenberg, Martin Luther lived in a thoroughly biblical world.[31] Indeed, over the course of his rather tumultuous career, one central constant in his life was a tireless dedication to the work of biblical interpretation and, a bit later, translation. From the young

---

[30]This is the definition of saving faith as found in Philip Melanchthon's *Apology of the Augsburg Confession*. BC, 128. The views of Luther and Melanchthon on this matter are in my view distinct but compatible.

[31]For a broad presentation of Luther's early acquaintance with the Bible, see Mattox, *"Defender,"* introduction.

friar's pious lectures on the Pauline epistles (1514–1518) to the elder professor's massive lectures on Genesis (1535–1545; his "swan song"), Luther remained furiously occupied with biblical exposition. In 1521, during the period of his exile at the Wartburg ("my Patmos"[32]), he threw himself into the painstaking task of making the biblical authors speak good German. His New Testament was published the next year. The year 1534 saw the publication of the first complete German Bible, which Luther continued to try to improve all the way up to 1545 when, with the help of his "Sanhedrin" (scholars who assisted with the translation), he saw the publication of its final edition. Either of these great accomplishments—the theological depth that marks his wide-ranging work as an expositor or the linguistic genius of his work as a translator—would easily qualify him as a leading figure in the history of the Christian Bible. Together, they propel him into a class almost all his own.[33]

Of course, Luther had help. As a young professor of Bible, he eagerly availed himself of the new tools that were being developed in sixteenth-century biblical scholarship. He gladly appropriated, for example, Erasmus's Greek edition of the New Testament, the *Novum Instrumentum*, complete with the editor's learned remarks on matters textual and theological, the so-called *Annotationes*. He taught himself Hebrew using the grammar of Johannes Reuchlin, Philip Melanchthon's uncle (by marriage). He also took extraordinary steps to realize the pedagogical potential inherent in these new tools and exegetical approaches by taking advantage of the latest technology: the printing press. When Luther began his early lectures on Paul's writings, he arranged with the Wittenberg publisher Grünenberg to have the biblical text printed in the manner of the glossed medieval Bible, but without the standard medieval apparatus—that is, without either the "interlinear glosses" in small type printed at the center of the page between the lines of biblical text, or the "marginal glosses" in large type arranged in columns at the sides of the biblical text, in which the collective exegetical wisdom of the church fathers and medievals was traditionally set forth. His students began, in other

---

[32]LW 48:246. Luther used the phrase often.
[33]Perhaps only Origen of Alexandria was truly his equal, though obviously the two men were separated both by temperament and by theological outlook. For an overview of Luther's work, see Siegfried Raeder, "Luther als Ausleger und Übersetzer der Heiligen Schrift," in *Leben und Werk Martin Luthers von 1526 bis 1546*, ed. Helmar Junghans, vol. 1 (Göttingen: Vandenhoeck & Ruprecht, 1983), 253–78.

words, with the bare biblical text in hand, but with sufficient space between the lines and around the margins to take down verbatim Luther's brief textual remarks (glosses) as well as his lengthier theological analyses (scholia).

In preparation for his lectures, Luther consulted not only the standard exegetical sources but also some of the most recent humanist biblical commentary, particularly that of the French humanist Jacques Lefevre D'Etaples (Faber Stapulensis). The young Luther, in short, worked very much at the cutting edge of sixteenth-century biblical scholarship.[34] He also clearly understood that this scholarship had significant revisionist implications not just for biblical interpretation but for the theology and practice of the church as well. In the very first of his celebrated Ninety-five Theses, for example, Luther cited from the traditional Latin biblical text Jesus' words "Repent, for the kingdom of God is at hand." Jerome had translated the crucial term *repent* with the Latin "poenitentiam agite" ("do penance"), and this was typically understood as Christ's own urging of the sinner to the sacrament of penance. In the Ninety-five Theses, Luther cited the text from Jerome's translation but drew intentionally on the proper meaning for the Greek *metanoeo* ("repent"; which he had learned from Erasmus)—that is, the decisive change of heart and mind that denotes the turn from self-will to authentic discipleship. The new biblical scholarship, it turns out, had everything to do with the controversy that ultimately propelled Luther onto history's center stage.

Twenty or so years later, however, when he wrote the words cited at the beginning of this chapter, he perceived clearly that the new exegetical tools themselves posed a theological problem that cried out for solution. In response, Luther argued forcefully that scriptural interpretation should neither be separated from nor superordinated to living Christian faith. The grammarians and historians could not be allowed to dictate to the theologians the meaning(s) of Scripture. If the meaning or translation of the biblical text was to be determined by textual analyses that ignored the rule of faith, then as Luther forthrightly admitted in the words cited above, the church would be better off relying on Jerome's Latin translation, faulty though it was. This is a stunning admission from a man who had dedicated much of his life's work to revisionist biblical com-

---

[34]On this issue, one may consult Helmar Junghans, "Luther als Bibelhumanist," *Zeitschrift der Luther-Gesellschaft* 53 (1982): 1–9.

mentary and translation. As will be shown below, the elder Luther had become deeply concerned that the presumed advances in biblical studies made possible by the new critical tools had destabilized the long-settled results of Christian scriptural interpretation, particularly in the sensitive matter of the relationship between New Testament and Old. He also seems to have been aware that the doctrine of the Trinity was coming under attack, based not only on the cover that had been provided by his own reforming movement but also on the study of the Hebrew Scriptures.[35] Having played a not inconsiderable role in letting this particular critical cat out of the bag, the elder Luther insisted that authentic Christian exegesis depends first and always on the authentic knowledge of God.

The catholicity of Luther's bold exegetical claim—its deep agreement, in other words, with convictions about the relationships between theology and church, Scripture and tradition, broadly characteristic of patristic and medieval Western theology—has long been obscured. Indeed, the tendency to paint the distinctions between Protestant and Roman Catholic thought in the colors of stark contrast is particularly pronounced in Luther scholarship itself, not least of all in research on Luther's biblical exposition. Studies almost too numerous to count have examined Luther's distinctive hermeneutical principle(s) and his allegedly unique insight(s) into particular biblical texts.[36] Some have considered the patristic and medieval background of his approach to the Bible. Often, however, they have done so only to set the stage for presenting Luther's unique hermeneutical insight(s) into the biblical text. Thus, Luther is set over against the traditions in which he was formed as a theologian, and his christocentric reading of the Bible is presented as something almost completely new, a departure from the patterns of patristic and medieval interpretation. Turned in upon its fascinating subject, Luther scholarship remains perennially underappreciative of the deep continuity

---

[35]In the *Tischreden*, Luther seems to indicate an awareness of the *Dialogi de Trinitate* (1532) of Michael Servetus (Nr. 237; WATR 99.18–21). According to Martin Brecht, in the 1540s Luther was concerned to defend the trinitarian dogma against both Servetus and John Campanus. See vol. 3 of Brecht's massive biography, *Martin Luther: The Preservation of the Church, 1532–1546*, trans. James L. Schaaf (Minneapolis: Fortress Press, 1993), 133.

[36]The most prominent study of the last generation of scholarship is still Gerhard Ebeling's *Evangelische Evangelienauslegung. Eine Untersuchung zu Luthers Hermeneutik* (Munich: Chr. Kaiser, 1942; 3rd ed., [erweitert um ein Nachwort], Tübingen: J. C. B. Mohr [Paul Siebeck], 1991).

between Luther's biblical exegesis and that of his patristic and medieval predecessors, particularly when it comes to the exegetical role of trinitarian faith.[37] This problem begins, of course, not with scholarly assessments of Luther's exegesis but in the usual Protestant working assumption that the doctrine that made Luther *different* from the tradition must serve as the *starting point* for evangelical theology itself. Focusing on the doctrine of justification as the "article by which the church stands or falls," prominent Lutheran theologians have long tended to exaggerate the situation.[38] To be sure, there have always been good reasons to focus on the distinctive aspects of Luther's hermeneutic and his remarkable insights into the Scriptures. Luther was an astonishingly creative reader of the Bible. As noted above, the study of his exegesis has been an important resource for biblical renewal in the divided Christian churches, and for an impressively diverse group of renewal movements. In practice, however, it is crucial to recognize

---

[37]Much the same could also be said of Luther's use of traditional exegetical helps. For a revealing glimpse at the use of just one of the more popular resources available in the early sixteenth century, see Karlfried Froehlich, "The Fate of the *Glossa Ordinaria* in the Sixteenth Century," in *Die Patristik in der Bibelexegese des 16. Jahrhunderts*, ed. David C. Steinmetz and Robert Kolb (Wiesbaden: Harrassowitz Verlag, 1999), 19–48.

[38]See David Yeago, "Lutheran-Roman Catholic Consensus on Justification: The Theological Achievement of the Joint Declaration," *Pro Ecclesia* 7 (1998): 449–70. Yeago notes that for these theologians, Lutherans and Catholics are divided by "two incompatible understandings of reality" (461). The German debate over the "Joint Declaration on the Doctrine of Justification" (JDDJ, 1999) provided an illustrative case in point. Eilert Herms of Tübingen University argued against the JDDJ on account of what he saw as a "foundational disagreement" (*Grunddissens*) between Protestants and Roman Catholics. The object of evangelical faith, he argued, is "God's self-presentation in the embodied Word of the Gospel through the Holy Ghost" (*Selbstvergegenwärtigung Gottes im leibhaften Wort des Evangeliums durch den heiligen Geist*). For Roman Catholics, he claimed, the "ground and object of faith" (*Grund und Gegenstand des Glaubens*) is not the God revealed in the Gospel, but the presentation of revelation in the "traditionary activities" (*Traditionstätigkeit*) of the bishops under the pope. Thus, evangelicals believe in God; Catholics, in dogma. See his "Die ökumenische Beziehungen zwischen der evangelischen und der römisch-katholischen Kirche im Spätsommer 1998," *epd-Dokumentation* Nr. 37/98 (August 31, 1998): 1–23; this line of reasoning is further elaborated in Eilert Herms, "Lehrkonsens und Kirchengemeinschaft," in *Von der Verwerfung zur Versöhnung*, ed. Johannes Brosseder (Neukirchen, 1996), 81–110. Herms's argument was met by the incredulous response of his Tübingen colleague Bernd Jochen Hilberath: "Catholics too believe in the triune God!" See his "Katholisch-lutherischer Grunddissens?—Zu Eilert Herms' Bestandsaufnahme der ökumenische Beziehungen," pts. 1 and 2, *Katholische Nachrichten Agentur* 48 (November 24, 1998): 5–10; 51 (December 15, 1998): 5–11.

that Luther read the Bible equipped with much more than a christo-centric hermeneutic and a deep confidence in its clarity. Most important, he relied on *the Christian faith itself* as a means for opening up the meaning of Scripture. In addition, throughout his career he read widely in patristic theology and exegesis, so much so that one could even say that Luther self-consciously read the Scriptures in the company of the church fathers.

Of course, scholarship on Luther's relationship to the church fathers typically stresses just the opposite point, emphasizing the freedom with which he criticized and even rejected the fathers' opinions when he found them in conflict with the Scriptures.[39] That is true. But it tells only half the story. As a biblical theologian, Luther thought of himself as doing his work not just in the company of the fathers but on a level playing field with them as well. The ease with which he sometimes argued with them reflected not critical distance (Luther against the fathers) but a profound sense of nearness and of kinship in the faith. He did not hesitate to say so when he thought their opinions were wrong or had even been damaging to the church, but at the same time he recognized them as heroic men of faith, that is, as saints (*heilige Väter, sancti patres*), and he saw himself as one too.[40] He argued with the dead, in short, as if they were living, and as if they were his brothers.

---

[39]See, for example, the late Leif Grane's model study *Modus Loquendi Theologicus: Luthers Kampf um die Erneuerung der Theologie (1515–1518),* trans. from the Danish by Eberhard Grötzinger (Leiden: Brill, 1975). Cf. Manfred Schulze's "Martin Luther and the Church Fathers," in *The Reception of the Church Fathers in the West: From the Carolingians to the Maurists,* ed. Irena Backus, 2 vols. (Leiden: Brill, 1997), 2:573–626.

[40]Luther's self-understanding seems to have undergone a decisive evolution during the period of his appearance before the Imperial Diet at Worms and subsequent period of isolation at the Wartburg Castle in late 1521. He saw himself recapitulating, for example, some of the experiences of the apostle Paul and, accordingly, self-consciously put himself forward in his letters as an apostle. Heiko Oberman remarks: "Of all the virtues, modesty is not one of which Luther can be accused. He did not hesitate to call himself a prophet, and thus to place himself in the tradition of Old Testament prophecy. He wanted to be heard as an evangelist who has taken the pure, unadulterated Gospel to the people as in the time of the apostles. And for this reason he is persuaded that he is himself an apostle, in direct succession from the Apostle Paul." In *The Reformation: Roots and Ramifications,* trans. Andrew Colin Gow (Grand Rapids: Eerdmans, 1994), 58. Further to this point, see Timothy J. Wengert, "Martin Luther's Movement toward an Apostolic Self-Awareness as Reflected in His Early Letters," *Lutherjahrbuch* 61 (1994): 71–92.

Luther's Anti-Judaism

In Luther's day no less than our own, the Old Testament presented the Christian expositor with innumerable questions and difficulties. The challenge of developing appropriate Christian readings of the Old Testament put expositors in conversation and potential conflict not only with one another but with Jewish readers as well. Scholars are now generally agreed that Luther's opinions regarding the Jews and Judaism were fairly consistent, and consistently negative, over the entire course of his career.[41] The regrettable anti-Jewish outbursts of his later years—which included his eerily prophetic recommendations that the Jews' property be confiscated, that their synagogues be burned, and that they be put into forced labor—seem to have been prompted by reports that in the territories where they were being tolerated, some Jews were successfully proselytizing Christians, including some former Jews who had previously converted to Christianity.[42] Sadly, Luther's anti-Jewish writings were filled with just the kind of hateful and vindictive language he often poured out on his enemies. For that reason, these writings seem to have strongly influenced the mentalities that fostered German anti-Semitism in the modern period.

Viewed from a contemporary perspective, one might say that Luther failed as a theologian in his attitudes and policy recommendations regarding the Jews because he was unable to imagine a tolerant society within which the civil authorities could allow religious freedom, including the freedom to convert from Christianity to Judaism. The fact that very few of Luther's contemporaries could have imagined such a society, and that many of them shared his antipathy for the Jews, in no way excuses Luther's failure, although it underscores

---

[41]For a wide-ranging introduction to these questions, see Thomas Kaufmann's "Luther and the Jews," in *Jews, Judaism and the Reformation in Sixteenth-Century Germany*, ed. Dean Phillip Bell and Stephen G. Burnett (Leiden: Brill, 2006), 69–104. Kaufmann underscores the continuity in Luther's views, although he also notes the changes in Luther's approach from 1523, when he counseled the friendly treatment of the Jews in hope of their conversion to Christianity, to 1543, when he recommended severe measures be taken to suppress them because he had become convinced that the exact opposite was occurring, that is, that the Jews were converting Christians to Judaism.

[42]Further to this point, see the introduction to Luther's treatise "Against the Sabbatarians: Letter to a Good Friend" (1538), in LW 47:57–63. Some fringe groups that developed at the time of the Reformation did in fact develop a Unitarian doctrine of God. Eventually, they also rejected adoration of Jesus and adopted Jewish rituals. On the development of these "Sabbatarian" groups, see Daniel Liechty, *Sabbatarianism in the Sixteenth Century* (Berrien Springs, Mich.: Andrews University Press, 1993).

that in this regard he was very much a man of his time. One might also observe that scholarship on Luther today more clearly recognizes the place and role of apocalypticism in his thought. Luther read the signs of his times as indicating that the end would come soon and that during this time the enemies of the gospel—among whom he counted the Jews, along with papists, Turks, and enthusiasts—would rage more than ever. Heiko Oberman's image of a man caught up in the fierce battle between God and the devil at the end of the age probably provides an appropriate framework for making at least some sense of Luther's harsh attacks.

As the quotation with which this chapter began clearly indicates, Luther spoke harshly about supposed Jewish interpretations of the Bible. In fact, however, he had little firsthand knowledge of Jewish people, and what he knew of their interpretations of the Old Testament came primarily through the writings of other Christian biblical commentators, particularly Nicholas Lyra. Still, in his exegesis Luther repeatedly postured himself as the defender of Christian truth, and the truth of the Scriptures, over against the Jews. The fact that Luther's trinitarian readings of crucial Old Testament texts include frequent and, typically, highly polemical mention of his Jewish opponents—often in terms that struck even some of his sixteenth-century readers as excessively harsh—suggests that any responsible effort to gain insight for theological exegesis from Luther will need simultaneously to recognize and reject consistently aspects of his exegesis that may reflect little more than anti-Jewish prejudice. At the same time, it will be crucial to keep in mind, as stated above, that the exegetical argument in which Luther participated so vigorously was being carried on almost exclusively with other Christian expositors—notably the Hebraist Sebastian Münster—and not with the Jews.

It is important to note that Christian expositors on all sides of the sixteenth-century exegetical debates not infrequently maligned the work of their opponents by labeling their theology or exegesis as "Judaizing." Luther's Roman Catholic opponents accused him of this "error,"[43] as Calvin's Lutheran opponents later did to him.[44] The

---

[43]For details on the charges or, more accurately, innuendos circulated against Luther, see Kaufmann, "Luther and the Jews," 80–81 n. 32.

[44]The case against Calvin was made by Aegidius Hunnius, *Calvinus Iudiazans, hoc est: Iudaicae Glossae et Corruptelae, quibus Iohannes Calvinus illustrissima Scripturae sacrae Loca & Testamonia, de gloriosa Trinitate, Deitate Christi, &*

term pointed toward allegedly sub-Christian defect(s) in a theologian's work. Regarding exegesis in particular, it suggested darkly that an expositor tended to compromise Christian readings of Scripture along exegetical lines that were consistent with (or even indebted to) presumed Jewish interpretations, ones that rejected Christ as Israel's Messiah and eliminated the trinitarian God from the Old Testament. In Luther's vocabulary, of course, it could also refer to "legalistic" readings of Scripture that failed to distinguish properly between law and gospel.[45] In fact, Luther's own bellicose remarks about Jewish exegesis were often intended not to engage in exegetical argument with Jewish expositors but to warn off Christian expositors. "The Jews" as the phrase occurs in Luther's exegesis is largely an abstraction, referring, to borrow an idea from Dean Phillip Bell and Stephen Burnett, to "abstract Jews" or "theological Jews" rather than to actual persons.[46] Luther's railings against "Judaizing" exegesis often amount to little more than an argument for guilt by association, the harsh terms of which tend to obscure the constructive side of his exegetical and theological work. It is also important to remember that Luther's work after 1518 (when he was a professor of Bible) was focused almost exclusively on the Old Testament. Furthermore, after 1522, he was perennially occupied with Hebrew translation problems in his work on the German Bible.

As we shall see below, Luther's exegetical arguments with "the Jews" often recapitulated classical disagreements between the church fathers and the Jews. Insofar as they do so, they reflect exegetical and theological arguments that go back to the period of the founding of

---

Spiritus Sancti, cum primis autem ascensione in caelos et sessione ad dextram Dei, detestandum in modum corrumpere no exhorruit. Addita est corruptelarum confutatio per Aegidium Hunnium (Wittenberg: Vidua Matthaei Welaci, 1593). Calvin's loyal follower David Paraeus answered in his *Libri Duo: I. Calvinus Orthodoxus de Sacrosancta Trinitate; et de aeterna Christi Divinitate. II. Solida Exposita XXXIIX. difficiliorum Scripturae Locorum et Oraculorum: et de recta ratione applicandi Oracula Prophetica ad Christum. Oppositi Pseudocalvino Iudaizanti nuper a quodam emisso* (Neustadt: Matthaeus Harnisch, 1595). For an analysis of this debate, see David C. Steinmetz's "The Judaizing Calvin," in *Die Patristik in der Bibelexegese des 16. Jahrhunderts*, ed. David C. Steinmetz and Robert Kolb (Wiesbaden: Harrassowitz, 1999), 135–45.

[45]For the Wittenberg critique of "Judaizing" exegesis, as well as Philip Melanchthon's role in it, see Timothy J. Wengert, "Philip Melanchthon and the Jews: A Reappraisal," in *Jews, Judaism and the Reformation in Sixteenth-Century Germany*, ed. Dean Phillip Bell and Stephen G. Burnett (Leiden: Brill, 2006), 105–35, esp. 119–25.

[46] Bell and Burnett, *Jews, Judaism, and the Reformation*, xxx.

the Christian religion. With those facts in mind, it seems fair to say that Luther's concern with Old Testament interpretation was in no way fundamentally anti-Jewish but was, to the contrary, constructively Christian. In short, Luther read and interpreted the Hebrew Scriptures as a Christian on behalf of Christian students and readers, and it is precisely here in his *argument for* trinitarian and christological exegesis—and not in his *argument against* the Jews—that we discover his genius as an expositor and his positive potential for today.

Recognizing Luther's exegetical genius need not come at the cost of legitimating his anti-Judaism. Contemporary advances in Jewish-Christian relations, especially in the years since the Holocaust, have been based largely on a rejection or, at the very least, a thoroughgoing reinterpretation of supersessionism, that is, the notion that the Christian church has superseded and therefore replaced Israel as God's chosen people.[47] These advances make it impossible to return, or even to wish to return, to anything like Luther's position on the Jews. Instead, we should keep ever in mind Luther's context in the sixteenth century, long before the experience of the Holocaust and without benefit of the contemporary rethinking of supersessionism. It would be a mistake for Christians today not to recognize and explicitly reject Luther's harsh words regarding the Jews, just as it would be a mistake not to recognize and reject similar words and ideas found in a host of other important contributors to the Christian tradition, patristic, medieval, and modern alike. At the same time, it would also be a mistake to imagine that Luther has no constructive contribution to make to the ongoing Christian exegetical tradition, or even to trinitarian theology proper, today. The doctrine of the Trinity has been the subject of vigorous research in recent years. As chapters 2 and 3 will show, moreover, there is good reason to believe that Luther can contribute significantly to contemporary conversations about the Trinity, and thus about the theological interpretation of Scripture as well. To be sure, bringing Luther's voice into this conversation is a delicate and a difficult task, but the depth of his exegetical insight and his position at the head of the theological stream that would become the Protestant tradition make the effort both worthwhile and necessary.

A final caveat before we proceed. Much contemporary research

---

[47]On this issue, one may consult *Jews and Christians: People of God*, ed. Carl E. Braaten and Robert W. Jenson (Grand Rapids: Eerdmans, 2003).

on the so-called new perspective on Paul presumes that Luther is at or
somewhere near the bottom of alleged classical Protestant misread-
ings of Paul, and especially of Judaism at the time of Jesus. Without
attempting to evaluate this idea, it should simply be noted here that
Luther clearly saw the religion of Israel up to the time of Jesus as a
religion of grace and faith that was founded on God's word of promise given to Adam and Eve even before their expulsion from the garden. Preus has shown that in his early Psalms lectures (*Dictata super
psalterium*, 1513–1515), Luther discovered the "faithful synagogue"
of the Old Testament, where men of faith like the patriarch David
truly *knew* and *referred to* the triune God, and where the men and
women of Israel struggled to keep their faith in the promises of God
despite the *contraria* of their difficult historical experiences.[48] The Old
Testament as Luther understood it was not a book of law, as opposed
to, say, the gospel of the New Testament. Luther was no Marcion.
The Old Testament contains both law and gospel, and it powerfully
teaches the latter. In fact, Luther frequently drew on the stories of the
Old Testament as preeminent examples of the subtle ins and outs of
the experience of God's judgment (law) and grace (gospel).

To put it in the negative, Luther tended to collapse the distance
between Christianity and the Judaism of the Old Testament by reading the Old Testament as a Christian book. But to state the case more
positively, Luther saw continuity between the faith of the patriarchs
and his own faith. Clearly he saw himself as a Gentile, by blood an
outsider, who had been grafted into the faith of the patriarchs and
prophets of the Old Testament. But he argued frequently and often at
length that the faith of the Christian church was in fact identical to
the faith of ancient Israel. On Luther's account, salvific inclusion in
the people of God is based on one's sharing in the faith of Israel, not
on one's blood heritage. They are the children of Abraham who imitate Abraham's faith. For all these reasons and more, Luther is probably most accurately labeled anti-Judaistic rather than anti-Semitic.
Any account of Luther's place in the history of the Christian (mis)
understanding of Judaism, moreover, should take account not only of
his hateful utterances about Judaism at or after the time of Christ but
also his love for the people and the religion of the Old Testament.

---

[48]See James Samuel Preus, *From Shadow to Promise: Old Testament
Interpretation from Augustine to the Young Luther* (Cambridge: Harvard University
Press, 1969). As Preus puts it, in Luther's thought, the faithful synagogue is "solidly
in its own time, *ante adventum*, yet *simul in spiritu*" (174).

Indeed, as George Lindbeck has pointed out, Luther himself somewhat paradoxically embodied a love for the law of God that is almost rabbinic.[49] In the Large Catechism, Luther uses the creed both to *identify* the Christian God—that is, the "object" of Christian faith—and also as a word of *gospel* that answers the Ten Commandments in their function as divine *law*. Because we are sinners, Luther explains, each of the commandments "constantly accuses us."[50] Understood as gospel, the creed answers the commandments in their perpetual accusatory function by setting forth "all that we must expect and receive from God."[51] Paradoxically, the knowledge of God and the gospel given in Christian faith and confessed in the creed results not in freedom *from* God's law but in a willing return *to* the law.[52] The creed shows the believer a gracious God and thus becomes the source of strength out of which a Christian existence shaped by the wisdom of the Ten Commandments freely flows. Faith enables the baptized believer to find also within the Ten Commandments a word of grace and promise—that is, "I am the Lord your God"—and to answer that word with an emphatic "I believe."[53] Enlightened by the right knowledge of God and enkindled by the flame of love for God made possible by the gospel, the Christian properly discerns in the Ten Commandments the foundation for the godly life.

2. The Substance of Scripture: Teaching the Traditions of Trinitarian Faith

From Luther's perspective, properly trained pastors were essential to perpetuating the trinitarian faith in the church. Thus, his classroom lectures constitute an important source for displaying his exegesis

---

[49]For Luther's work on the Ten Commandments in the LC, see George Lindbeck, "Martin Luther and the Rabbinic Mind," in *Understanding the Rabbinic Mind: Essays on the Hermeneutic of Max Kadushin*, ed. Peter Ochs (Atlanta: Scholars Press, 1990), 141–64.

[50]BSLK, 639; BC, 427.

[51]BSLK, 646; BC, 431.

[52]For a thoroughgoing theological demolition of the notion that Luther can be understood as an antinomian, see Reinhard Hütter, *Bound to Be Free: Evangelical Catholic Engagements in Ecclesiology, Ethics, and Ecumenism* (Grand Rapids: Eerdmans, 2004), 111–67.

[53]On Luther's interpretation of the First Commandment, see Althaus, *Theology of Martin Luther*, 130–32. According to Althaus, Luther takes this commandment as a word of gospel given in the form of a command. In the LC, Luther even goes so far as to put these words of fatherly grace into God's mouth, informing the catechist exactly what God requires of us here: "See to it that you let me alone be your God, and never search for another." BSLK, 647; BC, 387.

of many of the Old Testament passages that Christian expositors had traditionally understood as giving witness to the Holy Trinity. Lecturing through the book of Genesis (or, as the German title would have it, "First Moses") over the last ten years of his academic career, Luther frequently emphasized the idea that the Christian reader meets and knows the triune God in the Old Testament. As he did so, he also showed his deep sense of solidarity with the "holy fathers" of the church. Luther agreed broadly with the patterns of trinitarian exegesis found in patristic and medieval explications of these texts, but he thought the recovery of the Hebrew language and the recovery of the gospel in its clarity had made it possible for sixteenth-century exegetes to do the fathers one better, affirming that their exegesis was right and then confirming it through the application of those new tools, that clearer insight.

More often, however, Luther was content simply to follow the traditional readings of these texts and to use them as a springboard for teaching the rudiments of classical trinitarian theology. The *Lectures on Genesis* (1535–1545),[54] for example, provided Luther with many opportunities to school his students in solid trinitarian theology. Lecturing in 1535 on Genesis 1:26—"let us make man" (*faciamus hominem*)—for example, Luther modeled for his students the Christian exposition of the first-person plural verb (that is, "let us"). Luther's central point had been made by Augustine more than a thousand years earlier, and it could easily have been made by almost any Western catholic theologian after him.

> Therefore here [that is, in Genesis 1:26] the Trinity is clearly signi-fied, that in the one divine essence there are three persons, Father, Son and Holy Spirit; thus not even with regard to activity [of cre-ation] is God separated, for all three persons here agree together and say "let us make." The Father does not make any other man than the Son, nor the Son than the Holy Spirit, but the Father, Son and Holy Spirit, one and the same God, is the author and creator of the same work. Thus neither in this way can God be separated as a thing present to the mind [*obiective*]. For God the Father is not known, except in the Son and through the Holy Spirit. Therefore just as with regard to activity [that is, creation] so also as a thing present to the mind God is one, who nevertheless within himself

---

[54]*Enarrationes in Genesin*, WA 42–44. Translated as *Lectures on Genesis*, LW 1–8.

substantively or essentially is Father, Son, Holy Spirit, three distinct persons in one divinity.[55]

God the Creator, Luther teaches, is a Trinity of divine persons whose works are, as Augustine had famously put it, indivisible.[56] Moreover, this Creator is also the God known in Christian faith. The God Who acts in creation, the God Who is, and the God known in Christian faith—this is the one God. The revelation of God the Father in the Son through the Holy Spirit is therefore a revelation of God as God is. Trinitarian theology therefore means nothing less than the mystery of God made known.

Similar explanations of the ins and outs of basic trinitarian theology can be found in Luther's preaching, although he often put his own distinctive spin on his quite traditional points. He developed a

---

[55]WA 42:43–44: "Quare est hic certo significata Trinitas, quod in una essentia divina sunt tres personae, Pater, Filius et Spiritus sanctus, ita ut ne active quidem Deus separetur, quia omnes tres personae hic concurrunt et dicunt, 'faciamus'. Nec Pater facit alium hominem, quam Filius, nec Filius alium quam Spiritus sanctus, sed Pater, Filius, Spiritus sanctus, unus et idem Deus, autor et creator est eiusdem operis. Ad hunc modum neque obiective Deus potest separari. Neque enim Pater cognoscitur, nisi in Filio, et per Spiritum sanctum. Quare sicut active ita quoque obiective unus Deus est, qui tamen intra se substantive seu essentialiter est Pater, Filius, Spiritus sanctus, tres distinctae personae in [12] una divinitate." Translation mine; emphasis added. Cf. LW 1:58. I understand the Latin "active" here as a reference to God's action in creation. In the language of sixteenth-century philosophy, the term *obiective* denotes an *object* (i.e., a thing concerning which one may predicate) *present to the mind*; as such, it could be understood as a "subjective" reality. Thus, the term might be rendered, as is the case in the LW, with the English term *subjective*. However, to do so without further explanation severs the connection between the object present to the mind and the object as such, or, in this case, between the God who is present to Christian understanding and the God who is "substantive seu essentialiter." In medieval terms, this latter phrase again refers to God as "obiectum," but this time as an extra-mental reality whose existence clearly does not depend on the subjective presentation of this object to the mind for the purpose of understanding. On this philosophical issue and the medieval terminology, see Léon Baudry, *Lexique Philosophique de Guillaume D'Ockham* (P. Lethielleux: Paris, 1957), 182–84. See also Rudolf Eucken, *Geschichte der Philosophischen Terminologie* (Hildesheim: Georg Olms, 1879), 68. I thank Richard Muller for assistance with this problem.

[56]Luther explicitly agrees with Peter Lombard in rejecting the notion that the essence of God constitutes a fourth divine something, the so-called quaternity. On this point, as well as for a helpful analysis of the elder Luther's appropriation of traditional scholastic trinitarian terminology, see Graham White, *Luther as Nominalist: A Study of the Logical Methods Used in Martin Luther's Disputations in the Light of Their Medieval Background* (Helsinki: Luther-Agricola Society, 1994), 181–230. See also Risto Saarinen, "Die moderne Theologie und das pneumatologische Defizit," in *Der Heilige Geist*, ed. Joachim Heubach, Veröffentlichungen der Luther-Akademie Ratzeburg (Erlangen: Martin-Luther-Verlag, 1996), 245–63.

distinctive German-language terminology, for example, in which the terms *outward* (*von aussen*) and *inward* (*von innen*) denote what are commonly referred to today as the economic and the essential Trinity.[57] Preaching on John 1 in 1541, Luther said:

> We should not consider God only from the outside, in his works; to the contrary, he also wants to be known as he is inwardly; internally he is one essence and three Persons, the Father, Son, Holy Spirit, and not three gods; thus we pray only to one God. How can that be? It is ineffable; in their joy the beloved angels themselves cannot sufficiently rejoice at this; to us however it is grasped and proclaimed in the Word.[58]

While Luther's points are basic and traditional, they have profound implications. The twofold knowledge of the "outer" and "inner" God in turn makes possible the right praise of God. While for Luther the knowledge of God is not to be understood in such a strongly ontic sense as to make it dependent on a prior philosophy of being, it is nevertheless knowledge of God as God "inwardly" is.[59] This knowledge of God introduces one into a never-ending cycle that moves from the gracious actions of God to a graced humanity and back to God again. Having received the grace and gifts and right knowledge of God, the Christian joins with the angelic host and returns thanks and praise to the God Who is revealed as ineffable mystery. The knowledge of God, we might say, is properly doxological.

Some scholars have found in texts like this one a trinitarian theology that tends toward Byzantine "personalism" rather than the

---

[57]The distinction between the "essential" and "economic" Trinity is not Luther's own. Wolfhart Pannenberg credits J. Urlsperger (1728–1806) with having introduced this distinction into Western theology. See Pannenberg's *Systematic Theology*, vol. 1, trans. Geoffrey Bromiley (Grand Rapids: Eerdmans, 1991), 291 n. 111.

[58]WA 49:238–39: "Wir sollen aber Gott nicht allein ansehen von aussen in seinen wercken, sondern er wil auch erkant sein, was er inwerts ist, inwendig ist ein einig wesen und drey Personen, der Vater, Son, heiliger Geist, nicht drey Goetter, Beten derhalben nur ein Gott an. Wie gehets denn zu? unaussprechlich ists, die lieben Engel koennen sich nicht gnugsam darueber verwundern fur freuden, uns wirds ins Wort gefasset und furgeprediget." My translation. For the text in modern German, see Emanuel Hirsch, *Hilfsbuch zum Studium der Dogmatik* (Berlin: Walter de Gruyter, 1964), 21–22.

[59]For the trinitarian ontology of the young Luther, one may consult the interesting if inconclusive study of Tuomo Mannermaa, "Hat Luther eine trinitarische Ontologie?" in *Luther und Ontologie: Das Sein Christi im Glauben als strukturierendes Prinzip der Theologie Luthers* (Helsinki: Luther-Agricola Society, 1993), 9–27.

so-called Western "monism."[60] More will be said on this problem in chapter 2. For the moment, and without passing judgment on either that claim or the characterization of Western versus Eastern theology that it presupposes,[61] suffice it to say that for Luther the doctrine of the Trinity is grounded in God's creative, redemptive, and sanctifying work in human history. The knowledge of God is trinitarian with respect to its ontological ground, to the structure of God's self-revelation in history, and to the reality of Christian experience.

3. Taking the Fathers' Exegesis a Step Further: Sarah, Abraham, and the Holy Trinity

Returning to the lectures on Genesis, we move now to a case in which Luther thought he could improve on the exegesis of the "holy fathers." Genesis 18:1-15 tells the story of the appearance of three mysterious visitors to Abraham and Sarah at the Oaks of Mamre.[62] The story of Abraham and Sarah's mysterious encounter was much loved by the church fathers and by Luther. In his interpretation of this text, Luther made plain his debt to patristic exegesis by appropriating, and even intensifying, hagiographical traditions of interpretation that had been developed by the fathers. Much like the fathers, he adopted a principled insistence that the exegete should assume the best about the patriarchs and matriarchs.[63] The result, for Luther no less than his saintly predecessors, was a retelling of the stories of the biblical heroes and heroines that clearly has its place in the genre of

---

[60]See Albrecht Peters, "Die Trinitätslehre in der reformatorischen Christenheit," *Theologische Literaturzeitung* 94, no. 8 (August 1969): 561–70. Note well the near-absence of explicit mention of the immanent Trinity in the LC. On this problem, see Reiner Jansen, *Studien zu Luthers Trinitätslehre* (Bern, Germany: Herbert Lang and Peter Lang, 1976), 74–86.

[61]Augustine is the alleged source for a distinctive Western trinitarian theology that "begins" with the divine unity, as opposed to the economic approach characteristic of the Christian East. The origins of this construct have been thoroughly explored and convincingly critiqued in M. R. Barnes, "De Régnon Reconsidered," *Augustinian Studies* 26 (1995): 51–79; M. R. Barnes, "Augustine in Contemporary Theology," *Theological Studies* 45 (1995): 237–50. For a reading of Augustine's theology that challenges the view that he "begins" with divine unity, see Lewis Ayres, "'Remember That You Are Catholic' (serm. 52.2): Augustine on the Unity of the Triune God," *Journal of Early Christian Studies* 8, no. 1 (2000): 29–82.

[62]My presentation here follows the detailed analysis in Mattox, *"Defender,"* ch. 3.

[63]Augustine gives classical expression to this widespread conviction in his *De Doctrina Christiana*, 3.5.

"saints' lives."[64] For Luther as much as any of the church fathers, both Abraham and Sarah—along with nearly all the central characters in the Genesis narratives—were paragons of heroic *virtue*. It is important to reiterate that Luther's analyses of the ins and outs of stories like this one were not scratched out with a writing quill within the relaxed confines of his study but were delivered with pathos in the public space of his Wittenberg University classroom, where they were explicitly intended to build up faith in the triune God in young men who aspired to service in the church's public ministry.

Luther read this text very much in concert with the Western catholic tradition as the story of a meeting between Abraham, Sarah, and the Holy Trinity.[65] He did not reject the patristic trinitarian exegesis of this text; nor did he allow it only as a possible figural interpretation of the text. Instead, Luther defended patristic exegesis with vigor and insight and then attempted to set their argument on a more solid foundation. With the "holy fathers," he insisted that the full meaning of the text includes the teaching, if not the proof, of the Holy Trinity. Once again, then, knowledge of God the Holy Trinity is what Scripture gives. As I have tried to show elsewhere, Luther's hagiographical reading of the Old Testament as well as his trinitarian exegesis have their common source in patristic commentary. These elements coalesce with Luther's insights into the meaning of the gospel to produce an interpretation that is at once deeply catholic and authentically "Lutheran." Luther finds in the Old Testament stories of the triune God of grace mercifully at work in the lives of men and women struggling for faith and faithfulness. Put simply, Luther offers a reading of Holy Scripture that is enthusiastically consistent with the moral and theological exegesis of catholic tradition and at the same time expressive of his distinctive understanding of the gospel.

---

[64]The pioneering study of Luther's hagiography of Genesis is Juhani Forsberg, *Das Abrahambild in der Theologie Luthers: Pater Fidei Sanctissimus* (Stuttgart: Franz Steiner Verlag, 1984). On sainthood in the Lutheran tradition, see Robert Kolb, *For All the Saints: Changing Perceptions of Martyrdom and Sainthood in the Lutheran Reformation* (Macon, Ga.: Mercer University Press, 1987). More recently, see Marc Lienhard, "La Sainteté et Les Saints," *Études Théologiques et Religieuses* 72, no. 3 (1997): 375–87.

[65]Pace the argument of Heinrich Bornkamm in his *Luther and the Old Testament*, trans. Eric W. Gritsch and Ruth C. Gritsch (Philadelphia: Fortress Press, 1969), 114–20.

Patristic Readings of the Encounter at the Oaks of Mamre

The earliest Christian interpreters had read the divine appearance at the oaks of Mamre christologically. In his *Dialogue with Trypho*, for example, Justin Martyr proved against his Jewish interlocutor that the three visitors were not merely three angels but Christ in the company of two angels. For Justin, the decisive exegetical factor is the identification elsewhere in the text of a single "angel" as Lord and God. This "angel," he attempted to prove, must have been not only God but also a divine personage distinct from the "Maker and Father of all things."[66] Irenaeus intimated something similar in his *Against Heresies*.[67]

In his *De Trinitate*, Hilary of Poitier (315–367)—to whom Luther refers explicitly in his comments on this text—offered an expansive treatment of the Christian meaning of the appearances of God to the patriarchs. Probing with care these mysterious manifestations of the divine, with the Arian heresy never far out of his sights, Hilary crafted an interpretation of the appearance of the three visitors at the oaks of Mamre as a preincarnate appearance of the Son in the company of two angels. The preeminence of one of the visitors over the other two, Hilary argued, may be derived from Abraham's behavior, for although the patriarch "sees three, [he] worships [only] One, and acknowledges Him as Lord."[68] Later, Jerome referred offhand to Abraham as the "friend of God" who "entertained God and his angels."[69] Elsewhere, in a letter written to Eustochium to console her after the death of her mother, Paula, he told the story of the latter's pilgrimage to the Holy Land, noting that she had visited the "traces of Abraham's oak under which he saw Christ's day and was glad."[70] In Jerome's exegesis, the Johannine reference to Abraham's vision of the "day of Christ" (John 8:56)

---

[66]"Dialogue with Trypho," ch. 56: G. Archambault, *Justin, Dialogue avec Tryphon. Texte grec, traduction française, introduction, notes et index*, Textes et Documents 8,11, 2 vols. (Paris, 1909), 253; ANF 1.223.

[67]*Against Heresies*, 4.VII.4: PG 7.992; ANF 1.470.

[68]*De Trinitate*, book 4, ch. 25: CCSL LXII.128; NPNF2 9.78. Cf. Novatian, who also argued that it was the preincarnate Son who, in the company of two angels, appeared to Abraham. He rejects the theory that it was the Father who appeared with two angels, on grounds that it would be improper for the Father to be manifested in visible form. *De Trinitate*, ch. 18: PL 3.918–22; ANF 5.627–29.

[69]Letter CXXII, "To Rusticus": CSEL LVI.57; NPNF2 6.225.

[70]Letter CVIII, "To Eustochium": CSEL LV.319; NPNF2 6.200.

was fashioned into a hermeneutical key to unlock the text's hidden meaning.

Patristic interpretation took a trinitarian turn in the exegesis of Ambrose. In book 2 of his *On the Decease of His Brother Satyrus*, the bishop expanded on the trinitarian meaning of the text:

> Abraham, ready to receive strangers, faithful towards God, devoted in ministering, quick in his service, saw the Trinity *in a type*; he added religious duty to *hospitality*, when beholding Three he worshipped One, and preserving the distinction of the Persons, yet addressed one Lord, he offered to Three the honor of his gift, while acknowledging one Power. It was not learning but grace which spoke in him, and he believed better what he had not learnt than we who have learnt. No one had falsified the representation of the truth, and so *he sees Three, but worships the Unity*. He brings forth three measures of fine meal, and slays one victim, considering that one sacrifice is sufficient, but a triple gift; one victim, an offering of three.[71]

The key element in Ambrose's interpretation was the analogy he identified among the Trinity itself, the three visitors worshiped as one Lord, and the three loaves and one animal offered by Abraham to his guests. Ambrose also collapsed the christological meaning of the text into the trinitarian one, as the sacrifice prefigured in the "one victim" slain for the occasion was served as an offering to the three.[72] Abraham thus *sees* the Trinity, but only "in a type."

In book 2 of his *De Trinitate*, a treatise Luther and his contemporaries knew well, Augustine took up his former bishop's teaching, defending it grammatically and developing it theologically. Augustine cautiously rebutted the theory of Christ and the two angels, offering in its place the explanation that the three angels appeared as representatives of all three persons of the Holy Trinity. To Augustine, these were the salient facts: (1) the "Lord" Who visits Abraham is announced in the singular; (2) Abraham invites the three in the plural but addresses them in the singular; (3) the Lord speaks to Abraham

---

[71]*De Excessu Fratris sui satyri*, PL 16.1342; NPNF2 10.189–90. Emphasis mine.

[72]Addressing the issue of Abraham's conversations with God, John of Damascus writes, "Abraham did not see the divine nature, for no man has ever yet seen God, but he saw an image of God, and fell down and worshipped." PG 94.1346; ET in *On the Divine Images: Three Apologies against Those Who Attack the Divine Images*, trans. David Anderson (Crestwood: St. Vladimir's Seminary Press, 1980), 80.

in the singular. Since three appeared, Augustine suggested, "why should we not here understand, as visibly intimated by the visible creature, the equality of the Trinity, and one and the same substance [*unam eandemque substantiam*] in three persons."[73] Extending this grammatical argument, Augustine observed that Lot later addresses the two "angels" who journey on to visit him in Sodom with the singular "Lord." Since the text speaks of their being "sent," which he thinks could not properly be predicated of the Father, Augustine surmised that these two were the Son and the Holy Spirit.[74] In book 3, Augustine buttressed his argument theologically, arguing that it is perfectly reasonable to believe that all three persons of the Godhead manifested themselves to the patriarchs of the Old Testament. Admitting that the substance of divinity is in no way changeable and therefore cannot "in its proper self be visible," he argued nevertheless that the appearances of the deity to the patriarchs cannot be confined to the person of the Son. The God Who appeared to Abraham as "three men," therefore, was the Trinity, manifested in three angels.[75]

Luther's Reading

Luther's exegesis of this text shows at once how much he shared with patristic interpreters, particularly Augustine, and demonstrates again how extensively he relied on the fathers. Luther himself suggests this comparison, for he explicitly couches his trinitarian exegesis of this text in the form of a defense of patristic interpretation. In addition to other patristic interpreters, Luther refers to Augustine four times in his exegesis of Genesis 18:1-15, twice in the section devoted to his treatment of the Trinity. He approvingly notes Augustine's stricture against establishing a teaching based only on the figurative reading of a biblical text,[76] and he refers positively to Augustine's notion of the trinity of powers in humankind.

In a short section of his *Luther and the Old Testament* addressed to the problem of the Trinity in the Old Testament, Heinrich Bornkamm argued that Luther "openly agreed with the judgment of the Jewish interpreters, that the true, historical sense

---

[73]*On the Trinity*, II.XI.20: CCSL L.106–7; NPNF1 3.47.
[74]*On the Trinity*, II.XII.21–22: CCSL L.107–9; NPNF1 3.47–48.
[75]*On the Trinity*, III.X.22–25: CCSL L.150–56; NPNF1 3.65–67. Cf. Augustine, *City of God* XVI.29; CCSL 48.533–55.
[76]*De Doctrina Christiana*, III.5ff.: CCSL XXXII.82–83.

of this text knows nothing of the Trinity." Moreover, Bornkamm claimed, Luther renounced as "proof texts those favorite passages of the allegorists," such as Genesis 18.[77] Viewed in the context of the patristic exegetical conversation, however, Luther's examination of the trinitarian meaning and implications of this text proves subtler and more extensive than Bornkamm thought. A careful reading of Luther's argument in its entirety does not support Bornkamm's claims.

First, Luther argues here in favor of the limited use of allegorical interpretation. Alluding to Paul's use of allegory in Galatians 4, he offers several examples of what are easily recognized as "allegories" of the text: according to one, Abraham = God, Sarah = Church, Hagar = Synagogue; according to another, Ishmael = people of the flesh, Isaac = people of the Spirit. However, he does not take the trinitarian interpretation of this text itself as an allegory in the same sense that these are allegories. In other words, he is not content merely to allow that the trinitarian reading is a licit even if historically improper reading of the text. Instead, Luther relates trinitarian interpretation to the "hidden sense" (*occultus sensus*) of the text, a meaning to which the reader is alerted by attending to grammar and typology but that also reveals the truth about what happened at the oaks of Mamre.

Next, Luther deploys three crucial distinctions in defense of the patristic exegesis of this text. The first is the distinction between argument and adornment or, as they were known in Luther's day, between dialectic and rhetoric. This text does not teach the Trinity dialectically, as Luther sees the matter. It does not, in other words, set forth an argument that the one God is three persons. It does, however, add the persuasion of rhetoric to a truth that has already been established dialectically from other texts. Second, as mentioned above, Luther distinguishes between the text's historical meaning (*historica sententia, historicus sensus*) and its hidden meaning (*occultus sensus*).[78] The former has to do with straightforward assertions contained in a text and is useful in argument with the "enemies of the church." The latter relates to a text's implicit meaning, which can

---

[77]Heinrich Bornkamm, *Luther and the Old Testament*, 114–20; here, 114.

[78]WA 43:13; LW 3:194 (on Gen. 18:2-5). Luther's appeal to the "hidden sense" is reminiscent of the glossators' allegorical observation that Abraham "looked up" and then saw the Trinity. *Glossa Ordinaria*, 52. The glossators also cite Gregory the Great's *Moralia in Iob*. See CCSL CXLIII, Liber IX.LXVI, 137ff.

be discerned when the text is read in the light of other clear biblical texts or of doctrines taught in the church on the basis of such clear texts.[79] In this case, the occult meaning clearly leans more in the direction of typology (as with Ambrose, above) than of straightforward allegory.[80] Luther's remarks suggest a correlation between the historical sense and dialectics, and between the hidden sense and rhetoric. The text teaches the historical meaning dialectically, while it teaches the hidden meaning only rhetorically.

Third, Luther distinguishes between what is reasonable and persuasive to those who stand *inside* the household of faith, and what is reasonable and persuasive to those *outside* the faith.[81] A text like this, Luther complains, is not of the right sort to carry forth "into battle" with those outside the faith in order to *prove* the Holy Trinity. Instead, it is a text whose hidden meaning—which is no less true for being hidden—can be known to the faithful, and it should be preached and taught as trinitarian, even if its historical meaning should not be placed in the first line of defense against those outside the faith.

Armed with these distinctions, Luther sets out to defend the patristic trinitarian interpretation of this text. His defense of the fathers begins with the concession that they were sometimes guilty of blurring the distinctions between dialectic and rhetoric, and between insiders and outsiders to the faith. Cyprian and Hilary, he admits, "cited many things with little aptness" (*parum apte citata*).[82] "A good and pious spirit"[83] motivated them, however, and these "holy fathers" (*sancti patres*) were right in stating that because God appeared in these three persons, Abraham "had a knowledge of the Trinity from this appearance" (*cognovisse ex hac apparitione Trinitatem*).[84] Their claim for Abraham's explicit knowledge of the Trinity, while sound, was not based on the dialectical argument of

---

[79]WA 43:14; LW 3:194 (on Gen. 18:2-5).
[80]The distinction between typology and allegory is problematic. The greater the care with which one attempts to distinguish the two, the more the line between them seems to blur. On this problem in recent research, see Elizabeth Clark, *Reading Renunciation: Asceticism and Scripture in Early Christianity* (Princeton: Princeton University Press, 1999), 70–78.
[81]WA 43:11–12; LW 3:191 (on Gen. 18:2-5).
[82]WA 43:11; LW 3:191 (on Gen. 18:2-5). Luther seems to have had in mind Novatian's *De Trinitate*, attributed variously to Tertullian or Cyprian, and Hilary's *De Trinitate*. Cf. Delius, *Die Quellen*, 36–37.
[83]WA 43:11; LW 3:191 (on Gen. 18:2-5).
[84]WA 43:14; LW 3:195 (on Gen. 18:2-5).

the text. Instead, it is a rhetorical argument made possible when the text is viewed in the light of Christ. "Let us defend our doctors [*doctores nostros*],"[85] Luther exhorts his students.

Although Luther finds some of the fathers' Old Testament proofs for the Trinity careless or overdrawn, he is nonetheless convinced that in substance their argument was right. After all, he claims, the fathers never argued for a strict identification of these three visitors with the three persons of the Holy Trinity.[86] To do so, he points out, would be like identifying the three persons with the three "distinct species" present at the baptism of Christ, that is, the second person with the humanity of Jesus, the first person with the heavenly voice, and the third person with the dove. The fathers did no such thing, he observes. In fact, they did little more than draw out the implications from an intriguing set of coincidences: the Lord appeared to Abraham in three, not in four or two; although three appeared, only one spoke; and although Abraham saw three, he adored one.[87] Echoing Augustine, Luther says that the coincidence of these facts suggests that there is somehow a Trinity (*aliqua Trinitas*) in God, although he admits that without the corroboration of other firm and certain texts, it would be impossible on this basis alone to build a doctrine of the Trinity.[88] Of course, the idea that belief in the doctrine of the Trinity could or should be bracketed out of the interpretation of a text like this is utterly foreign to Luther, so his admission means only that when one initiates the process of constructing a biblical proof for the Trinity, this is not the text with which to begin.

As Luther reads the text, the knowledge that they were encountering the trinitarian reality of God dawned on Abraham and Sarah slowly. Their initial hospitality toward the three strangers was not motivated by an explicit recognition that the strangers represented the Holy Trinity. At first, Luther admits, neither Abraham nor Sarah recognized that the Trinity was somehow "in" these three. However, on the basis of Christ's assertion in John 8:56 that Abraham "saw the day of Christ," Luther argues, "he saw also His divine nature. But if he saw His divine nature, this could not have happened without a knowledge of the Trinity."[89] Mysteriously, in the encounter

---

[85]WA 43:13; LW 3:194 (on Gen. 18:2-5).
[86]WA 43:12–13; LW 3:193 (on Gen. 18:2-5).
[87]LW 43:13; LW 3:194 (on Gen. 18:2-5).
[88]Ibid.
[89]WA 43:13; LW 3:194 (on Gen. 18:2-5).

with these three visitors, Abraham and Sarah had a prophetic vision of the truth now known to every Christian. If one knows God, if one encounters the divine nature, then by definition one knows and encounters the triune God.

Thus, Luther asserts that the holy fathers did not speak stupidly (*crasse*) about this manifestation of the Trinity, because it was God's wish "to appear to Abraham in a trinity of angels."[90] The text magnifies the virtue of Abraham, who *by faith* discerned the true identity of his "visitor" only after he had extended hospitality to him as a stranger. Abraham *knew* that "he had the God of heaven and earth as a guest,"[91] and as Abraham and Sarah came to understand the divinity hidden under the human (or angelic) form of their "visitors," so the reader's faith should understand the divine truth hidden in the patriarchal history. For Luther, the true, historical sense of this text cannot be separated from the substance of faith by which the Christian reader, like Abraham and Sarah, sees things as they really are. The hidden sense thus holds the key to the right understanding of the historical sense, that is, to knowing what really happened. In sum, for Luther much as for Augustine, the text narrates an appearance to holy Abraham and Sarah of the Holy Trinity in the form of three angels: Abraham and Sarah saw three but worshiped them as one. Luther's assertion that patristic expositors themselves did not strictly identify the three visitors with the three persons of the Godhead rings true to the actual content of patristic exegesis, and his elucidation of the hidden meaning of the text as it may be known to the Christian is perfectly consistent with patristic exposition.

4. The Substance of Scripture: Old Man Luther's Parting Exegetical Advice

Luther also addressed the topic of the Trinity in the Old Testament aggressively in two important but comparatively little-known treatises written while he was lecturing through Genesis: "The Three Symbols of the Christian Faith" (1538) and "On the Last Words of David" (1543).[92] In "The Three Symbols," Luther listed several texts from Genesis to demonstrate his assertion that the "prophets

---

[90]Ibid. Luther qualifies his own opinion as follows: "It is my opinion that these angels had assumed the form of men and were not the Trinity in essence." WA 43:41; LW 3:232 (on Gen. 18:20-26).
[91]WA 43:15; LW 3:196 (on Gen. 18:6-8).
[92]See WA 50:262–83 (LW 34:201–29); WA 54:28–100 (LW 15:265–352).

in the Old Testament also understood this article of faith [that is, the Trinity]."[93] The plural name for God (*Elohim*) found in Genesis 1, he argued, demonstrates the plurality of persons in the Godhead, as do the plural verbs in Genesis 1:26.[94] Genesis 18 also appeared prominently in this treatise, and Luther affirmed that "the text says clearly that this vision or manifestation was God himself" so that Abraham "well recognized the Holy Trinity."[95]

Written five years later, "On the Last Words of David" extends Luther's argument for the trinitarian exegesis of the Old Testament, finding the trinity not only in David's "last will and testament" but also in a diverse collection of Old Testament texts, including Isaiah, Daniel, numerous psalms, and, perhaps most prominently, 1 Chronicles 17. In addition, Luther answers a theoretical objection to his exegesis on the grounds that the "holy fathers" did not find the Trinity in David's last words. First, he appeals to the restoration of the Hebrew language in his own day, excusing the fathers because they lacked proper access to the real riches of the Old Testament. In addition, he allows that apart from the noetic advantage of Christian faith, one might read David's last words as words merely about David rather than words about the Holy Trinity and Jesus Christ. Illumined by the New Testament, however, the Christian exegete is enabled to look the Old Testament "straight in the eye" (*recht unter die augen*), finding there the purest truths of the Christian faith.[96]

Luther was convinced that the knowledge of God given in authentic Christian faith could not be bracketed out of properly Christian biblical study, reflection, and exegesis. To put the matter in the terms Luther himself often used, the "substance of Holy Scripture" (*res Scripturae sacrae*) holds the key to the "words of Holy Scripture" (*verba Scripturae sacrae*). The strength of Luther's conviction that the substance of Scripture should exercise a regulative function over any of the particular words of Scripture seems to have grown over

---

[93] WA 50:278; LW 34:223.

[94] WA 50:279; LW 34:223. Note Luther's trinitarian hermeneutical advice that where Scripture speaks of God as if there were two, the exegete may assume the passage indicates the entire Trinity: "Aber wo du in der schrifft findest, das Gott von Gott, als werens zwo Personen, redet. Da magstu kuenlich auff gruenden, das daselbs drey Personen in der Gottheit angezeigt werden" ("On the Last Words of David," WA 54:39; LW 15:280).

[95] WA 50:280: "Darumb hat Abraham die heilige dreyfaltigkeit hie wol erkand, wie Christus spricht Joh. 8: Abraham hat meinen tag gesehen." Cf. LW 34:225.

[96] WA 54:45; LW 15:287.

the course of his career, particularly after he had observed some of the exegetical trajectories emerging among the South German and Swiss Reformers.

"On the Last Words of David" drew attention to a text very few today, or even in Luther's day, would have chosen as the basis for defending the trinitarian exegesis of Scripture. Seasoned by more than three decades in the classroom, most of it teaching Old Testament, Luther chose this text because he thought its rich potential for urging the catholic doctrines of God and Christ had been insufficiently recognized.[97] Here, in Luther's own translation, is 2 Samuel 23:1-3: "These are the last words of David. The oracle of David, the son of Jesse. The oracle of the man who is assured of the Messiah of the God of Jacob, the sweet psalmist of Israel. 'The Spirit of the Lord has spoken by me, His Word is upon my tongue. The God of Israel has talked to me, the Rock of Israel has spoken, He who rules justly over men, He who rules in the fear of God.'"[98]

Announced at the end of the virulently anti-Jewish "Vom Schem Hamphoras und vom Geschlecht Christi" (also written in 1543), "On the Last Words of David" contained a number of unflattering references to the Jews and some heavy-handed arguments against their exegesis. Thus, the treatise has long been classed among the elder Reformer's notorious anti-Jewish writings. There is no question that Luther wished in the most emphatic terms to reject Jewish readings of important Old Testament texts, much as he had insisted in his regrettable treatise "Against the Jews and Their Lies" (1542). Nevertheless, "On the Last Words of David" did not at all take the form of an extended argument with the Jews. Instead, it offered one example after another of how to discern the authentic grammatical and theological meaning of the Old Testament as Luther understood it. In short, it modeled the way Luther believed Christian exegetes informed by the latest developments in biblical studies ought to read the text.

Luther among His Predecessors and Peers

Before turning to Luther's treatise, we will find it instructive to cast a brief backward glance at premodern Christian interpretation of

---

[97] For an intriguing reading of Luther's interpretation that stresses its speculative elements, see Christine Helmer, "Luther's Trinitarian Hermeneutic and the Old Testament," *Modern Theology* 18, no. 1 (January 2002): 49–73.

[98] I have slightly altered here the LW translation. See WA 54:16–100; LW 15:265–352.

this text. Did Luther follow the church fathers in his exegesis of 2 Samuel 23 as he did in Genesis 18? Is this another case of Luther's building on the exegetical foundation of patristic trinitarianism? So far as I have found, none of the church fathers had attempted to read this text in such an expansively trinitarian way as Luther. Of course, many of the biblical intertexts on which he relied to support and develop his position had long been read as supporting the trinitarian faith. For example, 2 Samuel 7, which recounted at length the divine promise of a Messiah, had been mentioned prominently in Augustine's *City of God* (*Civitas Dei*, XVII.8–10). Few among the church fathers seem to have turned, however, to 2 Samuel 23, and the situation was much the same among the medievals.

Thus, the compilers of the *Glossa Ordinaria* left the text almost entirely uncommented, noting dryly that it was the last "song of David" and observing that the mention of the sunrise in verse 5 prefigured Christ's rising from the dead.[99] Nicholas of Lyra, whose exegesis we can reasonably expect Luther to have consulted,[100] discerned christological resonances in this text.[101] But instead of following them up, he digressed into a brief discussion of grace, observing somewhat laconically that the promise of a Messiah through David's posterity was given on account of God's liberality, not human merit.[102] Alone among the medievals, so far as I have found, the "Ecstatic Doctor," Denis the Carthusian, found here at least an oblique reference to the Trinity.[103] Mention of the "Spirit" and the "Lord" in such close proximity brought to Denis's mind a central principle of

---

[99]*Biblia Latina cum Glossa Ordinaria*, vol. 2 (Strassburg: Adolph Rusch, 1480/81; facsimile reprint edition, Brepols-Turnhout, 1992), 84, interlinear comment on 2 Samuel 23:1. Hugh of St. Cher also explored any theological implications in this text. See *Hugonis de Sancto Charo Primi Cardinalis Ordinis Praedicatorum*, Tomus Primus (Venetiis, apud Nicolaum Pezzana, 1732), 262r.

[100]Note Luther's own remarks confirming his consultation of Lyra, WA 54:25ff.; LW 15:336.

[101]I cite Lyra from the *Biblia Sacra cum postilla Nicolai de Lyra* (Venice: Renner of Heilbrunn, 1482). Here, page ffv, comments "h" and "l," on verse 1. I use here the Douay-Rheims translation of the Vulgate text of 2 Samuel 23:1. The Latin text (the same in Lyra and Douay-Rheims) is a bit awkward to bring into English: "dixit vir cui constitutum est de christo Dei Iacob." For Luther's own remarks on this translation difficulty, see WA 54:32.15ff.; LW 15:272.

[102]Lyra, ffv, comment "x," on verse 4.

[103]*Doctoris Ecstatici D. Dionysii Cartusiani Opera Omnia*, Tomus III: In Josue, Judices, Ruth, I-III Regum, (Monstrolii: 1897), 562: ". . . facta est revelatio atque promissio de incarnatione, adventu et mysteriis Messiae, Salvatoris mundi, qui est Christus Dei, unctus a Deo Patre omni charismate Spiritus Sancti plenissime, juxta illud in Psalmo . . ." Denis cites Psalm 44:8 and Isaiah 61:1 in support of his point.

classical trinitarian theology, that is, that the works of the Trinity toward the outside are indivisible. Although he did not spell out the significance of that principle for understanding the biblical text, he at least implied that where the Spirit and the Word were active, there all three persons could and should be found.[104]

Luther's Reading

Luther seems to have been well aware of the dimly recognized but as yet unexplored christological and trinitarian potential of this text in the antecedent tradition. Indeed, he said in several places that he knew his "new" grammatical interpretation went beyond the interpretations of the "holy fathers" and the medievals.[105] Here, then, was the point the old man was trying to make when he drew attention to this overlooked text, namely, to show how the sixteenth-century revolution in Hebrew studies could be used to buttress the properly Christian reading of the Bible as it had been pioneered by Luther's catholic predecessors.[106] To accomplish that goal, Luther believed he had to refute the "judaizing" interpretations he saw developing among Christian expositors.[107] Finding Moses "to be a Christian," Luther explicitly lumped together with the Jews those Christian Hebraists who failed sufficiently to factor

[104]Ibid., 562: "*Spiritus Domini*, videlicet Spiritus Sanctus, *locutus est per me*, tanquam per organum animatum et intellectuale, quoniam ex divina revelatione pronuntiavi Christi mysteria, et alia multa future ac divina praeconia. . . . *Et sermo ejus per linguam meam*, prolatus est, ita quod verba me sunt sermo ipsius, cujus directione locutus sum, et qui specialem gratiam componendi psalmos, dulciterque psallendi praestitit mihi, ut dicere queam: Dominus dedit mihi linguam eruditam. Denique Sermo Dei increatus, videlicet Verbum Patris aeternum, per os et linguam David locutus est. Nam opera superbeatissimae Trinitatis sunt indivisa. De quo sermone ad Hebraeos asseritur: Vivus est sermo Dei et efficax."

[105]WA 54:45.2–3; LW 15:287: "Wie gehets zu, das wedeer die heiligen Veter, noch kein ander Lerer, solchs gesehen oder jemals gerueret haben, und jr newen Jungen Ebresiten habts nu erst ersehen?"

[106]For a critical assessment of the use of Hebrew studies in support of Christian exegesis in Luther's Wittenberg, see Jerome Friedman, "Protestants, Jews, and Jewish Sources," in *Piety, Politics, and Ethics: Reformation Studies in Honor of George Wolfgang Forell*, ed. Carter Lindberg (Kirksville, Mo.: Sixteenth-Century Journal Publishers, 1984), 139–56. Friedman is particularly disparaging of the work of Luther's colleague and former student Johannes Forster, whose *Dictionarium Hebraicum Novum* attempted to read Christology into the grammar of the Old Testament.

[107]On Luther's concern with "judaizing" exegesis, note the helpful work of Stephen Burnett, "The Significance of the Biblical Languages at the University of Wittenberg" (Heidelberg: Ninth International Congress for Luther Research, 1997).

Christian truth into their interpretation: "All else, whatever Jews, Hebraists, and anybody else may babble against this to make it agree with their stippled, tormented, and coerced grammar, we must certainly consider sheer lies."[108] These allegedly false interpreters comprise those many "wiseacres [*kluegel*] who claim a mastery of the Hebrew tongue,"[109] and they include in their number "both Jews and Hebraists."[110]

Indeed, the prospect of the widespread Christian adoption of this new exegesis troubled Luther so much that he thought it would be better if the church had only Jerome's Vulgate than to endure the confusion caused by numerous, substantially different "grammatical" readings of the Hebrew text.[111] Instead of simply giving up the game and returning to the time-honored text, however, Luther argued for a more authentically Christian translation and interpretation of the text. "We Christians," he claimed, "have the meaning and import [*synn und verstand*] of the Bible because we have the New Testament, that is, Jesus Christ."[112]

Implicitly recognizing that one might more reasonably expect a trinitarian reading of the Old Testament from a Christian than from a Jew, Luther aimed his criticisms directly at "the old and the new Hebraists, who follow the rabbis altogether too strictly," and he included both Lyra and himself in the number of those who at one time or another had done so.[113] Those who persist in such interpretation, he complained, are "saucy prigs who make bold to instruct the Holy Spirit."[114] They "insist on imitating the Jews."[115] Arguing for his interpretation of Exodus 33:19, Luther staked out his ground over against both Jewish and Christian interpreters: "It is indifferent to me if rabbis or contentious Hebraists [*die Rabinen oder zenckissche*

---

[108]WA 54:55.4; LW 15:299. Luther's reference is to John 5:46: "Moses wrote of me."

[109]WA 54:28.12; LW 15:267.

[110]WA 54:46.2; LW 15:288. Burnett says that Sebastian Muenster figures prominently among the targets of Luther's criticism. According to Friedman, in the mid-1530s, "reports of sabbatarianism in Austria and Moravia led Luther to believe that Jews were corrupting the new reformed Church. Melanchthon and Calvin too expressed the same sentiments and fears." Friedman, "Protestants, Jews, and Jewish Sources," 145.

[111]WA 54:30.30–31; LW 15:270.

[112]WA 54:29.3–4; LW 15:268.

[113]WA 54:30.13–14, 26; LW 15:268.

[114]WA 54:39.6–7; LW 15:280.

[115]WA 54:41.37; LW 15:283.

Ebreisten] do not accept this."[116] For Luther, the Trinity in the Old Testament had become the dividing line between him and not just the Jews but the false Christian interpreters as well. "The devil," he fumed, "is their god and father, the father of all lies."[117]

That bellicose assertion notwithstanding, Luther's tone in opposition to the Christian Hebraists was comparatively mild. This rhetorical posture seems to confirm what was suggested above, that is, that Luther was serious about trying to turn the course of sixteenth-century Christian Hebraism in a more catholic direction. His anti-Jewish rhetoric thus functioned, at least in this case, as a rhetorical device that offered at least a measure of relief to Christian readers, presumably shaming them but at the same time making it less psychologically difficult to repent of their past errors and come over to Luther's way of thinking.[118] The constructive purpose that motivated Luther's destructive rhetoric, in short, was to exhort and encourage his Protestant fellows to recommit themselves to the catholic interpretation of the Old Testament.

The Trinity in 2 Samuel 23

As the Weimar editor, F. Cohrs, points out, Luther's dogmatic interest in 2 Samuel 23 as a potential basis for defending catholic teaching had been sharpened in part by continuing translation work carried out following publication of the 1541 recension of the "Luther Bible" and in preparation for the 1545 edition, the last published during his lifetime.[119] This interest took shape within a context in which Luther had reached deep convictions regarding the trinitarian and christological significance of such texts as 1 Chronicles 17:7 and Genesis 4:1, as well as the royal psalms (particularly 110). In these exegeses, as Christine Helmer points out, the crucial factor was

---

[116]WA 54:80.20; LW 15:329. Cf. his argument for his interpretation of Genesis 4:1. WA 54:73.33: "Eben so musten auch alle ander Ebreisten bekennen, wenn sie denn text recht ansehen und hielten, das dieser Weibs samen Jehova, das ist Gott und Mensch were . . ." Cf. LW 15:321.

[117]WA 54:68.32–33; LW 15:315. Cf. the strong rhetorical posture in WA 54:93.23–25; LW 15:344: "Therefore it behooves us to recover Scripture from them as from *public thieves* wherever grammar warrants this and harmonizes [*reimet*] with the New Testament." Emphasis mine.

[118]For John Calvin's attempt to chart a *via media* here, see David L. Puckett, *John Calvin's Exegesis of the Old Testament* (Louisville: Westminster John Knox, 1995).

[119]WA 54:18–19.

Luther's understanding of the semantic referent of the divine names, especially YHWH and Adonoi.[120]

Luther's study of Genesis 4:1, for instance, had convinced him that Eve's words reported in the text referred clearly and directly to the promised Messiah. In itself, this was a new conclusion made possible only by a grammatical analysis of the Hebrew text. As recently as his own revision of the Vulgate text (published in 1529), Luther had chosen the genitive to translate the final crucial clause in the words spoken by Eve at the birth of Cain: "I have gotten the man *Domini*."[121] In the 1545 recension of the *Deutsche Bibel*, Luther still translated this with the genitive; but he chose the accusative when he explained its proper meaning in the margin: "I have gotten the Man the Lord, the Seed [*Ich habe den Man den HERRN, den Samen*]." Moreover, in a lengthy examination of this text in "On the Last Words of David," Luther argued vehemently that the Hebrew article and noun that appear at the end of this sentence, "YHWH," should be translated not in the genitive but in the accusative. This locution, he claimed, should be understood as a clear indication that Eve believed she had given birth to the Messiah: "I have gotten the man, Jehovah."[122]

That exegetical solution fit well into the general translational schema Luther had adopted as a solution to the problem of the divine names.[123] It also aptly symbolizes the way Luther thought the new biblical studies could complement and deepen traditional catholic readings of Scripture. Catholic expositors had long held that chapter 3 of Genesis teaches that God promised victory over the serpent through the "seed of the woman," that is, the Messiah.[124] Luther's intensification of that traditional exegetical conviction was to show how Eve and her husband had been enlivened by faith in that promise from the very beginning, even to the point of somewhat overoptimistically identifying their firstborn with the promised

---

[120]Helmer, "Luther's Trinitarian Hermeneutic," 56–59.

[121]WADB 5:16.2.

[122]WADB 8:47. To be sure, Luther had long since reached this exegetical conclusion. Cf. WA 54:71.33, 73.24; LW 15:319, 321.

[123]In his German Bible, Luther translated the Hebrew *Elohim* with the German *Gott*; "YHWH Elohim" with "Gott der HERR"; "YHWH" with "HERR"; and "Adonai" with "HERR."

[124]For the history of interpretation of Genesis 3:15, see Tibor Gallus, "*Der Nachkomme der Frau*" *(Gen 3, 15) in der Altlutheranischen Schriftauslegung* (Klagenfurt: Carinthia, 1964).

Messiah. The exegete can perceive this identification, so Luther, in the Scripture's use of the accusative case with the term *YHWH* for "Lord" in Genesis 4:1.

Similarly, Luther argued that the interpretive key to 2 Samuel 23 consisted in properly identifying the divine persons mentioned in verses 2 and 3: "the Spirit of the Lord," "the God of Israel," and "the Rock of Israel."[125] However, he did not base his trinitarian interpretation of these names solely or even primarily on a grammatical analysis of the Hebrew text. To the contrary, he recognized that a reasonable interpreter shaped generically by any of what we today might call the "religions of Abraham" could miss this text's trinitarian significance, quite naturally assuming that the terms *God* and *Rock* and *Ruler* refer "to God in one person in a superfluity of words."[126] Against this admittedly more natural reading of the text, he argued that the Holy Spirit here introduces in the words *God* and *Rock* both the Father and the Son. The advance in Hebrew studies that Luther wanted to retain, in spite of the difficulties these studies admittedly caused, consisted in the grammatical analysis that showed that the diversity of divine names used here and elsewhere in the Hebrew text should not be understood as instances of a "superfluity of words" but as precious textual intimations—clear to the Christian—of the triune God.

Although Luther offered some comparatively flimsy grammatical evidences to support his conclusions relative to 2 Samuel 23, the decisive arguments were all theological and intertextual, including appeals to the New Testament. He seems to have been doing something quite similar to what we saw in the case of Genesis 18, that is, drawing out the text's hidden, rhetorical meaning as opposed to its dialectical teaching. Thus, in the treatise itself, Luther moved rather quickly from commentary on the text itself to analyses of other texts whose trinitarian significance had already been somewhat better recognized. In his review of the biblical evidence for the Trinity and the

---

[125]WA 54:35.28–30; LW 15:276ff. Luther's text reads: "Es hat der Gott Israel zu mir gesprochen, Der Hort Israel hat geredt, der gerechte Herrscher unter den menschen, Der Herrscher in der furcht Gottes."

[126]WA 54:37.6–7: "Und denckt nicht anders, es sey alles von Gott als von einer person geredt, mit vielen ubrigen worten." LW 15:278. Cf. WA 54:48.28–30: "Hie stoesset sich nu fraw kluglinne, die Vernunfft, die zehen mal Weiser ist, denn Gott selbs, und fragt: Wie kan Gott seine ewige Gewalt von sich einem andern geben?" The LW translator inexplicably renders "fraw kluglinne" with the masculine English "Mr. Smart Aleck." LW 15:292.

two natures in Christ, Luther ranged widely across the Testaments, from Isaiah to Psalm 2, Philippians 2, 2 Samuel 7, 1 Chronicles 17, John 1/Genesis 1, Luke 3, Colossians 1–2, and Daniel 7. In these texts, Luther found confirmation of his reading of 2 Samuel 23. The point of the Scriptures as a whole—what others might have called the *scopus Scripturae sacrae*—thus provided the theological framework within which he carried out his analysis of the grammar of the text. "All points to the Son"; everything "is pure Christ."[127]

As he worked his way through these texts, Luther commented at length on the subtle ins and outs of catholic trinitarianism, employing to good effect the conceptual tools developed in patristic and medieval tradition. In one rather lengthy section, for instance, he examined the question of whether the "Our Father" is addressed to the person of the Father or to the divine essence itself. In answer, he invoked the same trinitarian principle mentioned earlier by Denis. "The works of the Trinity to the outside are indivisible," he noted. Therefore, "the worship of the Trinity *from the outside*" is also the undivided worship of the one God.[128] Divine paternity in relation to the creation, moreover, may be predicated not only of the Father but also of the Son, of the Spirit, or even of the divine majesty as such. The "Our Father" is therefore addressed to the one God, both as to each of the divine persons and as to the undivided divinity itself.

To put this in modern terms, Luther sees the creation as the result of the "common action" of the tripersonal God, even if it is rightly appropriated to the person of the Father. Luther's deft employment of the trinitarian appropriations makes it clear once again that he utilized traditional methods of trinitarian analysis, arrived at more or less traditional trinitarian conclusions, and encouraged his readers to adopt them as well. In addition, Luther laid down a general principle for Old Testament exegesis, insisting that wherever two of the divine persons are mentioned, "you may boldly assume that three Persons of the Godhead are there indicated."[129] Proving himself consistent in the matter, in his interpretation of the texts examined in this treatise Luther consistently inserted the Spirit wherever he believed he could

---

[127] WA 54:88.11–12; LW 15:338, 339.

[128] WA 54:65.23–24; LW 15:311. Luther cites the principle in Latin: "Quia opera trinitatis ad extra sunt indivisa, Sic cultus Trinitatis ab extra est indivisus." Emphasis mine.

[129] WA 54:39.8–10: "Aber wo du in der schrifft findest, das Gott von Gott, als werens zwo Personen, redet. Da magstu kuenlich auff gruenden, das daselbs drey Personen in der Gottheit angezeigt werden." Cf. LW 15:280.

discern distinct references to the Father and the Son. Thus, for example, when the Father and the Son are spoken of without mention of the Spirit, the Spirit should be recognized as the speaker.[130]

Finally, it is crucial to note Luther's stance in relation to the antecedent exegetical tradition. He by no means intended to posture himself here as an exegetical innovator. While he could not cite the church fathers explicitly on 2 Samuel 23, he nevertheless attempted to take them with him theologically, claiming kinship with their faith tradition and at the same time vindicating medieval trinitarianism. The "dear fathers" (liebe Veter) he mentioned to support his case included Augustine, St. Anthony, Ambrose, Sedulius Scotus, Gregory I, Prudentius, Hilary, Cyril, and Athanasius.[131] "We have precious books on this subject by St. Augustine, Hilary, and Cyril at our disposal," Luther wrote, adding that "this article of faith [i.e., the doctrine of the Trinity] remained pure in the papacy and among the scholastic theologians, and we have no quarrel with them on that score."[132]

However, even the witness of men of heroic faith could not serve as the foundation for Luther's trinitarian reading of the Old Testament. Nor could the sheer authority of the church impose that reading, as it were, from outside the community of faithful readers— and still less from a position of authority over the word of God.[133] Instead, the faith given in holy baptism, the faith by which alone the trinitarian God is truly known, this faith enables the exegete rightly

---

[130]See, e.g., WA 54:39.14–16 (LW 15:280); WA 54:46.28–30 (LW 15:289); WA 54:48.19–20 (LW 15:291); WA 54:53.17–18 (LW 15:297); and so forth.

[131]WA 54:56.4; LW 15:300.

[132]WA 54:64.19–21: "Und ist solcher artickel im Papstum und bey den Schultheologen rein blieben, das wir mit inen darueber keinen zanck haben." Trans. LW 15:310. Hilary, Augustine, and Cyril are commended for their treatment of John 1. On these issues, one may consult Pekka Karkkainen, Luthers trinitarische Theologie des Heiligen Geistes, (Mainz: Verlag Philip von Zabern, 2005); see also Simo Knuuttila and Risto Saarinen, "Innertrinitarische Theologie in der Scholastik und bei Luther," in Caritas Dei: Beiträge zum Verständnis Luthers und der gegenwärtige Ökumene, ed. Oswald Bayer, Robert W. Jenson and Simo Knuuttila, (Helsinki: Luther Agricola Gesellschaft, 1997), 243–64.

[133]Luther criticized sixteenth-century Catholic trinitarian exegesis of the Old Testament (particularly that of Johannes Eck) because Catholic exegetes defended trinitarian theology not from Scripture but on the basis of the teaching authority of the church. Luther saw excessive reliance on the church's authority in this matter as playing into the hands of such critics as Servetus, who had rejected the Trinity in part because he believed that the doctrine had not been articulated until the fourth century. On this issue, see Christine Helmer, "Luther's Trinitarian Hermeneutic and the Old Testament," Modern Theology 18:1 (January 2002): 49–73.

to perceive the mysteries inscribed in the *verba* of the holy text. The fathers, then, are "dear fathers" precisely because they read the Scriptures with that same faith, while scriptural exegesis remains a task given to the people of faith, that is, the church.

5. Conclusion: The Substance of Faith, the Substance of Holy Scripture

In the end, then, Luther's trinitarian reading of the Old Testament as found in "On the Last Words of David" was grounded not in grammatical or historical interpretation but, as suggested above, in a distinctive use of the *regula fidei*, that is, in the exegetical application of the faith that grasps and knows the triune God, the very same faith Luther had sought to instill and encourage through his Large Catechism. This distinctive "rule of faith" consists not in an external list of theological truths on the basis of which one ought to interpret the Scriptures but in the simultaneous realities of the God Who is known and the act of faith in which God is known. These realities are given and summarized precisely in the creed. The creed itself is the *res* that controls the understanding of the *verba*, for right interpretation depends in the first place on the right knowledge of the God revealed in the words of Scripture.[134] The faith given in the church in the sacrament of baptism, in other words, is intrinsic to properly Christian exegesis. Indeed, Luther spoke harshly of exegetes who, apparently lacking this faith, could see the "letters" (*Buchstabe*) of the text but could not read "what they give" (*was sie geben*). These "illiterate," he complained, "cannot know or understand what Moses, the prophets, and the psalms are saying, what true faith is, what the Ten Commandments purport, what tradition and story [*die Exempel und Historien*] teach and prove."[135]

At the same time, however, Luther wanted to put the best of the new scholarship to work in support of a robustly Christian reading of the Old Testament. The point of his argument, at least insofar as it was directed at Christian expositors, had to do with the fate and ultimate meaning of the emerging discipline of Hebrew studies for the understanding of the Christian Bible. Luther believed that the truth of Christian faith as known through Word and Sacrament was itself the key to rightly understanding the truth that could be

---

[134]For an interesting further example of Luther's invocation of this rule, one may consult Mattox, "*Defender,*" 165–69.
[135]WA 54:30; LW 15:269.

found through the rapidly developing science of grammatical biblical exposition. Unlike some other sixteenth-century interpreters, then, Luther could never content himself to find and defend an irreducible minimum of clear and incontrovertible texts in support of central Christian claims. To the contrary, he wanted to show that the truth of the Nicene faith had been inscribed far and wide into every letter of Holy Scripture, and to insist that the explicit recognition of this truth should illuminate and inform every authentically Christian act of biblical interpretation.

The dynamic at work in the background of this treatise—the one that made necessary Luther's attempt to reinforce traditional Christian readings of the Old Testament—was what David Steinmetz has called the "destabilizing effect" of humanist biblical study in the Reformation era on previously settled exegetical issues. "On the Last Words of David" reveals an elder Luther ill at ease in the rapidly shifting exegetical world he had helped to create. Again, it really is a shock to see this accomplished biblical translator openly suggest that with the proliferation of faulty translations, the church would be better off with only Jerome's Vulgate—the position, it should be noted, adopted only two years later in the decree on Scripture at the Council of Trent. Nevertheless, Luther counseled not a retreat to the presumed securities of the old text but the vigorous application of Christian faith to the problem of translating and interpreting the Scriptures anew. We miss the point of his continuing appeal to Scripture "alone" as a theological court of last resort if we hear it as an appeal to the Scriptures as understood apart from the traditions of living Christian faith or, for that matter, outside the *mater ecclesia* within which faith itself is imparted through Word and Sacrament. Once again, the knowledge of God given and received in the church is at the same time the foundation and the goal of any properly Christian reading of the Scriptures, the Old Testament together with the New.

CHAPTER TWO

Luther's Late Trinitarian Disputations
Semantic Realism and the Trinity

Dennis Bielfeldt

Here, in fact, reason, corrupted by original sin, must be taken captive; moreover, it must be extinguished, with its own light and wisdom, through the obedience of faith.

MARTIN LUTHER, *PROMOTIONSDISPUTATION*
OF ERASMUS ALBERUS, 1543[1]

---

[1]WA 39 II, 253:9–11.

1. Luther, Theological Semantics, and Ontological Questions

My initial reading of Luther occurred at age thirteen when I encountered the Small Catechism for the first time. I readily admit that I was then decidedly pre-Kantian in my philosophical presuppositions. As a "precritical" thinker, I assumed (though could not articulate) a *realist semantics* with respect to Luther's theological language.[2] For example, I believed that the word *God* actually referred to a supreme being having a triune nature and that this being was externally, causally related to physical and mental actualizations within His creation. In other words, I thought that God could and did bring about events that would not have been brought about without His agency, and that the bringing about of these events did not change His essence—that is, God would still have been God even if He had not created the particular world He created.[3]

Because I thought that there was an entity to which "God" referred, and because I believed that this bearer had particular monadic properties—I was told in confirmation class that He had omniscience, omnipotence, and omnipresence—and because I considered that the divine entity also possessed certain relational properties (for instance, the divine entity was causally related to the universe as creator to creature), I supposed that sentences that correctly specified existing theological states of affairs were true, while those asserting nonexistent theological states of affairs were false. Furthermore, I assumed that no empirical methods could ascertain the truth of these statements. (I had learned that we are justified in making claims about God only insofar as those claims can be substantiated

---

[2]Minimally, we can regard realism as concerning a class of statements rather than a class of entities. See Michael Dummett, *Truth and Other Enigmas* (Cambridge: Harvard University Press, 1978), 146: "I shall take as my preferred characterization of a dispute between realists and anti-realists one which represents it as relating, not to a class of entities or a class of terms, but to a class of statements, which may be, e.g., statements about the physical world, statements about mental events, processes or states, mathematical statements, statements in the past tense, statements in the future tense, etc. . . . Realism I characterize as the belief that statements of the disputed class possess an objective truth-value, independently of our means of knowing it: they are true or false in virtue of a reality existing independently of us." A realist theological semantics thus claims that statements about God have a truth-value apart from our knowledge of them.

[3]At that time, I regarded God's action as both *sufficient* and *necessary* for bringing about the universe. I thought it impossible were God to act and the universe not to come into being, or the universe to come into being anyway and God not to act.

on the basis of God's biblical revelation.) I also thought that God's revelation in Scripture *did not change* the being of God. Simply put, I thought theological statements were true or false, despite the fact that I was in no epistemic position to know their truth-value. (While I did not think I could *know* them to be true on the basis of biblical revelation, I did think I could properly *believe* them to be true.)

I assumed, in other words, that Luther's theological language had *evidence-transcendent truth conditions*, that a statement like "God is in Christ reconciling the world to Himself" is true if and only if God is in Christ reconciling the world to Himself.[4] While my pastor gave no lectures on the importance of assuming a *realist semantics* in understanding Luther, I thought the Reformer did hold such a semantic theory—though I clearly did not have the words then to make explicit my assumptions.

Ten years after I read the Small Catechism, I tried my hand at Immanuel Kant's *Critique of Pure Reason*. Two things occurred to me on my first reading of Kant: (1) Kant was harder to read than Luther, and (2) Kant was not a realist about theological language. Kant claimed that there is a class of concepts that is widely employed, yet unlike both the pure and empirical concepts of the understanding, these concepts have no empirical intuitions falling under them. The notion of a supreme being is one of these regulative concepts of human reason, a concept that is nonetheless crucially important for human reason. Kant writes:

> Thus, while for the merely speculative employment of reason the supreme being remains a mere *ideal*, it is yet *an ideal without a flaw*, a concept which completes and crowns the whole of human knowledge. Its objective reality cannot indeed be proved, but also cannot be disproved, by merely speculative reason. . . . Necessity, infinity, unity, existence outside the world (and not as world-soul), eternity as free from conditions of time, omnipresence as free from conditions of space, omnipotence, etc. are purely transcendental predicates, and for this reason the purified concepts of them, which every theology finds so indispensable, are only to be obtained from transcendental theology.[5]

---

[4]For a good discussion of the arguments against semantic realism, see Bob Hale, "Realism and Its Oppositions," in *A Companion to the Philosophy of Language*, ed. Bob Hale and Crispin Wright (Malden, Mass.: Blackwell, 1997), 275–83.

[5]Immanuel Kant, *The Critique of Pure Reason*, trans. Norman Kemp Smith (New York: St. Martin's Press, 1929), B669–70.

Although we can use the term *God* and apply the "transcendental predicates," we are not thereby declaring that any divine states of affairs exist. There are no evidence-transcendent truth conditions; Kant effectively jettisons realist semantics for theological statements.

Because the concept of God has no empirical intuitions falling under it, it cannot be related via the pure concepts of the understanding to other empirical objects. For Kant, the two most important pure concepts are substance and causality. While the empirical concepts can be related by substance and causality, God cannot be. Thus the categories of substance and causality do not apply to God. But if these cannot properly be thought to apply to God, then statements in which God apparently is spoken about as a substance causally related to other substances are either false or misconstrued. For Kant, theological language that *appears* to be making statements about God and His causal-relatedness to other beings *really* is not making such claims. The problem after Kant was how to understand the assertions of theology without supposing that God is a real being with real properties, causally related to other beings.

The Luther renaissance followed Kant, Rudolf Hermann, Lotze, and Albrecht Ritschl in assuming that the "precritical" view of the world is no longer intellectually plausible. One cannot have knowledge of God; nor can one think of God as a transcendent substance causally relatable to other substances. Theologians returning to Luther research naturally sought to find in Luther themes that were intellectually defensible, themes that were consistent with this basic Kantian orientation. This meant that Luther was investigated by those inhabiting an intellectual horizon that denied divine substantiality and causality, by those discovering in Luther themes that could be *appropriated* upon the contemporary intellectual horizon. Just as Luther sought to make the Bible speak to the horizon of the sixteenth-century German peasant, so Luther researchers sought to make Luther speak to the horizon of late-nineteenth- and early-twentieth-century intellectuals. Simply put, as Christine Helmer has said, they privileged the "new" Luther at the expense of the "old."[6]

Important figures of the Luther renaissance (for instance, Karl Holl, Erich Vogelsang, Reinhold Seeberg, and Erich Seeberg) represent an orientation to Luther studies that does not want to admit that

---

[6]Christine Helmer, *The Trinity and Martin Luther: A Study on the Relationship between Genre, Language and the Trinity in Luther's Works (1523–1546)* (Mainz: Verlag Philipp von Zabern, 1999), 7–8.

Luther is "precritical," that his theological language presupposes a *realist semantics*. In fact, varieties of *nonrealist* semantics have been assumed by the majority of Luther commentators of the last hundred years. Some of these nonrealistic accounts include *expressivist*, *donational*, and *global holistic* approaches. Because ofto their popularity (and sometimes uncritical acceptance), I think it is useful to examine each of these approaches in more detail (I will do so in section 3). Unless we are clear about what semantic realism is (and is not), we cannot properly apprehend the nature of Luther's trinitarian assertions.[7]

The question of semantics is closely tied to that of ontology. The tendency in Luther research within Protestant circles since Kant has been to downplay any hint in Luther of *theological realism*. But Luther does believe that the triune God exists and that His existence is not dependent upon human awareness, perception, conception, and language.[8] Everything Luther says about the Trinity presupposes this view.[9] He holds that statements about the real trinitarian God

---

[7]Semantic realism is compatible with different kinds of realism about objects. For instance, *naïve realism* claims that the world exists basically in the way that common sense understands it. *Direct realism* is related to this view, claiming that the objects of perception are external objects, properties, and events. While *critical realism* claims an objective external world, it recognizes that criteria of truth like scope and coherence do not support a "naïve correspondence" between theory and the way the world is. Sometimes the term *metaphysical realism* is used to refer to the view that self-identifying objects exist apart from the human conceptual, epistemic apparatus. *Internal realism*, on the other hand, recognizes that an object's "objective" reality profoundly depends upon the conceptual/epistemic apparatus of the knower. Like most theologians of the tradition, Luther might be regarded as a critical realist with respect to the divine. (Thomas's doctrine of analogical predication is clearly incompatible with naïve realism.) However, critical realism is compatible with either metaphysical or internal realism. While one could claim that the divine realm is constituted in a particular way apart from human knowledge (metaphysical realism), she might still hold that human beings have no epistemic access so as to build a theory asserting a naïve correspondence with that world.

[8]See Panayot Butchvarov, "Realism in Ethics," in *Midwest Studies in Philosophy*, vol. 12, ed. French, Uehling, and Wettstein (Minneapolis: University of Minnesota Press, 1988), 395–412. Butchvarov makes the important point that realism is a *metaphysical* theory: "I shall mean by unqualified realism with respect to x the view that (1) x exists and has certain properties, a nature, and that its existence and nature are independent of (2) our awareness of it, of (3) the manner in which we think of (conceptualize) it, and of (4) the manner in which we speak of it" (396).

[9]Realism comes in many varieties, and this is especially so in theology and the philosophy of religion. Insole details "four criteria for a realist construal of religious discourse." He argues that one is committed to religious anti-realism if he or she desnies at least one of these claims: (1) "There is an indispensable core of religious utterances that are fact-asserting, not merely expressive"; (2) "Statements are made

are true or false and that their truth-value depends upon how this independently existing triune God is and acts. Luther assumes that evidence-transcendent truth conditions, not mere *assertibility conditions*, govern the employment of trinitarian language.[10] Because he believes that there is a fact of the matter in the constitution of the Trinity, he can employ linguistic variations in referring to these trinitarian facts. Luther's semantic realism parallels his theological realism.

I believe it is necessary for Luther scholars today to grasp the profound tension between the semantics of Luther's trinitarian assertions and the prevailing Kantian philosophical context that has underlain Luther interpretation these past two centuries. If Kant is right and God cannot be known as a substance causally connected to the universe, and if pure reason cannot even think how a causal linkage with God is possible, then the reality of God must be understood either as an abstract object or as an ideal of human reason. As is widely appreciated, Luther research and the theological tradition appropriating it have looked to the contours of human experience in order to make sense of theological statements. Accordingly, talk of God either is *reducible* to human experience or is figured *relationally* with respect to it.[11] Although Luther emphasizes the relation of the objects of faith to their existential appropriation, he manifestly does not wish to downplay the objectivity of theological truth. Although the practice of the scholastic method within late medieval tradition often ignored the so-called "existential element" Luther so adroitly

---

true by a non-epistemic state of affairs"; (3) "What is the case is independent of human cognition"; (4) "We can, in principle, have true beliefs about what is the case independent of human cognition." See Christopher J. Insole, *The Realist Hope: A Critique of Anti-Realist Approaches in Contemporary Philosophical Theology* (Burlington, Vt.: Ashgate, 2006), 2ff.

[10]To say that a proposition has *assertibility conditions* and not *truth-conditions* is to say that the proposition can be asserted when specified conditions are met. For instance, I might assert that "Johnny is a good boy" when I have a particular attitude toward Johnny. The proposition is not *true* because there is no state of affairs wherein there exists a property of goodness ascribable to Johnny.

[11]For instance, one might assert that "Bob is a creature" without claiming that there is some x such that x is divine, and $<x$, Bob$>$ is a member of the set $\{<x, y> \mid x \text{ creates } y\}$. This is possible, however, only if "creature" means something like "having been created by a creator," that is, if "Bob is a creature of God" is *assertible* on the basis of some existential attitudes and orientations present in Bob, for example, if psychological condition C is met by Bob, then "is a creature of God" is properly predicable of Bob.

highlights, he obviously does assume an objectivity to God and language referring to God.[12]

My contribution follows those of my coauthors, Paul Hinlicky and Mickey Mattox, in highlighting aspects of Luther's thinking that are decidedly "catholic." Clearly, Luther is a "catholic" thinker when engaged with traditional dogmatic trinitarian concerns. He employs a realist semantics to assert a realist theological perspective, for example, that God *really is* in Christ *causing* the world to be reconciled unto Himself. For too long within Protestant circles there has been a presumption that God needs no *causal powers* in order to be real and, concomitantly, that language about God can be fully performative without being constative. But to say that "God's word is what it does" is not to say that there is *no* "aboutness" to God's word, on the basis of which it *does* what it *is*.

Luther was a man of his time, a man who knew the late medieval semantic and ontological traditions and was comfortable working within them. I believe that his theological innovations are best understood against the backdrop of his profound acquaintance with these traditions. With Maddox and Hinlicky, I hold that Luther neither inaugurates a whole new way of interpreting Scripture nor grounds the entirety of his theology on a radically "thin" (forensic) sense of justification. Instead, Luther works out of the Catholic theological tradition in which he was educated and in which he preached, prayed, and worshiped. Not surprisingly, he engages traditional trinitarian problems, showing in his engagement the influence of the Augustinian and *via moderna* traditions he knew well, traditions that realized, in their own ways, that reason cannot penetrate into the trinitarian mysteries of the faith. For Luther, human beings can have only very limited epistemic access to the incomprehensibility of the Trinity. By faith, and through the incarnation, human beings approach this profound mystery only as a "line [that] touches the whole sphere but at a point, and thus does not comprehend the whole thing."[13]

As a late medieval theologian, Luther knew too much about the limitations of reason to be anything but humble in the face of incomprehensible trinitarian truths. Luther's ontological humility strongly parallels his own care in properly speaking about the

---

[12]Luther distinguishes subjective and objective faith clearly at LW 36:335; WA 19 482:25—483:19. See the introduction to this volume, p. 5.

[13]WA 39 II, 255:17–19.

divine. Theology's *nova lingua* talks about those divine things that human reason cannot deeply *know* but with which it is, nevertheless, faithfully engaged. Profound thoughtfulness is needed to speak such a language. By attending carefully to Luther's speaking, contemporary Lutherans can find a model for their own speaking of theological *truth* within a context of epistemic nonfoundationalism. Neither Scripture nor ecclesial structure or dogma provides a cadre of properly basic (nonemendable) foundational statements from which all theological truth can be derived. As both Hinlicky and Maddox have pointed out, Luther knows that the *sensus* of the text depends upon the *res*. Putative "foundational" statements always presuppose other statements that cannot be derived from the foundational statements alone. A hermeneutical circle forms that is driven by the activity of the Spirit.

We live in a time that assumes that *to be real is to have causal powers*. Our age is not a time when religious and theological language is presumptively, profoundly meaningful, a time when we might then option to salve our ontological scruples by affording such language a nonproblematic ontological construal. Rather, our time is a time when such language is but one option among many, an option that communicates to some and not to others. In such a time as ours, what is desperately sought and needed is the knowledge of whether such language is *true*, for only if the language is true can it be profoundly existentially meaningful. Just as at the beginning of the Christian tradition, the claim of theological truth is, for us now, logically prior to existential meaningfulness. Recovering Luther as a "catholic" thinker uncovers the requisite semantic and ontological basis that makes the claim of God's action in Christ a real claim about how the world is constituted, a claim having universal significance to all men and women regardless of their cultural and historical situatedness, a claim that can be *true* regardless of whether it is appreciated as such or not.

I shall argue that Luther holds to semantic realism, the view that theological language has robust *truth conditions*; that is, a theological proposition is true if and only if the divine exists in some way that makes true the proposition. After looking at some relevant parts of Luther's late disputations, and after laying out the general problem of the Trinity in the Western tradition, I shall distinguish between two different ways in which realist theological language might have meaning for Luther. The *new meaning* (NM) view claims that an intensional element underlies the distinction between Luther's theological and philosophical discourse; the *different inference* (DI) view argues that the distinction between the two discourses can be accounted for on the basis of semantic resources within late medieval nominalism. I shall explore the issue of whether or not Luther privileges the divine processions or the personal relations ontologically in conceiving the Trinity. On the basis of key propositions in the late disputations, I shall suggest that Luther can be read as advocating a position at least as friendly to the Franciscans as to the Dominicans. At the conclusion of the chapter, I shall follow Richard Cross in suggesting that Theodore de Regnon's thesis may be incorrect; there just may not be that much theologically different in the claims made by the East and West respectively.

2. Luther's Trinitarian Thinking

Helmer claims that in the last years of his life Luther searched "for comfort in the themes of eternal life and the eternity of God."[14] Perhaps this does motivate his trinitarian reflections in the doctoral disputations of Erasmus Alberus (August 24, 1543), Georg Major and Johannes Faber (December 12, 1544), and Petrus Hegemon (July 3, 1545).[15] Perhaps it is the contemporary challenge of nontrinitarian theology, or the specter of the Arian heresy, a heresy arising whenever the relationship between the Father and His Word is vitiated.[16] Whatever the motivation, there are a number of themes to explore in these fascinating disputations.

Luther engages such questions as the distinction between eternity and time, the ability of tensed propositions to refer to eternity, the relationship between the actual and potential infinite and God, the legitimacy of John Duns Scotus's formal distinction in understanding how three things can be one, and the question of whether the divine essence generates. That these rather technical topics are important

---

[14]Helmer, *Trinity*, 58. It is, of course, always difficult to know what is in the mind of another, especially a man separated from us by five centuries.

[15]For a historical study of the disputations at Wittenberg, see E. Wolf, "Zur Wissenschaftsgeschichtlichen Bedeutung der Disputationen and der Wittenberger Universität Im 16. Jahrhundert," *Studien zur Reformatorischen Theologie Zum Kirchenrecht und zur Soizialethik*, vol. 2, Peregrinatio (München: Ch. Kaiser, 1965).

[16]Helmer, *Trinity*, 67: "For Luther, a common front is represented by the heretics, the theologians, and the philosophers . . . who deploy reason to reduce the theological subject matter to the temporal domain."

for Luther may come as a surprise to those who have not read Luther's disputations. But to anyone taking the time to read through volume 39 of the Weimar edition, it should not be surprising that Luther has some rather definite, analytical things to say about how one refers to, and thinks about, the trinitarian persons.

There is no doubt that the Reformation tradition has tended to leave Luther's theology of the Trinity relatively unexplored. Perhaps scholars have assumed that a man who rejected the scholastic method so thoroughly would not seriously engage a topic so closely associated with scholasticism.[17] But Luther did reflect on the Trinity; in fact, as Helmer points out, he thought deeply about the nature of the immanent Trinity, the Trinity in its eternal nature.[18] Moreover, he reflected upon the Trinity within a definite context of intellectual precursors. Given Luther's preparation in philosophy, it is perhaps not surprising that he could be conceptually concise and analytically precise in what he had to say about the *tres res sunt una res* of the Trinity.

Luther's Last Disputations

On August 24, 1543, Erasmus Alberus debated theses on the unity of the divine essence written by Martin Luther. Luther's theses here speak of the incomprehensibility of the triune God and God's intratrinitarian relations. For Luther, reason simply cannot grasp how one God can be three.[19] Scotus's formal distinction is of no help. Reason is oriented to things below it, and thus cannot comprehend eternity: "Although it is certain in divinity, since he is eternity itself, there is no place in grammar or philosophy where past, present and future is the same."[20] Accordingly, reason cannot conceive infinity— whether actual or potential. Knowledge of God by reason is obscure and partial. It is as a "line [that] touches the whole sphere but at a point, and thus does not comprehend the whole thing."[21] Though reason cannot penetrate to the divine, limited epistemic access is

---

[17]Perhaps they agree with Werner Elert that the Trinity is "an erratic block in Luther's theology." See Werner Elert, *Morphologie Des Luthertums*, 3rd ed., vol. 1 (Munich: C. H. Beck, 1965), 191.

[18]This is a point Christine Helmer has made repeatedly; e.g., Helmer, "God from Eternity to Eternity: Luther's Trinitarian Understanding," *Harvard Theological Review* 96, no. 2 (2003), 129ff.

[19]WA 39 II, 253:9–10.

[20]Ibid., 254:30–32.

[21]Ibid., 255:17–19.

possible by faith: "Whoever in searching wishes not to err, nor to be crushed by the glory of his majesty, let him by faith touch and lay hold of the Son of God manifest in the flesh."[22] Far from attaining the standpoint of the divine, limited human beings have access to God only by faith through the incarnate Son of God.

In early December 1544, Luther wrote forty-eight theses for the doctoral disputations of Georg Major and Johanes Faber. The set of theses for Major deals with trinitarian issues, while those assigned Faber are concerned with justification and Christology. After discussing the importance of truth generally, thesis 5 states boldly the trinitarian claim: "The truth is indisputable that God is one and threefold, and the sole creator of all things outside Him." This unity is very profound: "This unity of the Trinity (as we say it) is a greater oneness than that of any other creature, or even of mathematical unity." Yet Luther warns that "this distinction of persons is so strong that only the person of the Son assumed human being."[23] Luther hits some of the same themes as the Alberus disputation: thesis 13 denies that mathematics can be used in thinking the Trinity, and thesis 14 attacks Scotus's formal distinction. Other theses repudiate Lombard's claim that the essence neither generates nor is generated. We shall have more to say on this later.

In his final disputation for Petrus Hegemon, Luther explicitly treats the distinction between theology and philosophy, claiming that "a relation pertaining to the divine ought to be understood in a far different way from any which is in the creature or in philosophy."[24] Hegemon must defend some tricky claims; he must argue that "a relation does not here demonstrate a distinction of things, but three distinct things prove to be a relation,"[25] and at the same time must defend the identity of the relation and the hypostasis: "In divine matters a relation is a thing, that is, a hypostasis and subsistence, truly, the same as divinity itself; there are three persons, three hypostases and three subsistences."[26] Hegemon must then address an already familiar theme: the inadequacy of reason to grasp trinitarian truths. From the standpoint of reason, the highest things are nothing, but

---

[22]Ibid., 255:20–21.
[23]Ibid., 287:24–25.
[24]Ibid., 339:26–27.
[25]Ibid., 339:6–7.
[26]Ibid., 340:3–5.

from faith's perspective all things are spoken and known rightly.[27] The same incomprehensibility attaches to the incarnation because, next to the Trinity, "it is the highest, for here the finite and the infinite were placed in proportion—which is impossible."[28] Luther reiterates that the only epistemic access humans have to the Creator is through the incarnation of Christ. Near the end of the disputation, Luther engages again the question of the generation of the divine essence, claiming now that "personally" God can be said to generate God, but "essentially" God cannot be said to do so.[29]

Luther and the Trinitarian Processions

Simo Knuuttila and Risto Saarinen suggest that Regnon's century-old thesis may be wrong. The so-called Augustinian conception of the Trinity may not be as different from the Cappadocian view as has been supposed. Regnon argued that for the Cappadocians, the distinct persons of the Trinity are ontologically primary, while for Augustine, the unity of the Trinity is primary.[30] Knuuttila and Saarinen further claim that Luther emphasizes the procession of persons rather than their differentiation through relations in the last promotional disputation in which he was in charge. Simply put, Luther, the Augustinian monk, follows the Franciscans generally in adopting a position closer to the Cappadocian rather than the Augustinian view, thus demonstrating again that Regnon's general distinction may be problematic.[31]

What textual evidence is available for the claim that Luther gives the procession of the persons logical priority over the presence of relations in understanding the trinitarian claim that *tres res sunt una res*? I think Knuuttila and Saarinen are correct to indicate that Luther's last disputation does suggest that the relations of the persons are logically grounded in the nonrelational nature of these persons in procession. It is also true, however, that the rather loose way that

---

[27]Ibid., 340:12–13.

[28]Ibid., 340:14–15.

[29]Ibid., 370:8–14.

[30]Theodore de Regnon, *Etudes de Theologie Positive sur la Sainte Trinite*, vol. 1 (Paris, 1892).

[31]Simo Knuuttila and Risto Saarinen, "Innertrinitarische Theologie in Der Scholastik und bei Luther," in *Caritas Dei. Festschrift für Tuomo Mannermaa Zum 60. Geburtstag*, ed. Simo Knuuttila (Helsinki: Luther-Agricola-Society, 1997). Simo Knuuttila and Risto Saarinen, "Luther's Trinitarian Theology and Its Medieval Background," *Studia Theologica* 53, no. 1 (1999).

Luther discusses persons and relations suggests that Luther himself would be quite uncomfortable with the distinction Regnon suggests. The distinction of persons cannot be easily separated from that which the relations individuate. The question as to whether the persons are first individuated and then relatable (or are instead individuated by the relations) seems not to be important for Luther theologically.

The relevant text is the disputation of Peter Hegemon, from July 3, 1545. Theses 1 through 17 discuss in what sense one can apply the term *wisdom* of the Father. The important points arise in theses 14 through 16. They run as follows:

14. A relation does not here demonstrate a distinction of things, but three distinct things prove to be a relation.

15. This does not follow: "The Father is wise in Himself, therefore the wisdom of the Father in Himself—since wisdom is relative to Him—is a distinct thing from Him."

16. Nevertheless, just as it is properly said that the Son is relative to the Father, therefore He is another hypothesis from the Father, so too is this rightly said of the Holy Spirit.[32]

In thesis 14, Luther seems to claim the logical priority of persons over relations. He is, in effect, stating that the persons are related *externally*, that the persons are who they distinctly are, and that the distinctness of the *relata* grounds the nature of the trinitarian *relationes*. Thesis 15 denies that Christ as wisdom, relative to and distinct from the Father, can be derived from wisdom as an essential attribute of God. Just because there is some being (God) having the property of wisdom does not entail that there is some being (wisdom) hypostatically distinct from the Father. Luther here points out that one cannot derive the persons of the Trinity from the essential properties of God. While thesis 15 claims that the "wisdom of the Father" is Christ, thesis 16 argues that because this wisdom is relative to the Father, that is, not absolutely predicated of Him, then this "wisdom" names the hypostasis of the Son of God.

Luther's claim that the relations of the persons are grounded in some prior distinction follows a number of theses in which he clarifies that the Word as the second trinitarian person just is the wisdom of the Father and that the distinct persons just are these relations.

---

[32]WA 39 II, 340:6–11.

11. Really, nevertheless, a relation pertaining to the divine ought to be understood in a far different way from any which is in the creature or in philosophy.

12. A relation in things does not affect the thing; as they say, the relation is a minimal entity and does not subsist through itself; moreover, it is nothing according to the Moderns.

13. In divine matters a relation is a thing, that is, a hypostasis and subsistence, truly, the same as divinity itself; there are three persons, three hypostases and three subsistences.[33]

In thesis 11, Luther claims that the meaning of "relation" differs when applied theologically (to divine things) or philosophically (to creaturely things). "Relation" in a philosophical context connotes a "minimal entity" that does not "subsist through itself." In Ockhamist-inspired thought, only particular objects exist and relations must be defined externally over those objects. However, when considering the Trinity, a relation is identifiable with a hypostasis or subsistence. As it turns out, in theology a relation is not a "minimal entity" at all, but one of the very persons of God.

Thesis 13 seems to be in tension with thesis 14. In 13, Luther appears to side with the Dominican tradition in claiming that a relation is a hypostasis or subsistence, while in 14 he asserts that three already distinct things prove to be a relation. But this latter claim seems to be more at home in the Franciscan tradition (and the Eastern tradition generally), which assumes that individuation of the persons is metaphysically prior to the trinitarian relations. It is significant that Luther can speak with the Dominicans in thesis 13 and with the Franciscans in thesis 14. Luther apparently finds no important theological difference in the two trinitarian traditions. While dogmatic trinitarian statements have truth conditions for Luther, he is not interested in speculative ontological trinitarian reflection. Whether relations, or nonrelational monadic properties, individuate the persons is not an issue of salvific import. Because the Trinity is incomprehensible, the best that human beings can do is simply to try to use language that does not lead to heresy. What is important is that trinitarian language clearly asserts that the three divine persons are really one God. Because this theological concern is primary for

---

[33]Ibid., 339:26—340:5.

Luther, he is liberated to think more in terms of the processions than many of his contemporaries.

A crucial question pertains to how the term *relatio* in theology differs from its employment within philosophy. One can *say*, of course, that in theology a relation just is a person of the Trinity. But the question is whether one is using the term *relation* in a way consistent with traditional usage, and if so, in what way is it consistent? Is the way it is employed in theology *incommensurate* with the way it is employed within the nominalistic philosophical context? If not incommensurate, then in what way exactly can it be translated into the language of philosophy? What is the semantics of Luther's theological *nova lingua*, the "new language" of theology? If it is semantically independent from philosophy, then how do the two relate? Is there semantic discontinuity between the two? We shall examine these questions in section 5 below.

Luther on Infinity

Luther is convinced of the ineffability of the Trinity, and in the *Promotionsdisputation* of Alberus, he questions the usefulness of the concept in conceiving the Trinity.[34] Key theses in this *Promotionsdisputation* read as follows:

30. Aristotle also perceives that eternity or infinity, in however many of its modes, is not known and is incomprehensible.

31. Moreover, he affirms that infinity or eternity, in however many of its modes, cannot exist, and he appears to speak rightly according to reason.

32. But he does not see the consequence, or rather does not wish to see it, namely, that it follows from reason that God neither is, nor can He be.

33. For that reason, he disputes so coldly about religion, and is completely Epicurus in the skin.

34. He concedes nevertheless that the infinite is potential and can be known, even if again the eternity of the world confounds him.[35]

---

[34]Helmer, *Trinity*, 80ff.
[35]See WA 39 II, 255:7–13.

Thesis 31 questions whether or not the infinite can be real. Aristotle
had denied that an actual infinity is possible.[36] By "actual infinite,"
he meant the greatest possible collection, a set to which no other
member can be added.[37] On the assumption that God is such an
actual infinite, Luther concludes that God neither exists nor could
exist: "*Deum non esse, nec esse posse.*"[38]

As Helmer points out, however, this Aristotelian-inspired notion
of the actual infinite (*infinitum est quo nihil est maius*) was not uni-
versally accepted in the medieval tradition. In fact, Robert Holcot,
Gregory of Rimini, and William of Ockham all seem to hold that the
actual infinite need not be accepted as an infinite series but, rather,
as that which is "beyond all finite number and proportion."[39] Scotus
distinguishes *intensive* and *extensive* unity in his effort to infer divine
infinity from the finitude of creatures. He understands extensive
infinity as that which explains "how a finite effect is produced over
an infinite amount of time." Intensive infinity is that by virtue of
which the first mover has the power to produce "the sum total of
an infinite series of effects."[40] In this disputation, Luther effectively
conflates the actual infinite with intensive infinity and thus deduces
the denial of God.[41]

Turning to the potential infinite, Aristotle defines it as follows:

---

[36]See *Metaphysics* II, 994b 20–28.

[37]Helmer quotes Anneliese Maier: "Infinitum est quo nihil est maius" or "tot
quod non plures." See Helmer, *Trinity*, 84.

[38]He proceeds as follows, reading "◊" as "it is possible," "□" as "it is necessary," and "~" as "not."
(1) It is impossible that infinity exists.   ~◊I
(2) God is infinity.   G = I
(3) Therefore, it is impossible that God exists.   ~◊G
It follows, of course, from (3) that "~G" holds as well, for if God does not
obtain in any possible world, then God does not obtain in the actual world.
Possible world semantics grants an interpretation of modal notions. Reading
"∃x" as "there is some x," "∀x" as "for all x," and "∈" as "is a subset of," to say
"◊P" is to say "∃w(P ∈ w)"—"There is some world w such that P obtains in that
world"—and to say "□P" is to say "∀w(P ∈ w)"—"P obtains in each and every
possible world w."

[39]Helmer, *Trinity*, 84 n. 161.

[40]Ibid., 85.

[41]One must distinguish the following where "$=_{df}$" means "is defined as":
Infinity$_1$ $=_{df}$ a series such that one cannot add any other number to it.
Infinity$_2$ $=_{df}$ that unbounded reality lying beyond all number and proportion. (Helmer, *Trinity*, 84 n. 161.)
Obviously if the first sense of infinity is employed in (1)—the Aristotelian actual
infinite—and the second sense in (2)—Scotus's notion—the conclusion of the impos-
sibility of God does not follow. There is an equivocation on notions of infinity. It

"A quantity is infinite if it is such that we can always take a part of it outside of what has already been taken."[42] The idea of the potential infinite is connected to the notion of a continuum. One can always take a finite whole and divide it into an infinite number of parts or add another member to a finite collection. But this is not so with an actual infinite. Here there is already an infinite number such that no more members can be added. An example of the potential infinite is the natural number series because it can never be completed; it is impossible to imagine the entire series as a completed thing. An actual infinite, on the other hand, would be a definite something that is not constructed from a finite set through recursion.

Just as Luther argued that reason must hold that because there is no actual infinite there is no God, so must it claim the same of the potential infinite. Over and against Aristotle, Luther argues that the potential infinite also cannot be grasped. Because it cannot be conceived, one must simply admit that there is no God. The relevant theses run as follows:

34. He concedes nevertheless that the infinite is potential and can be known, even if again the eternity of the world confounds him.

35. St. Paul says rightly in Romans I: "The knowledge of God is manifest to all people, that is, his eternal power and divinity."

36. But this knowledge is obscure and partial (although the knowledge of faith is also in its own way partial), as a line touches the whole sphere but at a point, and thus does not comprehend the whole thing.[43]

What one can know of God is the point of intersection between a sphere and a line tangent to that sphere. This is the same with the potential infinite. In any infinite series generated by recursion, one "knows" each member generated in that series as but a "point"

---

does not follow from there being no greatest collection that there is nothing that lies outside of each and every collection.

[42]Aristotle, *Physics*, book 3.6:207a7. He says in Book 3.7:207b12: "The infinite is potential, never actual: The number of parts that can be taken always surpasses any assigned number. . . . Since no sensible magnitude is infinite, it is impossible to exceed every assigned magnitude; for if it were possible there would be something bigger than the heavens."

[43]WA 39 II, 255:13–19.

compared to the whole series generated. Human beings cannot grasp the infinite by reason and thus cannot grasp God. The Trinity is truly an incomprehensible thing.

The Question of the Divine Essence Generating

In the *Promotionsdisputation of Georg Major and Johannes Faber* (December 12, 1544), Luther discusses whether or not the divine essence can be said to generate. After a general statement of three distinct persons being one undivided divine essence, Luther moves into this rather technical discussion. Starting with thesis 15, he writes:

15. Indeed, the Master of the *Sentences* taught not correctly enough, that the divine essence neither generates nor is generated.

16. But he was rightly repudiated by Abbot Joachim, because he asserted a quaternity in divine matters.

17. Neither does the Canon *Firmiter de Trinitate* accomplish anything, proving the Master and condemning the Abbot.

18. While, in fact, on the basis of Augustine, the Master could not deny that substance is generated from substance and wisdom from wisdom.

19. In no way could he deny that essence is generated from essence, and whatever could be said of the true God, could be said in a similar way.

20. Especially since everything is suspect which this abomination, standing in the holy place, has determined.

21. It seems that the Master feared that if one essence were born from another, then one would be speaking of two or three essences.

22. But similarly he would have to worry that if one god were generated from another, there would then be two or three gods.

23. We concede that there is an essence in the creature, not talking "relatively" (as Augustine uses the term), but solely "absolutely."

24. But since it seems substance, wisdom, nature and similar terms in divine matters are taken "relatively" by Augustine and Hilary,

25. There was no reason why he should deny that "essence" is spoken relatively, and why one word should move such crowds.

26. And so, not without reason, this determination greatly displeased Cardinal Cambrai, the most learned among the Scholastics.[44]

Thesis 15 takes aim at Peter Lombard, who claims that we cannot say "the divine essence generates." Lombard seems on prima facie solid ground, however, for the divine essence comprises such essential divine properties as omnipotence, omnipresence, omnibenevolence, omniscience, and immutability. Since the divine essence is immutable, it cannot generate anything or be generated by anything, including itself. As Hinlicky points out in chapter 3, the notion that the divine essence does not generate seems to follow from the "axiom of impassibility."[45]

Luther believes that Lombard is wrong. He reasons that since Augustine allows "substance generates substance" and "wisdom generates wisdom," there is no reason to deny "essence generates essence." But Luther understands Lombard's uneasiness with the locution. If "essence generates essence" is true, then it seems "God generates God" is true, and divine unity is thus compromised.

To solve the problem, Luther invokes the standard Augustinian distinction between taking terms "absolutely" or "relatively." To speak of the essence absolutely is to speak of it as it is common to all three persons; to speak of the essence relatively is to speak of it as it is with respect to each individual person.[46] Luther explains that Lombard thought that allowing "essence generates essence" commits one to a quaternity in God. The problem is that he supposes that "essence" must be taken "absolutely." But this need not be. Luther writes, "It is certain that 'essence does not generate', taken absolutely, but taken relatively, it certainly generates."[47] He goes on to explain: "If one says 'the Father generates' then, since I am under our article of faith, I must say that this is not a substantial distinction, but a personal one. Dialectic did not invent this distinction. The thing itself [the subject matter] equivocates. To be God is absolute, but to

---

[44]Ibid., 287:31—288:22.
[45]See Hinlicky, 137 below. While the axiom of impassibility entails the divine essence does not generate, the converse is not true.
[46]See WA 39 II, 307:20–23.
[47]See ibid., 316:16–25.

generate is relative; there is nothing similar to this in the nature of things, etc."[48]

In the doctrinal disputation of Peter Hegemon, Luther uses the distinction "personally/essentially" instead of "relatively/absolutely": "If we take 'God' personally, then 'God generates God' is true; but if we take 'God' essentially, then God neither generates himself nor some other thing. The essence does not generate, but the person does."[49] But Luther was not always convinced of the permissibility of "the essence generates the essence." He writes in 1539: "Therefore, it is more fitting and, from the standpoint of a professional theologian, safer and better to say that 'the Father generates' than to say 'the essence generates' or 'the Trinity generates'. One should not understand some personal essence, but one common to the three persons of the Trinity, and that God is one in essence and a Trinity in persons."[50]

Here Luther seems to admit that "essence generates essence" can be mistaken to assert that *each* person of the Trinity has its own

---

[48]The argument is this:

(1) The Father generates the Son.
(2) The Father is the essence.
(3) The Son is the essence.
(4) Therefore, the essence generates the essence.

More perspicaciously, we write:

(1') Gfs   [The Father and the Son stand in the relation of generation.]
(2') f = e   [The Father is the divine essence.]
(3') s = e   [The Son is the divine essence.]
(4') Therefore, Gee [The essence stands to itself in the relation of generation.]

The difference between "absolute" and "relative" in this context can be easily seen. Taken absolutely, "f = e" and "s = e," and thus we conclude "Gee," the statement of God generating God. But taken "relatively," e and f become coreferential expressions used to mention the first person of the Trinity. Accordingly, they *supposit* for the same entity—even though each retains a different *significance*. (We shall have much more to say about this critical distinction later.) "Gee" is false if "f = e" and "s = e," and thus the one essence is reflexively related by generation, but "Gee" is true if e is another name for that to which f refers, and e is another name for that to which s refers. On the second construal, the Father and the Son each are "picked out" by the description, "essence." On the first interpretation, "Father" and "Son" both name the divine essence; on the second, "essence" names both the Father and the Son. This second reading, here adopted by Luther, fits quite naturally with a processional understanding of divine persons.

[49]WA 39 II, 370:8–14.
[50]Ibid., 18:4–12.

individual essence, and thus speaking in such a way can compromise the unity of God. There are different ways of speaking, and it is a problem if one is using essence "relatively" and one's hearers take it "absolutely." It is a *pragmatic* decision to employ particular locutions in particular situations. Certain locutions might be "more fitting" even though others are *formally* correct. The question is whether they shall be properly understood.[51]

It is important to grasp what is presupposed in this discussion on the divine generation. Language can refer to trinitarian "facts" in different ways. Since it is possible to say "the essence generates the essence" because there are two *particular* persons referred to by the two uses of "essence" in the locution, language about the Trinity clearly does not change the constitution of the Trinity. Thus, the trinitarian structure exists independent of human conception and language; simply put, the Trinity is *real*.[52] In order to understand the importance of this claim of *semantic realism*, it is useful, I think, to compare it to other semantic options that have surfaced in the tradition of Luther scholarship. In the following section, I develop four semantic models and point to some problems in each. While I support semantic realism, I do believe that a case can be made for *semantic holism* with respect to the two languages of theology and philosophy in Luther. Hinlicky's approach to the distinction between these two languages places him closer to the holistic position than does mine.

---

[51]It is important to recall that it was indeed standard in the late-medieval tradition to give the following truth-conditions for a true statement: a statement is true just in case its subject and predicate stand (or supposit) for the same thing. Luther's teacher Unsingen puts it this way: "Every affirmative is true in which the extreme terms supposit for the same thing, as in 'a man is an animal.'" See Unsingen, *Tract* I, f. a4: "Omnis affirmitiva est vera cuius externa supponunt pro eodem, it 'homo est animal.'" For a universal affirmative statement like 'every man is an animal', each and every man supposits for something that is an animal. For a singular affirmative statement like 'Howard is an animal' 'Howard' supposits for something that is a man. In 'the Father generates the Son' the term 'Father' supposits for something that generates that for which the term 'Son' supposits. From the standpoint of set theory 'every man is an animal' is $\forall x (x \in M \rightarrow x \in A)$, and 'Howard is an animal' is $h \in \{x| x \text{ is an animal}\}$."

[52]See Graham White, *Luther as Nominalist: A Study of the Logical Methods Used in Martin Luther's Disputations in the Light of Their Medieval Background* (Helsinki: Luther-Agricol Society, 1994), 202–3: "Thus, Ockam's work on the Trinity gave Luther the freedom to modify the usual semantics of Trinitarian language, and thus to say that 'essence' was a term that could stand for the persons of the Trinity."

3. Four Semantic Models

How does Luther's theological language have meaning? Do theological terms, phrases, and statements have meaning because they *express* some fundamental, subjective, phenomenological-ontological, experiential truth before God? Do they have meaning because they *refer* to present, past, or future existing objects, properties, events, or states of affairs? Are theological terms and statements meaningful by virtue of the *donation* of a mode of being in a linguistic event? Or are theological terms, phrases, and statements only meaningful in that they are internally related to, or are implicitly defined with respect to, other theological expressions within a rule-governed context of meaning or *language-game*?

Wilhelm Link is representative of those who suggest that theological utterances are expressions of the believer's immediacy before God. Instead of stating theological facts about a being's having divine attributes, and the relation between that being and human being, such utterances "speak out" or "ex-press" a fundamental relation of the individual before God. Like prayer, theological expressions function as confessions made in the subjectivity of faith. They show one's standing *coram Deo* (before God) without saying or specifying exactly what that "place" is. Link's work suggests what contemporary philosophy might call an *expressivist* or *projectivist* semantics of Luther's theological assertions.[53]

Bengt Hägglund contends that while theology, for Luther, retains a practical orientation, it nevertheless still claims a *knowledge* of the divine and the divine/human relationship. Against Link, Hägglund argues that theological statements are not merely expressions of a relationship before God true only in the subjectivity of faith. Rather, theological words and phrases have extensions, and theological sentences possess definite truth conditions. Hägglund's work exemplifies a *realist semantics* of Luther's theological language.

Gerhard Ebeling holds that theological language for Luther functions to establish a "word event" (*Wortgeschehen*) in which the reality of freedom and future is donated to the reader or hearer. In this linguistic event, words no longer have definite referents; rather, they function in the presentation of their own referent, the referent of the existential forgiveness and liberation of the sinner. Theological

---

[53]For a discussion of projectivism, see Simon Blackburn, *Spreading the Word: Groundings in the Philosophy of Language* (Oxford: Clarendon, 1984).

language as human language about the word of God is figured as a vehicle for the donation of God's grace. Ebeling's view is more difficult to locate within the contemporary philosophical context, but it might be called a *donational semantics*.

Ulrich Asendorf suggests that Luther's theological expressions acquire their meaning within a larger theological context of meaning, which itself presupposes a set of determinate semantic rules. Different semantic rules, associated with differing "fundamental presuppositions," ground the employment, and the meaning, of words in different contexts of meaning. The theological context is autonomous in that its primitive terms are semantically discontinuous with primitive terms within other contexts. Importing a term whose meaning was determined within a different context may result in semantic confusion and a concomitant loss of meaning. There is no overarching "grammar" containing the discourse of philosophy and theology; there is no common semantic field supported by common semantic rules. This view presupposes a *holistic semantics* of Luther's theological language. We shall look at each model in turn.

Expressivist Semantics

Before his tragic death at age thirty, Wilhelm Link completed his major work *Das Ringen Luthers: Um die Freiheit der Theologie von der Philosophie.* In this book, Link deals with the central content of Reformation knowledge, the *simul iustus et peccator*.[54] Instead of being "an objective and general description of what human beings are," the *simul* is *not* true "for each person in every place and situation" but is "true only in the subjectivity of faith, . . . but not for one who does not stand prayerfully before God."[55] The confession of God's holiness and human wickedness, constituting the heart of the *simul*, arises only in a person's encounter with God. The confession expresses the individual's place before God and seeks to move others toward a similar standing *coram Deo*.[56] Instead of a metaphysical description of the human relation to God, the confession is a preobjec-

---

[54]Wilhelm Link, *Das Ringen Luthers um die Freiheit der Theologie von der Philosophie* (München: Chr. Kaiser Verlag, 1955), 73.

[55]Ibid., 78.

[56]Ibid., 79: "It is always a confession in the sight of God, and it has essentially the form of the address, 'against you only,' whether it does or does not come to expression in outward form. Furthermore, with all of its content-rich assertions [*nhaltlichen Aussagen*] it has no other purpose than to express the believer's standing before God [*Vor-Gott-Stehen*], and in the same way to place before God the person

tive knowledge of the "I" as it stands before God.[57] The "subjectivity of the address constitutes the essence of the confession."[58]

While philosophy attempts to *describe* the relationship of the believer before God, theology *expresses* the immediacy of the believer *coram Deo*.[59] No philosophical reflection can undermine the expression of this immediacy. Confession is neither the object of critical reflection nor a judgment about existing states of affairs.[60] The immediate experience of the "I" before God generates both the confession of human forlornness and the confession of divine mercy. Thus, theological assertions do not refer to mental or phenomenological states but merely express those states. They are a "speaking from" rather than a "speaking about."

Although Link claims that theology is free from philosophy, he acknowledges that theological language cannot be wholly separated from philosophical categories. Even the statement "God has given Himself in Christ" presupposes the philosophical concepts of transcendence and immanence, the infinite and finite, and the interpenetration of one into the other.[61] Philosophy must be able to understand theological language, reflect upon it, and interpret it as mythological.[62] Accordingly, philosophy can only judge theological statements to be false. But while the *what* of a theological statement is bound to philosophical representations and meaning, *that* to which the sentence attests is free from philosophy. Simultaneity, eternity, and simplicity constitute the "form" of a theological assertion; they do not state a divine ontology but rather express the event of divine encounter.

The expressivist model suggested by Link is consonant with the general attitude toward theological language of logical positivism and its intellectual successors.[63] David Hume is the grandfather of

---

for whose ears the confession is spoken. This distinguishes the expression of confession [*Aussagen des Bekenntnisses*] from every objective description."

[57]Ibid., 81.

[58]Ibid., 82.

[59]Ibid., 98.

[60]Ibid., 104. Link lists three fundamental characteristics of the *simul*: (1) its assertion is impervious to relativization; (2) it is an assertion both of God's act and of our forlornness (*Verlorenheit*); (3) the assertion is not spoken from a philosophically objective standpoint but is uttered out of the reality of life itself.

[61]Ibid., 382.

[62]Ibid., 383.

[63]For a classical logical positivist treatment of the meaninglessness of theological language, see A. J. Ayer, *Language, Truth, and Logic* (New York: Dover, 1952).

modern expressivist views because of his antirealist understanding of moral language as expressing sentiment. Hume writes of the human "productive faculty," which gilds or stains "all natural objects with the colours, borrowed from internal sentiment," and thus "raises in a manner a new creation."[64] While realism understands assertions of a particular kind (for instance, theological, moral, aesthetic) as having genuine *truth-conditions*, expressivism claims that these assertions merely evince the *attitude* of the one doing the asserting.[65]

George Lindbeck's 1984 work *The Nature of Doctrine* identifies "an experiential-expressive approach" to theological language.[66] Accordingly, one "interprets doctrines as noninformative and nondiscursive symbols of inner feelings, attitudes, or existential orientations."[67] More generally, the experiential-expressivist discovers "whatever is finally important to religion in the prereflective experiential depths of the self and regard[s] the public or outer features of religion as expressive and evocative objectifications (i.e., nondiscursive symbols) of internal experience."[68] For the experiential-expressivist, the "prereflective experiential depth" of religion is indeterminate, and traditions are individuated by the symbols that express and inculcate that depth experience.

Unfortunately, practitioners of the experiential-expressive approach have not been generally clear on whether they advocate expressivism without truth-conditions or a subjectivism with truth-conditions. For instance, does the Judeo-Christian God, which symbolizes "the God above the God of theism," enter into states of affairs that could comprise truth conditions for theological language?[69] That Paul Tillich, the great experiential-expressivist, is willing to talk about the "truth" of symbols in terms of the degree to

---

[64]David Hume, "Enquiry concerning the Principles of Morals," in *Enquiries concerning the Human Understanding and concerning the Principles of Morals*, ed. L. A. Selby-Bigge, 169–323 (Oxford: Clarendon, 1966), 294.

[65]For Frege and followers, a truth condition is that which determines what it is that the sentence expresses. Accordingly, the conditions under which a sentence is to count as true determines what it is that the sentence expresses. See David Wiggins, "Meaning and Truth Conditions: From Frege's Grand Design to Davidson's," in *A Companion to the Philosophy of Language*, ed. Bob Hale and Crispin Wright, 3–28 (Oxford: Blackwell, 1997), 5.

[66]George Lindbeck, *The Nature of Doctrine: Religion and Theology in a Postliberal Age* (Philadelphia: Westminster, 1984), 18.

[67]Ibid., 16.

[68]Ibid., 21.

[69]See Paul Tillich, *The Courage to Be* (New Haven: Yale University Press, 1952), 186ff.

which the power of being is manifest in the life of the believer does suggest that theological language has truth conditions—though not conditions that most believers would know how to identify.[70] We can conclude from just this one example that what Lindbeck calls "experiential-expressivism" cannot merely be equated with expressivist theories. In fact, Lindbeck's category has elements of both the *expressive* as well as the *donational* (and perhaps the *propositional* as well).

A BRIEF RESPONSE

Difficulties for the model arise when trying to think through the radical discontinuity Link suggests between philosophy and theology. Is such a discontinuity even conceivable? Recall Link's suggestion that the *simul* specifies the place of the "sinner before God," and his view that theological assertions employ the vestments of philosophy. Both claims make considerable difficulties for this position.

The *simul* putatively expresses both the believer's forlornness before God and her experience of divine mercy *coram Deo*. However, the phrase "the believer's experience of sin and righteousness *coram Deo*" employs the notion of standing before God. But what is the nature of "x stands before God"? Is it merely an expression of an existential attitude, or is it the assertion of a state of affairs? If it is the former, then the phenomenon of the confession is not in principle connected to God—that is, the expression is just the expression of a pro-attitude and con-attitude that could take many different nontheological forms. But if it is the latter, then it seems that the expressivism is logically dependent upon the objective existence of God, a fact involving truth conditions. Taking either horn seems to undermine the radical discontinuity between the two.[71]

---

[70]See Paul Tillich, *The Dynamics of Faith* (New York: Harper & Row, 1957), ch. 5.

[71]The problem is in the reference of "sinner before God." Assume that x means "sinner before God" taken in a philosophical sense and y means "sinner before God" taken in a theological sense. For every confessional statement w, w must assert something about either x or y. But if w asserts something about y, then y claims some particular situation to obtain and denies others. But what would be the content of this assertion? If it asserts only a particular existential orientation, then y is reducible to the philosophical language of phenomenological description. But if it is not reducible, what constitutes the criterion for the identity of y? On the other hand, if w expresses something about x (if "sinner before God" has ontic reference), then there is no theological assertion hiding underneath the philosophical statement after all. If "sinner before God" is a philosophical assertion, then such an assertion would

The expressivist model is also suspect when Link talks about the "truth" of theological assertions. He claims that one "theological truth" is proclaimed through different "philosophical representations."[72] But what is the status of this "truth" that can never be a representation? If it is supposed to be an "existential truth," then how does the particularity of the language relate to the truth being expressed? Can any words at all express the "believer's standing before God"? If so, the particularity of confessional statement has no ground at all. If not, then there must be particular theological words that are functioning philosophically, that is, as representations asserting a relationship between God and human beings.

Two questions naturally arise for the expressivist: (1) How does one locate theological language with respect to other types of discourse? (2) How does one know exactly what is expressed? The first question asks whether theology is relatable to other disciplines. How do expressions of the subject relate to the states of affairs talked about in science and philosophy"? For instance, if one construes "God is in heaven reconciling the world unto Himself" as the evincing of a pro-attitude toward my life, how does it relate to "the universe began fifteen billion years ago"? The second question is particularly tricky. In addition to expressing emotion, what is it for theological language to express the pre-reflective depth experience of the believer? How does one know what is expressed without employing descriptive categories? In the absence of a map of the depth experience, theological assertions express something whose ultimate significance is actually unknown.

The expressionist model also fails in its adequacy to Luther's employment of theological language. Doctrinal formulations are extremely important for Luther.[73] As Eeva Martikainen has commented, for Luther, doctrine "show the objects" humans are to

---

presuppose other philosophical assertions, and there would seem to be no place for a theological assertion. If "sinner before God" is a theological assertion, then a philosophical assertion hides a theological assertion which itself is another theological assertion, and so forth. Where is the self-identical "what" being expressed?

[72]Link, *Das Ringen*, 385.

[73]Luther speaks often of the importance of doctrinal "articles of faith." Any knowledge one has about divine things is grounded in these articles, which transcend what reason can affirm. See, for instance, LW 37:36; WA 23, 101:11–22 ("This Is My Body"); LW 38:239; WA 39 II, 4:2–3 (the disputation *The Word Was Made Flesh*); WA 39 II, 382: 6–8 (Promotionsdisputation von Petrus Hegemon); and WA 39 II, 137:2–3 (Promotionsdisputation von Joachim Mörlin).

believe and "helps them in appropriating that object."[74] But according to the expressionist model, the radical incommensurability between theological and philosophical assertions precludes the possibility of theological language ever asserting determinate states of affairs. On this model, theological assertions cannot declare God's relation to particular historical events; they cannot speak about the union of the divine and human in the person of Christ, the real presence in the bread and wine, or the movement of persons in the Trinity. Surely Luther would claim that there is a great difference between the phrases "expressing the believer's standing before God" and "expressing the believer's existential orientation." The first clearly cannot be reduced to the second. For Luther, theological language prima facie retains an ontological reference over and above the expression of the believer's own existential-ontological situatedness.

Semantic Realism

Hägglund believes that Luther's theological language has objective reference.[75] Theological statements assert the way in which things can stand between God and His creation. Although theology is not concerned with the objective, rational knowledge (*Wissen*) of the philosopher, it nevertheless speaks about reality (*Wirklichkeit*) through the propositions of faith.[76] "The Word describes human beings in their total situation before God."[77] Instead of an expression of one's

---

[74]See Eeva Martikainen, "Der Doctrina-Begriff in Luthers Theologie," in *Thesaurus Lutheri. Auf der Suche nach neuen Paradigmen der Luther-Forschung*, ed. Tuomo Mannermaa, Anja Ghiselli, and Simo Peura (Helsinki: Luther-Agricola-Gesellschaft, 1987), 123ff.

[75]Hägglund holds that for Luther, theological language both states what is the case and inculcates a response from that pronouncement. See Bengt Hägglund, *Theologie und Philosophie bei Luther und in der occamistischen Tradition*, vol. 51, *Lunds Universitets Årsskrift* (Lund: C. W. K. Gleerup, 1955). Over and against any subjectivist theory, Hägglund declares: "It would be completely false to understand everything as a content of faith having only putative subjective reality [*subjective Realität*], a reality that is related only to [the believer's] own experience, and outside this experience has no validity [*Gultigkeit*]. In this connection, when one speaks of something 'that only in the subjectivity of faith is true—that is not true for the one who does not stand prayerfully [*betend*] before God'—one possesses a mistaken limitation of Luther's concept of faith" (62).

[76]Hägglund, *Theologie und Philosophie*, 62.

[77]See Bengt Hägglund, "Theologische und philosophische Anthropolgie bei Luther," *Studia Theologica* 37 (1983): 101–24. Hägglund claims explicitly that the character of the Word as address is grounded in its descriptive nature: "The 'address character' [*Anredecharakter*] is a consequence of the fact that this Word describes human beings [*Menschen*] in their total situation before God" (117).

existential state before God, a theological statement describes the state of affairs of human beings before God. Such a description is a "re-presentation" (*Darstellung*) of the revealed truth of the *doctrina divinita inspirata*.[78]

Hägglund supposes that there must be some kind of correspondence between the content expressed in a true theological statement and objective reality. Although justification for believing a theological expression true is provided by the Holy Spirit working through the word of God in Scripture, the *content* of theological language is not determined by the Holy Spirit in the interpretive act.[79] The referential model declares that the theological language can denote divine reality itself. The word *God* refers to a divine bearer; *Trinity* denotes an actually existing Godhead comprised of three distinct persons in one essence; and *incarnation* refers to an actual state of affairs in which the bearer of "God" is joined to the bearer of "Jesus." Accordingly, the semantic realist asserts that the condition for meaningful discourse about God is that the word *God* denotes a divine being within the totality of being—regardless of whether or not reason can grasp the properties of that being.

Hägglund's view is consonant with Lindbeck's "cognitive-propositional" approach. Accordingly, "church doctrines function as informative propositions or truth claims about objective realities."[80] The existence of such objective realities constitute the truth conditions of theological discourse. I believe that Luther is a *semantic realist* and that he is committed to a cognitive-propositional position.

A Brief Response

Any model suggesting that theological language can, in Ludwig Wittgenstein's words, "be laid against reality like a measure" is open to criticism.[81] If the truth of a statement is its correspondence to extralinguistic reality, then what of the truth of the statement "True

---

[78]Hägglund, *Theologie und Philosophie*, 9.

[79]Hägglund claims that for the Ockhamists, the will is free either to believe or to disbelieve revealed truth: "Faith is therefore an act of the free will and presupposes the participation of the will." The situation differs for Luther: "Faith is a grasping of the evangelical promise through the whole will. It can never come into existence through the powers of man, but is worked by the Holy Spirit, and is therefore more than a human power or virtue." See ibid., 84.

[80]Lindbeck, *The Nature of Doctrine*, 16.

[81]See Ludwig Wittgenstein, *Tractatus Logico-Philosophicus*, trans. D. F. Pears and B. F. McGuinness (London: Routledge & Kegan Paul, 1961), 2.1512.

statements are those that correspond to extralinguistic reality"? What is the reality mirrored by this latter statement? If one can isolate some state of affairs to which it corresponds, then what about "it is true that there is some state of affairs to which the statement 'True statements correspond to extralinguistic reality' corresponds"? To avoid such unwanted regresses, many reject truth as correspondence between propositions and reality.[82]

Even if this objection can be met, further problems arise when one tries to specify the criteria for the relation of correspondence. What is the nature of the correspondence? How can a proposition, expressed in sentence tokens, correspond to physical facts, to relationships among ideas, propositions, and facts?[83] Obviously, we can do no more than merely mention the general semantic problems of correspondence views. There is ample literature elsewhere.[84]

Anthony Flew asks what possible state of affairs is negated by "God loves his children." Finding that the true believer cannot (or will not) specify instances falsifying the statement, Flew declares, "If there is nothing which the putative assertion denies, then there is nothing which it asserts either."[85] But if it asserts nothing, then the terms comprising it have no determinate reference. Moreover, how can earthly language ever "say what is so" about divine reality? Earthly language consists of earthly words having bearers, the properties of which are picked out on the basis of natural reason and experience. To assume that theological language can straightforwardly picture divine truth demands that human beings have a pregrasp of the context of those divine facts, that they have a conceptual apparatus that could conceive the properties individuating such objects as God, God's love, the incarnation, and the Trinity. Saying that a language denotes divine objects requires a way to individuate those objects denoted apart from that language. But what kind of prelinguistic capability would this be?

It is not merely a question of human language failing to speak univocally about earthly and divine properties—the medieval doctrine of analogy was formulated to address just such a concern.

[82]See Blackburn, *Spreading the Word*, 226–29.

[83]See Gottlob Frege, "The Thought," *Mind* 65, no. 259 (1956): 289–311, esp. 291.

[84]See Blackburn, *Spreading the Word*, 224–35, or D. J. O'Connor and Brian Carr, *Introduction to the Theory of Knowledge* (Minneapolis: University of Minnesota Press, 1982), 169–75.

[85]Anthony Flew, "Theology and Falsification," in *The Philosophy of Religion*, ed. G. J. Warnock (Oxford: Oxford University Press, 1971), 15.

Rather, for Luther, it is that human language runs into contradiction when it attempts to state divine truths. Since the logic of theological language does not permit a correspondence to divine facts, it seems that all theological language can do is point to the divine reality it can never completely picture. Yet, paradoxically, Luther holds that this language does refer. Theology says what is so about the heavenly realm, though it says it by means of language whose logic is oriented only to states of affairs within the earthly realm. Despite its internal problems, semantic realism is, I believe, Luther's own understanding of theological language.

Donationalist Semantics

Ebeling stresses those aspects of Luther's theology that deal with practical discernment in preaching the word of God. For Luther, theological language is meaningful because it brings "assurance, certainty, life, and salvation."[86] Existential appropriation is not separate from intellectual assent: "For Luther, theology as the object of intellectual and theology as the sphere of a personal encounter, form an indivisible unity."[87] In interpreting Scripture, one does not apply "objective" exegetical tools that then ground abstract articles of faith; rather, true interpretation is "identified in Luther's mind with the question which constantly pursued him of his standing in the sight of God."[88] Intellectual inquiry into the articles of faith revealed in Scripture occurs only upon the horizon of preunderstandings comprising the reader's own existence. Theological language finds its deepest meaning at the level of existence, at the level where life, assurance, and salvation are at issue, at the level of the primordial experience of truth prior to the question of the *criterion* of truth. It is this level that Ebeling believes Luther has uncovered in his use of theological language, a language that *gives* reality to the hearer or reader.

Ebeling denies the traditional metaphysical view of self-contained substances, possessing determinate properties, externally related to

---

[86]Gerhard Ebeling, *Luther: An Introduction to His Thought* (Philadelphia: Fortress Press, 1970), 93.

[87]See ibid., 95–96. Ebeling claims that Luther disallows the distinction employed since the Enlightenment between the *explicatio* and the *applicatio* of a passage. The first is the approach of knowledge as "objective presentation and exposition of material"; the second is the approach of faith as "one's own subjective involvement, one's personal response or the appeal and challenge to make such a response" (93–94).

[88]Ibid., 96.

one another. According to him, the Reformer's close reading of the biblical text inaugurated the turn in theology from the "intellectual-metaphysical" conception of scholasticism to the "realistic" view of the Reformation.[89] Human being is a relationship that is sustained with other things.[90] Thus, human existence is always incomplete, always dynamic, always be-ing in its orientation toward the other—regardless of whether that other is human or divine. Human being stands at the crossroads between the *coram mundo* and the *coram Deo*. Because the situation of the person at the crossroads is ultimately *linguistic*, the contradictory orientation *coram mundo/coram Deo* is a word situation in which the word of promise is heard simultaneously with the word of demand, in which existence is opened in promise to freedom and future while yet oriented in demand to guilt and death.

Theology does not primarily "talk about" the distinction between law and gospel but is itself the process of that distinction. It is not primarily descriptive but rather inculcates the proper relationship between law and gospel. Theological language presents the word of God to the hearer, the word "which sets a person free from imprisonment within himself," and "reveals to the person a hope not founded upon himself," a hope that "promises the person a courage not derived from himself."[91] Theological language brings about justification through the word alone through faith alone in evoking faith—that *donation* of grace and the promise of freedom—through the *presencing* of the Word working grace within the historicity and linguisticality of existence.

Ebeling claims that existence is a linguistic phenomenon: "*Sein is Sprachlichsein* [To be is to be linguistically]."[92] For Ebeling, it is the "word event" *Wortgeschehen* that accomplishes this transformation

---

[89]Gerhard Ebeling, *Lutherstudien* (Tübingen: Mohr, 1971), 24: "The Holy Scripture does not concern itself with the 'whatness' of things [*quidditates rerum*], but only their qualities. What does this mean? Substance does not mean in scripture the essence of thing in and for itself, but, rather, what the thing means for the person associated with it; that is, how the person takes it, how he understands himself in his relation to it. Therefore, substance is not that which things are, but is that which a person has in relation to things. When he exists in such-and-such-a-way [*so oder so existiert*], he relates himself in such-and-such-a-way to things."

[90]Gerhard Ebeling, *Evangelische Evangelienauslegung* (Darmstadt: Wissenschaftliche Buchgesellschaft, 1969), 297.

[91]Ebeling, *Luther*, 120.

[92]Gerhard Ebeling, *Dogmatik des christlichen Glaubens I* (Tübingen: J. C. B. Mohr, 1979), 352.

of the web of primordial, existential significations into an existential orientation toward the future. Whereas the theological language of scholasticism always confronts the individual as demand, Ebeling emphasizes that for Luther, the language of theology becomes the believer's own language in the word event of existential appropriation: "Whereas someone else's dogmatic construction offers at best a dwelling place in which one can find shelter as a guest and a stranger, a 'linguistic innovation' [*Sprachereignis*] provides a place to live and make one's own home."[93] In the event of language, there is an "opening up of revelation and disclosure."[94] When words address me with a "decisive utterance about my existence as a human being,"[95] then the word of God is spoken, which sets me "free from myself and to all the powers to which I sold myself."[96] Now the external word becomes *my* word, for it is God's word for me. It strikes me in the horizon of my preunderstanding of what it is to be free from myself before God.

God's word authenticates man and woman within the human existential situation. The new reality is "in, under, around, and beyond" the old. It is the liberty of the gospel bounded by the law. The word event does not have meaning because of its reference to divine objects, properties, relations, or states of affairs, but rather it "donates" or "gifts" to the person a new orientation, a new way of understanding, a new way of be-ing in the world, a way of be-ing in which one actively anticipates the future and remembers the past, a way of be-ing in which one sees the future pregnant with the possibility of justice for a sinner and of love for the unworthy one.

A Brief Response

While Ebeling's view is plausible as a phenomenological *description* of the existential significance of theological language for the believer, it fails to take seriously the salvific relevance of the propositional understanding of such language within the believer's structure of significances constituting her world. While language having no extra-linguistic referent may, in some situations, empower a person who has become self-consciously aware of that lack of reference, many times this would not happen. Consider the thirty-year-old terminal

---

[93]Ebeling, *Luther*, 28.
[94]Ibid., 28.
[95]Ibid., 98.
[96]Ibid., 121.

cancer patient empowered by the words "You will be resurrected to live with Christ eternally." It is likely the words will empower her only if she believes that they speak about some postmortem state of affairs in which there will be self-conscious existence with God after death. Accordingly, she lives with hope for the future, freed (at least in part) from the power of death's despair. However, were she to become aware that "You will be resurrected to live with Christ eternally" does not refer to a future state, she will likely respond differently.

Accordingly, the model is clearly inadequate to Luther's own use of theological language. The Reformer thought that phrases such as "You will be resurrected to live with Christ eternally" point beyond themselves to a real future. In very moving passages from his *Table Talk*, Luther speaks about the death of his young daughter, Magdalene. While she was gravely ill, Luther cried out, "Dear daughter, you have another Father in heaven. You are going to go to him."[97] After her death, he declares, "Ah, dear child, to think that you must be raised up and will shine like the stars, yes, the sun."[98] Later, at the burial, Luther remarks, "There is a resurrection of the flesh. My daughter is now fitted out in body and soul. We Christians now have nothing to complain about. We know that it should and must be so, for we are altogether certain about eternal life."[99] A semantic model of theological language that fails to take account of *what* is believed cannot be adequate to Luther. Although it correctly models the empowering function of theological language, it fails to deal with the *truth conditions* necessary for empowerment, that is, that Christ really did die for human sins so that all who believe might live with God eternally—even little Magdalene.

Another problem must be mentioned. By emphasizing that the letter is law and that God's word is gospel, by declaring that the prelinguistic horizon of preunderstandings is determinative of whether a word or phrase will be experienced as law or gospel, and by advocating such a sharp dualism between spirit and letter, Ebeling seems to be in danger of compromising the externality of God's word. The very meaning of the external language is made contingent upon the horizon of the hearer. No longer is the Holy Spirit girded by the medium of the external word; rather, the external word becomes a documentation of spirit—not, of course, the ontic "spirit" of the Enthusiasts,

---

[97]LW 54:432; WATR 5 (*Table Talk*, 1543), 192–93, #5497.
[98]Ibid., 193, #5498.
[99]Ibid., 194, #5500.

but rather the existential-ontological "spirit" of the preunderstood structure of meaningfulness comprising Being-in-the-World.

Semantic Holism

In *Luther und Hegel*, Ulrich Asendorf suggests that we can best understand Luther's distinction between philosophy and theology as between autonomous "contexts of meaning," between independent, overarching semantic fields each presupposing rules by which meaning obtains.[100] He points out that Luther scholars have neglected to pay enough attention to Luther's own "linguistic analysis" in distinguishing the languages of theology and philosophy. Accordingly, Luther's views on language resemble in some ways those of the later Wittgenstein.[101] The meaning of words, phrases, and statements of theology and philosophy respectively are determined by their overarching contexts of meaning. Asendorf writes:

> The meaning of a word or proposition is therefore dependent upon the relation arrangement (*Beziehungsgefüge*) in which the word or proposition is employed. This is exactly the relevant theme for Luther in the question of the relation between philosophy and theology. Words and propositions are not abstractly valid nor do they have invariant meanings as the Parisian theologians supposed when they presupposed the same meanings for terms of theology and philosophy and declared the syllogism to be universally valid.[102]

On this model, words and sentences are not meaning-invariant across philosophy and theology—for example, *righteousness* means something different in theology than it does in law and politics.[103]

---

[100]Ulrich Asendorf, *Luther und Hegel* (Wiesbaden: Franz Steiner, 1982).

[101]Ibid., 108: "For contemporary philosophy the position should be considered that Luther's thought in many regards touches that which philosophers of linguistic analysis from G. Frege and L. Wittgenstein have made the object of their investigations. Except for Nygren's philosophy of religion the attempt has hardly been undertaken to make the philosophical tradition culminating in Wittgenstein at home in theology, and especially to employ that tradition fruitfully for the interpretation of Luther."

[102]Ibid., 119.

[103]Cf. Christopher Peacocke, "Holism," in *A Companion to the Philosophy of Language*, ed. Bob Hale and Crispin Wright, 227–47 (Oxford: Blackwell, 1997), 227: "[Global holism claims that] the meaning of an expression depends constitutively on its relations to all other expressions in the language, where these relations may need to take account of such facts about the use of these other expressions as their relations to the non-linguistic world, to action and to perception."

Asendorf's analysis rests on the legitimacy of the notion of a context of meaning. If a word has meaning only within an autonomous context, and if different contexts of meaning are alternate linguistic frames of reference by which reality is grasped and experienced, then a simple referential view of theological language linking itself to an already determinate experience or reality must be jettisoned, for experience becomes determinate only *within* a given context of meaning. The linguistic context is logically prior to that which is thought or spoken through it.

But the logical priority of the context means that it must be contingent, for there can be no *justification* for the adoption of a particular context. Anders Nygren, in fact, claims that no context of meaning is truer than another, for there is no "ultimate self-validating principle from which to derive the validity of all that is valid."[104] As Wittgenstein says of a "language-game" (which Nygren holds as equivalent to a context of meaning): "It is not based on grounds. It is not reasonable (or unreasonable). It is there—like our life."[105] Instead of searching for an explanation for the employment of a language-game, "we ought to look at what happens as a 'proto-phenomenon.'"[106] Simply put, we ought to look to the fact that "this language-game is played."[107] Wittgenstein declares, "If I have exhausted the justifications I have reached bedrock, and my spade is turned. Then I am inclined to say: 'This is simply what I do.'"[108]

If the context of meaning of theology is simply and contingently "there—like our life," then the statements of theology do not make necessary reference to some extralinguistic reality as a condition for their meaningfulness. The meaning of a name need not be a bearer, nor the meaning of a sentence its possibility of referring to certain configurations in the world. As Wittgenstein says, "for a large class of cases" the meaning of a word can be defined as "its use in the language."[109] Accordingly, "God" has meaning not on account of its

[104]Anders Nygren, *Meaning and Method*, trans. Phillip Watson (Philadelphia: Fortress Press, 1972), 276.

[105]Ludwig Wittgenstein, *On Certainty*, trans. G. E. M. Anscombe and G. H. von Wright (Oxford: Basil Blackwell, 1969), #559.

[106]Ludwig Wittgenstein, *Philosophical Investigations*, trans. G. E. M. Anscombe. (New York: Macmillan, 1953), #654.

[107]Ibid., ##655–56: "Look on the language-game as the *primary* thing. And look on the feelings, etc., as you look on a way of regarding the language-game, as interpretation."

[108]Ibid., #217.

[109]Ibid., #43.

reference, but rather because of "the place of the word in the grammar" of theology.[110] The phrase "resurrection of Christ" possesses meaning because of its role in a theological grammar.[111]

Comparing language to a "calculus" serves to illuminate its rule-ordered structure. One might claim that words, like numbers, are implicitly defined through their relatedness to one another in the customary patterns of their usage. To understand an expression is not to grasp some discrete mental content; rather, it is the ability properly to respond linguistically to the expression in the various situations in which it occurs. If Luther's theological language is successfully modeled by this approach, then the meaning of "God" must be construed as a function of its use in the matrix of rule-ordered relationships of customary usage within a theological grammar.

The autonomy model links to the "cultural-linguistic" model discussed by Lindbeck.[112] On this view, dogmatic theological expressions are rules (customs) controlling the "play" of religious and theological expressions and meaning. Lindbeck writes that "for a rule theory . . . doctrines qua doctrines are not first-order propositions, but are to be construed as second-order ones: they make . . . intrasystematic rather than ontological truth claims."[113] Instead of meaning being found in the subject, it is found in the *use* to which that language is put by a community of language users. Thus, the expression "we are justified by grace alone" becomes a community-

---

[110]Ludwig Wittgenstein, *Philosophical Grammar*, trans. Anthony Kenny (Berkeley: University of California Press, 1974), 59.

[111]Ibid., 65: "A name has meaning, a proposition has sense in the calculus to which it belongs. The calculus is as it were autonomous. Language must speak for itself. I might say: the only thing that is of interest to me is the *content* of a proposition and the content of a proposition is something internal to it. A proposition has its content as part of a calculus. . . . The meaning is the role of the word in the calculus." It should be noted that although Nygren and Asendorf appeal to Wittgenstein in asserting that the meaning of an expression is a function of the place that expression has in an autonomous context of meaning, Wittgenstein never went this far in his published work. In the *Tractatus* and the *Investigations*, he spoke only of a *word*'s meaning defined in terms of use. See Garth Hallett, *A Companion to Wittgenstein's Philosophical Investigations* (Ithaca: Cornell University Press, 1977), 123. Hallet does cite an unpublished manuscript from 1938 in which Wittgenstein asserts, "We must understand that the meaning of a proposition lies in the use we make of it" (91). In the posthumous *Philosophical Grammar*, he also declares that "the role of a sentence in the calculus is its sense" (130).

[112]We have previously seen how the expressive and donational models link to "experiential-expressivism" and how the referential model connects to the "cognitive-propositional" approach.

[113]Lindbeck, *Nature of Doctrine*, 80.

embedded rule governing the customs of use of religious language for a particular group. Truth conditions are not important on this construal, for the concern is with the context of customs of use for a community, not with the existence of objects, properties, relations, or states of affairs making true that language.[114] Because different "grammars" operate in different religious traditions, there is no point-by-point translatability among them.[115] There can be no recipe of translation because such a recipe or schema would presuppose a broader context of meaning encompassing both contexts.[116] Nygren claims that the inability to translate these different contexts of meaning is a "fundamental insight to which contemporary philosophy has come."[117] Failing to attend to the "distinctive character" of contexts of meaning produces "category mistakes" and "category mixing," and a concomitant loss of meaning.[118]

Two recent Luther commentators assume somewhat similar views

---

[114]The truth conditions of any sentence are the conditions under which that sentence has the semantic value of truth. Theology must speak of the possibility of evidence transcending truth conditions. This is possible on a Tarskian formulation: Just as "snow is white" if and only if snow is white, so too "God is the creator of the universe" if and only if God is the creator of the universe. The sense of "God is the creator of the universe" gives the conditions under which the sentence is true, that is, God is the creator of the universe.

[115]Nygren, *Meaning and Method*, 292.

[116]For a discussion of the difference between a "recipe" and a "schema" of translation, see Arthur Pap, "Philosophical Analysis, Translation Schemas, and the Regularity Theory of Causation," *Journal of Philosophy* 49 (1952). For a discussion of the indeterminacy of translation, see Willard Van Orman Quine, *Ontological Relativity and Other Essays* (New York: Columbia University Press, 1969). Quine argues that even the specification of the reference of terms in one language presupposes a background language needed for correlation (49). He claims that it "makes no sense to say what the objects of a theory are, beyond saying how to interpret or reinterpret that theory in another" (50). It is only by presupposing a background theory that any translation, reduction, or reinterpretation of theories in terms of each other is possible: "Within this background theory we can show how some subordinate theory, whose universe is some portion of the background universe, can by a reinterpretation be reduced to another subordinate theory whose universe is some lesser portion. Such talk of subordinate theories and their ontologies *is* meaningful, but only relative to the background theory with its own primitively adopted and ultimately inscrutable ontology" (50–51). For Quine, what words mean in any given linguistic framework is relative both to the background language in which the specification is made *and* to the choice of how to interpret the given linguistic framework in terms of the background language.

[117]Nygren, *Meaning and Method*, 292.

[118]Ibid., 287: "Category mixing, no matter of what kind, always leads to meaninglessness, or at any rate to loss of the meaning intended. The meaning of a statement can only be preserved if it is seen in the light of the presuppositions which obtain in its context of meaning."

in claiming incommensurability between theology and philosophy in Luther. Stefan Streiff declares of Luther, "Theology is an incommensurable context of meaning." It "has its own presuppositions and rules, its own prescriptions, it own thinking, its own specific language. Theology must therefore be distinguished from other contexts of meaning, from philosophy."[119] Streiff discerns incommensurability in the difference between the instrumental character of everyday philosophical language and the medial character of the "unusual" language of theology.[120] Thomas Wabel also finds incommensurability between philosophy and theology. He declares that for Luther, "it follows that by means of the syllogism no comprehensive reality of theology and philosophy can be formed. To attempt to do so is to soften the distinction between law and gospel."[121] In developing his position on the crucial role of metaphor in the incommensurability of the two discourses, Wabel cautions that the presence of commensurability would take away the tensions between the two kingdoms, "between works and faith, between law and gospel."[122]

A Brief Response

The semantic holism model is open to internal criticism. What is the relationship among the various contexts of meaning, and what putatively stands over and against them and is expressed through them? In a crucial section in *The Nature of Doctrine*, Lindbeck explores the "truth" of religion. He claims that "intrasystematic" truth is necessary, but not sufficient, for ontological truth. In order to have ontological truth, he offers, what is required of the system as a whole is to be "categorially true" (or adequate) to that which lies outside the system, for instance, God's being and will.[123] But what precisely does "categorial truth" mean here? What sense can be made of "God's being and will" if it supposedly exists outside any "system"? If language is the necessary condition for determinate experience, then

---

[119]Stefan Streiff, *"Novis Linguis loqui": Martin Luthers Disputation über Joh 1,14 "verbum caro factum est" aus dem Jahr 1539*, ed. Wolfhart Pannenberg and Reinhard Slenczka, *Forschungen zur systematischen und ökumenischen Theologie*, Band 70 (Göttingen: Vandenhoeck & Ruprecht, 1993), 225.

[120]Ibid., 126.

[121]Thomas Wabel, *Sprache als Grenze in Luthers theologischer Hermeneutik und Wittgensteins Sprachphilosophie*, Theologische Bibliothek Töpelmann, Band 92 (Berlin: Walter de Gruyter, 1998), 320.

[122]Ibid., 321.

[123]Lindbeck, *Nature of Doctrine*, 65ff.

how is God's being and will possible outside language? Furthermore, if there is nothing external to the contexts that the contexts express in differing ways, then how are the contexts *relatable*? Either one must postulate a determinate reality outside of the contexts that is completely unknowable (yet functions to give unity to the divergent contexts), or one must assert that there is nothing outside of the contexts grounding any possible integration of them and that life is, after all, "divided up into a series of parallel lines of meaning which never meet."[124] The model fails to clarify the relationship between the contexts of meaning and that which is *independent* and *prior to* those contexts. If contexts determine the contour of experience, then there is no sense in talking about any objectively subsisting "facts" awaiting interpretation by the various contexts.

Clearly, Nygren's repudiation of "category mixing" diminishes the possibility of metaphor. I believe this is particularly disastrous for a proper understanding of Luther's theological language.[125] If words have meanings only within existing contexts, then how exactly can new meanings be generated, for do we not employ words in unusual ways within a context in order to create new meanings? How is it possible without category mixing that the word *father* (belonging to the language of everyday life) could have been applied to the word *God* (belonging to the language of religion) such that we can now say "God the Father"? Do we wish to reject contemporary category mixing between religion and other contexts while yet implicitly supporting its legitimacy at earlier times?[126]

Summary

While there are problems with all of the models, I believe that *semantic realism* is most accurate of Luther. Luther lived in the sixteenth

---

[124]Nygren, *Meaning and Method*, 294.

[125]For more on these last two points, see Earl MacCormac, "Anders Nygren's Philosophy of Religion: A Critique of *Meaning and Method*," *Scottish Journal of Theology* 27 (1974): 208–21, esp. 219–20.

[126]For example, Nygren rejects Tillich's assertion that "God is Being-Itself" because predicating "Being-Itself" of "God" mixes categories and destroys religious meaning (Nygren, *Meaning and Method*, 233). But what about Augustine's equation of God with the *summum bonum*? Is that also a mixing of categories producing a loss of meaning? And if "God" and "good" is a category-mixing, destroying meaning, where would one go to find the pristine religious context of meaning prior to this destruction? Is it found in the New Testament itself? But why allow metaphor there while rejecting it in the later tradition? Why does identifying "Jesus" with "Logos" not constitute a destruction of meaning?

century and was trained in the semantic traditions of his time. It would have been very odd for him to have departed significantly from the presuppositions of his period and to have embraced views that only became popular in the twentieth century. Unfortunately, there is a marked tendency among Luther scholars to attribute to the Reformer positions adumbrating the contemporary horizon. Graham White has called this tendency within Luther research the fallacy of *descriptive foundationalism*: "The secondary literature approaches this problem by attempting to find some single metaphysical concept, which Luther had and which the scholastics did not (or vice versa), and from the presence or absence of which the differences between Lutheran and scholastic methods can be derived."[127] Much Luther research has simply supposed that Luther wholly rejected a theology of lifeless, abstract propositions in favor of a theology of lived experience. But with this emphasis on human experience, Luther becomes almost a proto-Enlightenment figure, a man more at home 250 years after the time in which he lived.

But this subjectivized Luther bears little resemblance to the real Reformer. Luther clearly retained medieval interest in the theological problems of trinitarian formulation. While I believe that Luther adopts a semantic realist position generally consistent with Lindbeck's *cognitive-propositional* approach, Hinlicky suggests a type of semantic holism in his acceptance of the Lindbeckian cultural-linguistic approach. Although Hinlicky does not embrace the particularities of the Asendorf-Nygren proposal, the cultural-linguistic approach nonetheless presupposes the problematic of having to determine the "adequacy" of holistic theological language to nonlinguistic reality.

4. The Trinitarian Problem in Context

The idea that three persons are one God is a profound philosophical problem, for one must somehow steer a course between *modalism* and *tritheism*. The first claims that God is one thing and that the three persons are various ways that the one substance shows itself. Analogously, I am father of my son, son of my father, and the "spirit" of the Bielfeldt household. (The last is surely debatable.) The second asserts that because the three distinct persons are so similar with respect to certain features, they can be called one thing. Thus, John, Paul, and Luke are similar with respect to being my sons and

---

[127]See White, *Luther as Nominalist*, 37.

thus *are* Bielfeldt in some way. Various trinitarian positions fall somewhere on the continuum between these extremes, with some emphasizing the unity of the divine substance and others emphasizing the distinctiveness of the persons. In order to appreciate better Luther's trinitarian claims in his late disputations, it is important to review some of the major trinitarian players. Luther's trinitarian thought is deeply indebted to Augustine, even though the Reformer is, in many respects, a late medieval nominalist.

Augustine

Augustine declares that the persons are constituted by the relationships each have with the other persons. He calls these persons "relative entities" (*relativa*) and distinguishes them from the divine substance: "For this reason, although being the Father and being Son are different, there is not a different substance, because here one does not talk according to a substance but according to a relative entity; but it is a relative entity (*relativum*) and not an accident because God is immutable."[128] The *relativum* that is a person is neither substance nor accident, for if the *relativa* were different substances, there would no longer be divine unity, and if the *relativa* were accidents, then God could not be immutable and divine simplicity would be compromised. Although this notion of a *relativum* has important theological work to do, it clearly is philosophically problematic, for how can something be neither substance nor accident? Nonetheless, the distinction is crucial for subsequent trinitarian thinking. After Augustine, one can talk about God "substantially" (with respect to His divine nature) or "relatively" (with respect to the divine persons). Luther's trinitarian work in these disputations does not depart greatly from this Augustinian starting point. He regards the persons as *relativa*; they are neither substance nor accident. "Wisdom" is not a quality for Luther, nor is it a substance; it is the *relativum* itself.

Dominican Relations and Franciscan Processions

In the thirteenth and early fourteenth centuries, two different trinitarian traditions developed in the West. The tradition grounded in Thomas Aquinas claims that relations themselves individuate the

---

[128]*De Trinitate*, book 5, ch. 5, 210f. (PL 42, 914): "Quamobrem quamvis diversum sit patrem esse et filium esse, non est tamen diversa substantia quia hoc non secundum substantiam dicuntur sed secundum relativum, quod tamen relativum non est acciedens qui non est mutable."

persons of the Trinity; that is, the Father is the Father because he bears a particular relation to the Son.[129] The personal processions and the divine relations are thus identical, differing only in their

---

[129]The medieval tradition distinguished relations according to speech (*relationes secundum dici*) from relations according to being (*relationes secundum esse*). In general, they rejected any ontological correlate to polyadic predicates: there are no extramental relations; things are related *in mente* due to the particular accidents they have. (I am indebted to the work of Jeffrey Brower. See *Medieval Theories of Relations*, 2005, Stanford Encyclopedia of Philosophy, available at http://plato.stanford.edu/entries/relations-medieval/#3 [accessed October 30, 2007].) But if this is true, then it seems that they must assume *anti-realism* with respect to relations. It thus becomes problematic to identify the persons with subsistent relations. Yet the medieval tradition rejected anti-realism. Aquinas, for instance, claims that "nothing is placed in a category unless it is outside the soul" (Aquinas, *De potentia*, q. 7, a. 9).

How can these two views be reconciled? Jeffrey Brower distinguishes *reductive* from *nonreductive* realism with respect to relations. According to *reductive realism*, the putative relations are simply the nonrelational accidents each related object supposedly has. Thus, "*a* is taller than *b*" is construed as *a* has property F (a certain length) and *b* has property G (another length). Given the properties F and G, *a* is thus taller than *b*. There is nothing more to the relation than F*a* and G*b*. Nonreductive realism claims that *a* being taller than *b* is due to *a* and *b* having accidents that are necessitated by the heights of *a* and *b* but which are not themselves identical to the heights. These accidents are sui generis and hold by virtue of the relation itself. According to his *nonreductive* view, the relation is not identical to its foundations: there is something "more" to R*ab* than merely F*a* and G*b*. The medieval tradition divides on the question of relational reduction, with Abelard and later Ockham holding the reductive position, and Albert the Great and Scotus claiming nonreductionism. Reductive realism nicely mirrors the intuition that *a* doesn't change in any way if *b* gets taller. It seems that rejecting the reductivist position commits one to claiming that *a* has properties that change as *b* changes, even though there is no intrinsic change in *a* at all. Accordingly, nonreductive realism understands that the "foundation" by which the relation is had is different from the relational property itself.

The medieval philosophers discussed relations of reason (*relationes rationis*). There are beings of reason (*entia rationis*) that do not have extramental existence but that nevertheless must be thought. For instance, Bob is thinking about Mary. While we can point to an extramental property in Bob by virtue of which Mary is thought about, there is no extramental property in Mary by virtue of which Mary is thought about. Yet we may conceive the "thought-aboutness" of Mary as a property of Mary. This "thought-aboutness" is an *entia rationis*, and the relation between the two constitutes a *relatio rationis*. Relations of reason saved medieval philosophers from having to claim that substances were relations. But this cry of "no substances are relations" cannot apply to the Trinity, for here the relations of the persons cannot simply be *relationes rationis*. If we grant real relations in God and yet hold that God is divinely simple, then we must concede that the substance God is a *relation*. Aquinas declares, "Whatever is in God is his nature. . . . It is thus clear that a relation really existing in God is identical to his nature according to reality, and does not differ from it except according to a concept of mind" (*ST* I, q. 28, a. 2). For Scotus, on the other hand, relations are real accidents inhering in the things related. If *a* and *b* are similar with respect to whiteness, then whiteness inheres in *a*, whiteness inheres in *b*, and inhering in *a* is the accident of being similar to *b* with respect to whiteness, and inhering in *b* is the accident of being similar to *a* with respect to whiteness.

modus significandi et intelligendi.[130] The Son is generated because he is the Son; he is not the Son by virtue of his being generated. The second tradition, developing in and through the work of Richard of St. Victor, Bonaventure, Henry of Ghent, Duns Scotus, and others, claims an emanationalist model in which origins individuate the trinitarian persons. The person of the Father is innascible—He is not able to be born—and *is* the Father by virtue of this innascibility. On the first model, relations themselves individuate the trinitarian persons; on the second model, the persons possess particular monadic properties, on the basis of which relations among the persons are established.[131] The first view, because it is committed to individuation through the relations, understands "Word" metaphorically. "Word" can be spoken of this Son metaphorically because the Son is "like a Word" in being an expression (issue) of the one who expresses (issues) it. The emanationalist view, on the other hand, regards "Word" as specifying more or less the individuating property of the second person. Because the second person is Word, he is called the Son of God.

The distinction between internal and external relations is useful. An external relation R holds of a with respect to b if and only if R does not change the entity a in its relation to b. For example, I am externally related genetically to my son because I remain who and what I am genetically regardless of whether the relation "being the parent of" obtains or not. An internal relation R' holds of a with respect to b, however, if and only if the tokening of R' changes what a is in relation to b. For example, my son is internally related to me because his genetic material depends upon whether or not the relation "being a son" obtains.

On the Franciscan model, the trinitarian persons are *externally* related with respect to "being the Father of x" because the dyadic relation of Father to Son is grounded on the existence of nonrelational, mondadic properties such as innascability, which themselves individuate the persons. For the Dominican, however, the persons are *internally* related by dyadic relational properties such as "being the Father of x," for the Father could not be the person He is apart from the relation in question. The Dominican claim is that the One called "Father" is the One having two dyadic relations: "being the Father

---

[130]Knuuttila and Saarinen, "Luther's Trinitarian Theology," 5.

[131]For a thorough discussion, see Russell Friedman, "Divergent Traditions in Later-Medieval Trinitarian Theology: Relations, Emanations, and the Use of Philosophical Psychology, 1250–1325," *ST* 53 (1999): 13–25.

of the Son" and "being the One from Whom the Spirit proceeds." For the Franciscans, the One called "Father" is the One having the nonrelational monadic quality of innascability, a property presupposed by the relation of Father to Son. While the Dominicans start with the relations, move to the persons, and then proceed to talk of the processions, the Franciscans begin with the personal processions, move to the persons, and then speak about the trinitarian relations.

Difficulties arise when trying to conceive how either account avoids the trinitarian problematic. If we say that there are either *real relations* or *real intrinsic qualities* in the persons, we seem to claim that there is a real ontological constituent to individuation, a *modus essendi*, not merely a *modi intelligendi*. If this is so, it appears that divine simplicity, and hence the divine essence itself, is compromised, and tritheism follows. On the other hand, if we say that the trinitarian individuaters are mere *modi intelligendi*, then the ontological distinctiveness of the trinitarian persons is undermined. There is one divine essence ontologically, although human beings might distinguish that essence into persons. But if this is so, then the persons arise because of human conceptuality, and modalism follows.[132]

---

[132]The logical problem of the Trinity is that there are three divine persons but only one God. But how is this possible? If there are three divine persons, they must be *numerically distinct*, for numerical distinction is presumably a necessary condition for personhood. But if there is only one God, then the persons must be *identical*, for nonidentity entails plurality and God is not a plurality. But nothing can be both identical and distinct, and thus there can be no Trinity. This is the reductio argument against classical trinitarianism. In the contemporary philosophical literature, two general strategies are used to combat this reductio, both of which deny the absolute identity of the persons and God: one is the social trinitarian position (ST); the other, the relative identity strategy (RI). (See Michael Rea, "Relative Identity and the Doctrine of the Trinity," *Philosophia Christi* 5.2 [2003]: 431–46.) RI tries to provide a model that allows the persons to be God-identical and person-distinct. Peter Geach claims that genuine identity statements are always relative identity statements; that is, if *x* is identical to *y*, then *x* and *y* will be identical with respect to some property F, even though they might not be identical with respect to some other property G. (See Peter Geach, "Identity," *Review of Metaphysics* 21 [1967]: 3–12; Peter Geach, "Identity—A Reply," *Review of Metaphysics* 22 [1969]: 556–59; and Peter Geach, "Ontological Relativity and Relative Identity," *Logic and Ontology*, ed. Milton Munitz [New York: New York University Press, 1973], 287–302.) On this view, "identical" marbles could be identical with respect to size and shape even though they are not identical with respect to position or mass. Accordingly, the three persons are identical with respect to the divine nature F, but not with respect to innascibility G. According to ST, the relation between the persons and God is not identity but must be either a relation of *mereology* (together the three parts comprise the whole God) or a relation of *class membership* (the Son *s* is God, because *s* ∈ {Father, Son, and Holy Spirit}). Obviously, the first of these is problematic because it denies that God is entirely present in each and every person. The second avenue is even more

The problem of the identity in difference of the trinitarian persons is not solved by either the Dominicans or the Franciscans. I believe that Luther recognized the intractability of this logical problem of the Trinity and was thus led to assert that the three-in-one nature of the Trinity forms a paradoxical, theological state of affairs that cannot be conceived within standard philosophical categories. Accordingly, Luther is free to emphasize the distinctiveness of the persons at least as much as the unity of the divine essence. In fact, in his late disputations, we find him often thinking more like a Franciscan than like a Dominican on the issue of the processions of persons.

The Trinitarianism of the *Via Moderna* and the Late Medieval Traditions

In his *Commentary on the Sentences*, the founder of the *via moderna*, William of Ockham, writes that by its own powers reason "would say that in God there cannot be three persons with unity of nature."[133] It is only through the revelation of Scripture that we know that the divine Trinity exists.[134] Alfred Freddoso discusses the role of reason as it relates to Ockham and the Trinity, pointing out that Ockham departs significantly from Aquinas's position that claims that although reason seemingly rightly concludes that there can be no real relations within the Trinity, the light of natural reason can nevertheless find the flaw leading to this conclusion and rectify it. Ockham, on the contrary, denies that the light of natural reason can find and rectify the flaw, for only through revelation can human beings even begin to discern that there is a flaw. Ockham thus holds that there is no possibility of uniting faith and reason in a synthesis.[135] Instead, reason and philosophy seem to deal with objects, properties, and states of affairs that are quite different from those of faith and theology. This distinction between the epistemic deliverances of faith and those of reason is bequeathed to Luther, and he presupposes such a separation in developing his view of theology and philosophy comprising distinctive *semantic regions*. There is a

---

problematic, however, because *monotheism* becomes almost impossible: $\exists x(Gx \leftrightarrow x \in \{f, s, h\})$. Something has the property of being God if and only if it is a member of the set of those entities that are God, that is, the Father, the Son, or the Holy Spirit.

[133]Ockham, *Sent.* I, d. 30, q. 1, B.

[134]Ibid., d. 2, q. 1, F.

[135]See Alfred J Freddoso, "Ockham on Faith and Reason," in *The Cambridge Companion to Ockham,* ed. Paul Vincent Spade (Cambridge: Cambridge University Press, 1999), 326–49.

way of speaking theologically that is quite unlike that of speaking philosophically. Theology, in fact, constitutes a *nova lingua* (a "new language") over and against philosophy, a language requiring that all terms must first be "taken to the bath" (*zum die Baden füret*) in order to function properly within theology.

5. Theology, Philosophy, and the *Nova Lingua*[136]

Commentators frequently overlook the fact that Luther was adept at logic, semantics, and argument.[137] In his late disputations, he is frequently concerned with questions of semantics. These reflections are really "meta-theological," for they deal with the meaning and truth of normative theology.[138] The following syllogism is illustrative:

(1) Every human being (*homo*) is a creature.
(2) Christ is a human being.
(3) Therefore, Christ is a creature.[139]

Although the premises are true and the syllogism valid, the conclusion is false. But how can this be? What makes the conclusion true in philosophy but false in theology?[140] One "solution" follows the early-sixteenth-century theologians at the Sorbonne who suggested

---

[136]In this section, I am relying heavily on two of my former articles, "Luther and Language," *Lutheran Quarterly* 16, no. 2 (2002): 195–220, and "Luther and the Strange Language of Theology," in *Caritas et Reformatio: Essays on Church and Society in Honor of Carter Lindberg*, ed. David Mark Whitford, 221–44 (St. Louis: Concordia Academic Press, 2002).

[137]The practice of conducting public disputations in Wittenberg seems to have revived after 1533 (WA 39 II, xiii). In these academic disputations taking place between 1535 and 1545—and collected in WA 39 I and II—Luther clearly demonstrates agility in the use of logical and semantic tools in the construction of arguments. Twenty-four of these disputations are examinations of candidates for higher degrees in which the candidate defends theses written by his teacher against attacks from faculty *opponens*. (The responses to arguments given by Luther himself are of particular interest.) Three "circular" disputations find Luther himself writing and defending theses. See E. Wolf, "Zur wissenschaftsgeschichtlichen Bedeutung der Disputationen and der Wittenberger Universität im 16. Jahrhundert," in *Peregrinatio* (München: Ch. Kaiser, 1965).

[138]Luther is not doing something new in reflecting on the meaning and truth of theological language. Such metatheological investigations characterized much of scholasticism.

[139]Disputation concerning the passage "The Word Was Made Flesh," 1539, LW 38:246; WA 39 II, 10:4–5 (my translation).

[140]For Luther, *philosophy* is a broad term referring to the general project of knowing and acting according to the rational criteria of autonomous man. See Althaus, *Theology of Martin Luther*, 9–11, and Gerhard Ebeling, *Luther*, trans. R. A. Wilson (London: Collins, 1970), 76–92.

that the term *human being* (*homo*) simply equivocates between the major and minor premise. Luther, however, denies that equivocation can solve the problem, for four terms result and there is then no syllogism at all. In his 1539 disputation, *The Word Was Made Flesh*, he claims that though there is no equivocation, "the same thing is *not* true in philosophy and theology." But how is this possible?

One response is that the syllogism does not hold in theology because key terms within theology assume a nonstandard signification. Accordingly, the linguistic distinction between theology and philosophy is due to the fact that new meanings of terms emerge within theological contexts. This view is consistent with semantic holism but does not entail it. I call this the *new meaning* (NM) view.

A second response claims that while there is no real difference in *meaning* between terms within the two languages, there is a difference in the *inferences* permitted. Although theology and philosophy are not *semantically* distinct, they are *inferentially* differentiated. I call this the *different inference* (DI) position. The semantic status of theology's "new tongue" is at stake in this controversy. Are theology and philosophy finally semantically commensurate? Or are theological assertions in principle reducible to their philosophical counterparts? DI is consistent with semantic realism but does not entail it.

The difference between NM and DI is related to the question of Luther's connection to late medieval philosophical and theological streams. NM assumes that theological language retains some of the important semantic and ontological commitments of the *via antiqua* tradition. DI, however, understands Luther's theological semantics to be nominalistic in the *via moderna* tradition of Ockham and his school. I have advocated NM, while White defends DI.[141]

Luther begins the 1539 disputation, *The Word Was Made Flesh*, by declaring against Sorbonne that "what is true in one field of learning is not always true in other fields of learning."[142] While theology regards "the Word was made flesh" as true, in philosophy "it is simply

---

[141]See White, *Luther as Nominalist*. See also Dennis Bielfeldt, "Luther, Metaphor, and Theological Language," *Modern Theology* 6 (1990): 121–35; "Luther on Language," *Lutheran Quarterly* 16, no. 2 (2002): 195–220; and "Luther and the Strange Language of Theology: How New Is the *Nova Lingua*?" in *Caritas et Reformatio: Essays on Church and Society in Honor of Carter Lindberg*, ed. David Mark Whitford, 221–44 (St. Louis: Concordia, 2002).

[142]LW 38:239; WA 39 II, 3:2.

impossible and absurd."[143] Semantically, "God is a human being [*homo*]" is more disparate than "a human being is an ass."[144] Luther believes that by assuming that the same thing is true in philosophy and theology, Sorbonne effectively places the articles of faith (*articuli fidei*) under the judgment of human reason.[145] If God is man, then God must be "a rational, living being, capable of feeling, alive, having a body, actually a created substance."[146] But since Christians speak according to a different rule (*praescriptum*) than this, "such conclusions are simply to be rejected."[147] Philosophy impinges more on theological rules (*regulae*) than theology does on philosophy.[148] Consider the following pertinent syllogism:

(1) The Father generates within the divine.
(2) The Father is the divine essence.
(3) Therefore, the divine essence generates.[149]

The syllogism is sound (*bonus*)—it has true premises and is formally valid—and yet theologically it is neither sound nor valid.[150] (Notice that Luther here argues that it is false that the divine essence generates. But as we have seen, in his final disputations he advocates— and has the doctoral students argue—that it is true that the divine essence generates.) The inference from true premises to a false conclusion is due not to syllogistic form but to the "power and majesty of the subject matter [*materiae*] which cannot be comprehended by narrow reason or syllogism."[151] Instead of contradicting philosophy, this is "*extra, intra, supra, infra, citra, ultra omnem veritatem dialecticam.*"[152]

Different rules seemingly govern theology and philosophy. Just as different rules apply in regions within philosophy, so too do

---

[143]LW 38:239; WA 39 II, 3:3–4.
[144]LW 38:239; WA 39 II, 3:5–6.
[145]LW 38:239;WA 39 II, 4:2–3.
[146]LW 38:240; WA 39 II, 4:10–12.
[147]LW 38:240; WA 39 II, 4:13–14.
[148]LW 38:240; WA 39 II, 4:22–23.
[149]WA 39 II, 4:24–25; LW 38:240 (my translation).
[150]LW 38:240; WA 39 II, 4:26–27.
[151]WA 39 II, 4:32–33; LW 38:240–41 (my translation).
[152]WA 39 II, 4:34–37; LW 38:241: ". . . but is outside, within, above, below, and beyond all logical truth. . . . In the same way the following syllogism is sound in philosophy, but not in theology: Whatever was made flesh was made a creature; The Son of God was made flesh; Therefore, the Son of God was made a creature."

they operate in philosophy and theology generally. There is an incommensurability of lines and weights.[153] While moisture becomes even wetter in air, it does not in fire. Luther summarizes, "You will never discover that the same thing is true in all of them."[154] He thus concludes, "How much less is it possible for the same thing to be true in philosophy and theology, for the difference between them is infinitely greater than that between liberal arts and crafts."[155] Luther counsels that philosophy be left in its "own sphere" (*sua sphaera*) and that we learn to speak "the new tongue [*novis linguis*] in the realm of faith outside every sphere [*extra omnem sphaeram*]."[156] If this is not done, we shall be guilty of putting new wine into old wineskins, resulting in a loss of both (*utrumque perdamus*).[157] But what is the nature of the differing rules within each?

Extension, Intension, and Luther's Theological Semantics

NM claims that key terms in both languages are defined by their respective contexts, that is, that the meanings of primitive terms differ in philosophical and theological contexts. Accordingly, incommensurability arises because there is no point-by-point translation of sentences from one discipline into sentences of the other.[158] The language of theology thus becomes radically new; no recipe of translation can reduce its sentences to nontheological counterparts.[159] On the other hand, the nominalist-inspired DI declares that the difference between theological and philosophical "rules" concerns

---

[153]WA 39 II, 5:15–28; LW 38:241–42.

[154]LW 38:242; WA 39 II, 5:31–32.

[155]LW 38:242; WA 39 II, 5:33–34.

[156]WA 39 II, 5:35–36; LW 38:242 (my translation).

[157]WA 39 II, 5:35–36; LW 38:242 (my translation).

[158]Basically, two languages are incommensurable if and only if there is no language, neutral or otherwise, into which they can be translated without loss. Contingent proposition p in language L is point-by-point incommensurate with contingent propositions $p_1, p_2, p_3 \ldots p_n$ in T', if and only if the truth or falsity of p cannot be in principle derivable from the truth or falsity of $p_1, p_2, p_3 \ldots p_n$ in T .

[159]Broadly speaking, the view has a number of sympathizers. See Thomas Wabel, *Sprache als Grenze*; Eberhard Jüngel, *Gott als Geheimnis der Welt. Zur Begründung der Theologie des Gekreuzigten im Steit zwischen Theismus und Atheismus* (Tübingen: 1977); Streiff, *Novis Linguis loqui*; Risto Saarinen, "Metaphor und biblische Redefiguren als Elemente der Sprachphilosophie Luthers," *Neue Zeitschrift für Systematische Theologie und Religionphilosophie* 30 (1988): 18–39; and Bielfeldt, "Luther, Metaphor, and Theological Language." .

only the inferences sanctioned in each. Although terms retain their meanings across theology and philosophy, their rules of inference change.[160] While philosophy supposes that "God is man" entails "God is created," the inference is blocked in theology. But what grounds the existence of divergent rules in theological contexts? DI responds that normal entailments are blocked because there are new references of terms in theological contexts. To appreciate this, we must examine the crucial distinction between *signification* and *supposition*.[161] Understanding this distinction is important if we are to grasp fully what is going on in Luther's disputations.

Signification and Supposition

The notion of signification develops from Boethius's translation of Aristotle's *De interpretatione* 3, 16[b] 19: "Moreover, [words] spoken in themselves are names and signify something. In fact, the one who speaks them establishes an understanding and the one who hears [them] rests."[162] Paul Vincent Spade claims that "a term signifies that of which it makes a person think, so that, unlike meaning, signification is a species of the causal relation."[163] Most logicians held that there are three kinds of terms (and thus three kinds of languages): written, spoken, and conceptual. While the latter signifies the thing "naturally," spoken terms signify the conceptual (or are subordinate to the conceptual in signifying the thing), while written terms signify

---

[160]White, *Luther as Nominalist*. See also White's "Luther's Views on Language," *Journal of Literature and Theology* 3, no. 2 (1989): 188–218, and his "Theology and Logic: The Case of Ebeling," *Modern Theology* 4, no. 1 (1987): 17–34.

[161]Paul Vincent Spade, "The Semantics of Terms," 188–96 in *CHLMP*, 188.

[162]Boethius, *Commentarii in librum Aristotelis PERI EPMHNEIAS pars prior versionem continuam et primam editionem continens*, ed. Carl Meiser (Leipzig: Teubner, 1877), 5:5–7: "Ipsa quidem secumdum se dicta nomina sunt et significant aliquid. Constituit enim qui dicit intellectum et qui audit quiescit."

[163]Spade, "Semantics of Terms," 188–89. As Spade points out elsewhere, signification is primarily an epistemological notion because to signify is "to constitute an understanding of [*constituere intellectum*]." See "Ockham's Distinctions between Absolute and Connotative Terms," *Vivarium* 13 (1975): 55–76; here, 56. De Rijk defines *significatio* this way: "A word's actual meaning (its meaning on a particular occasion of its use) ultimately is, or can be reduced to, its fundamental 'significance' (*significatio*), which as the word's natural property constitutes its essence or form (*essentia, forma*), in virtue of which it is at the root of every actual meaning of that word." See L. M. De Rijk, "The Origins and the Theory of the Properties of Terms," in *CHLMP*.

the spoken conventionally (*ad placitum*) and, in this manner, signify the object.[164]

It is important to understand that signification is not logically equivalent to meaning.[165] While meaning is a relation between terms, signification involves reference to minds as in this late-scholastic definition: "To signify is to *represent* (a) something or (b) some things or (c) somehow to a cognitive power."[166] Moreover, signification is a *causal* relation, while meaning is not.[167] However, although signification and meaning are not equivalent, signification nonetheless does possess *intensional* elements. This is true both in the early- and high-scholastic traditions, as well as in the later Ockhamist theory of absolute and connotative terms.[168] As L. M. De Rijk points out,

---

[164]Spade, "Semantics of Terms," 189. The written term *immediately* signifies the spoken, and the spoken *immediately* signifies the conceptual. While the latter *immediately* signifies its natural object, the written and spoken *mediately* signify that object. But there is no unanimity on this understanding of signification—though Aristotle, Augustine, Boethius, and Buridan seem to have held it. Ockham and Burley claim that spoken words do not signify the conceptual at all but rather signify natural objects through being *subordinate* to the conceptual. For later thinkers also, spoken words make one think not of concepts but of the object itself. The spoken expression thus signifies something "in the world through the mediating signification of a mental term or proposition [*subordinari idem est quod mediante alio significare*]." See Gabriel Nuchelmans, *Late-Scholastic and Humanist Theories of the Proposition* (Amsterdam: North Holland, 1980), 21.

[165]See Paul Vincent Spade, *Thoughts, Words and Things: An Introduction to Late Mediaeval Logic and Semantic Theory*, 83, available at http://www.pvspade. com/Logic/docs/thoughts1_1a.pdf (accessed October 30, 2007).

[166]". . . *significare est repraesentare potentiae cognitivae aliquid vel aliqua vel aliqualiter.*" Nuchelmans, *Late-Scholastic and Humanist Theories*, 14.

[167]Nor can mental language be conflated with Frege's notion of "sense," though synonymy is accounted for by both in parallel ways. On Ockham's view, spoken term x is synonymous with spoken word y if and only if both x and y are subordinate to the same mental concept m. For Frege, word x is synonymous with y if and only if both x and y have the same sense. There are two major differences: (1) while concepts are terms in a mental language, Frege never spoke of senses as being terms in a language; and (2) while concepts are private and dependent on the mind, senses are public and independent of the mind. See Spade, *Thoughts, Words and Things*, 102.

[168]See Jan Pinborg, *Logik und Semantik in Mittelalter. Ein Überblick* (Stuttgart-Bad Cannstatt: Friedrich Frommann Verlag, 1972). He points out that this is especially true of the modistic theory of semantics. See "Speculative Grammar," 254–69 in *CHLMP*, 264–65. In the modern discussion, the *intension* of an expression is commonly distinguished from its *extension* as follows: (1) with respect to *sentences*, the intension is the proposition expressed and the extension is the truth-value of that proposition; (2) for *predicate symbols*, the intension is the property or relation expressed while the extension is the ordered set of n-tuples satisfying the predicate; (3) finally, for *individual terms*, the intension is the sense of the term, while the extension is that term's denotation. See Joseph Bessie and Stuart Glennan, *Elements of Deductive Inference* (Belmont, Calif.: Wadsworth, 2000), 216–26. The distinction

a word's signification depends on its imposition, on its original application.[169] A single imposition has a single signification. A word is *univocal* if and only if it has the same signification each time it is used. A word is called *equivocal* if it has more than one imposition, if it has different significations on different occasions.[170] But univocal words can apply to different things. An appellative term might "stand for" different things in different propositions.[171] This "standing for" relation is called *supposition*.

Supposition is a semantic relation between the terms in a proposition and the things to which those terms refer (their extension).[172] Specifically, supposition is the referring property of categorematic words serving as subjects or predicates in propositions.[173] According

---

is often made less formally, as in this characterization from Pinborg: "Ich verwende den Ausdruck 'Denotierung' oder 'Extension' (Carnap) für die Beziehung, die zwishen dem Terminus und den von ihm bezeichneten konkreten Gegenständen besteht, also gleich reference, Bedeutung (Frege), während ich für die Beziehung des Terminus zum gemeinten Inhalt, also sense, Sinn (Frege) den Ausdruck 'Konnotierung' oder 'Intension' (Carnap) verwende." See Pinborg, *Logik und Semantik*, 12. "Extension" is thus the set of objects a term is true of, while the "intension" is the meaningful content by which the term denotes its object. Two different intensions can thus have the same extension. While having a heart is a different property than having a kidney, the same class of objects satisfies both. The intension of a term is sometimes conceived as a function assigning an extension to that term in all possible worlds.

In discussing signification, one must distinguish *categorematic* and *syncategorematic* terms. While the first can stand by themselves in a strict sense (e.g., substantival and adjectival names, personal and demonstrative pronouns, and nonauxiliary verbs), the latter relate the categorematic terms within the context of a proposition (e.g., conjunctions, disjunctions, adverbs, and prepositions). Strictly speaking, in the medieval tradition only categorematic terms have signification.

[169]De Rijk, "Origins," 164.

[170]Ibid.

[171]*Appellatio* is a central semantic notion at one stage of the development of medieval logic. De Rijk points out that in the important twelfth-century logical work, the *Ars Meliduna*, the "appellative noun 'appellates' (*appellat*) each thing comprehended under it but signifies (*significat*) it only in an indeterminate way; thus the word 'man' signfies the species (universal nature) *man* indeterminately, not as *this* or *that* man, and it may appellate a man who actually exists as well as one who does not exist." See De Rijk, "Origins," 165.

[172]De Rijk points out that by the twelfth century, "*supponere*" was thought to be equivalent to "*significare substantiam*." See De Rijk, "Origins," 164.

[173]That supposition and signification are different semantic relations can be clearly seen in this passage from Peter of Spain: "The signification of a term . . . is the representation of a thing by an utterance, according to a convention. . . . But supposition is the taking of a substantive term for something. Now supposition and signification are different. For signification occurs through the imposition of an utterance for signifying a thing. But supposition is the taking of the term itself, already significant, for something. . . . Hence signification is prior to supposition. . . . For to signify belongs to an utterance, but to supposit belongs to a term already . . .

to Ockham, the predicate term supposits for (refers to) "everything of which it is truly predicable."[174] This definition holds both for *proper* and *improper* supposition. The first occurs when a term refers literally, while the second happens when it supposits figuratively. An important question thus arises: Does Luther's *nova lingua* result (at least in part) from improper supposition, or can it be accounted for entirely on the basis of proper supposition?

While there are some divergences, the tradition generally distinguishes *personal, material,* and *simple* supposition. The first is the standard supposition of individual things; the second, the supposition of a spoken or written expression itself; and the third, the supposition of a universal (realist construal) or a universal concept (nominalist construal). Simply put, personal supposition involves reference to particulars; material supposition, to language; and simple supposition, to universals or universal concepts.[175]

Significatio and *suppositio* are intimately connected in Ockhamist-inspired, late-medieval semantic theory. For Ockham, spoken and written terms are subordinate to concepts in the mental language and *primarily signify* whatever those concepts signify. Since he rejects the existence of real universals or common natures, written and spoken terms must "primarily" signify individuals, that is, "the things they can be truly predicated of."[176] Thus, for Ockham, personal supposi-

---

put together out of an utterance and a signification." See Spade, *Thoughts, Words and Things,* 245. Supposition and signification also differ because whereas terms can signify outside of a propositional context, supposition occurs only within a context. A second difference is that within propositions, terms can supposit for that which they do not ordinarily signify.

[174]Spade, "Semantics of Terms," 192. De Rijk argues that reference was more important than signification well prior to William Ockham: "What is primarily meant by a term is the concrete individual objects the term can be correctly applied to; that the term may also be taken to mean what those things have in common is of interest in a secondary way only." See De Rijk, "Origins," 167. Yet the notion of signification remained important in a number of authors. William of Conches claimed that substantive nouns do not signify *substantia* and *qualitas* as Priscian held, "but only that which is intelligible, the universal nature (*intelligibile*), not this or that existing thing (*actuale*)" (De Rijk, "Origins," 168). For Peter of Spain, signification applies both to the connotation of the universal nature and the denotation of the individuals having this nature.

[175]Spade, "Semantics of Terms," 193. There are many ways in which personal supposition happens: discretely, determinately, and merely confusedly.

[176]Spade, *Thoughts, Words and Things,* 251. The Ockhamist tradition differs from the *via antiqua* in that the latter held that the immediate significate of the word *homo* is either a universal or a universal concept representing the numerically distinct natures inhering in individual things.

tion occurs when a term supposits for the things it primarily signifies. A term is said to be "taken significantly" when it supposits for everything it primarily signifies.[177] Accordingly, in " 'the cow is red' is true" the term *cow* supposits for the same individual for which the term *red* supposits. ("Red" supposits for each and every red thing.) In " 'the cow is red' is false," the terms *cow* and *red* do not supposit for the same individual. The general statement "all men (*homines*) are rational" is true if and only if the term *rational* supposits for each and every individual for which the term *man* supposits. Late-medieval supposition theory understands the truth conditions and meaning of statements *extensionally*, that is, by whether or not they supposit for the same individual or individuals.[178]

Intensions and Extensions

While the *via moderna* emphasized an *extensionalist* semantics, the earlier *via antiqua* school was more *intensionalist* in its approach, claiming that " 'all men are rational' is true" if and only if "man" signifies (causes the mind to think about) a property inexorably instanced only if the property signified by "rational" is instanced.[179] An intension of a predicate specifies all and only those properties a thing must have in order for the predicate truly to apply to it. An extension, on the other hand, is the class of things to which the predicate rightly applies. In an intensionalist semantics, the intension establishes the conditions by virtue of which extension is determined. Because a complete specification of the property of being a man includes the properties of rationality and animality, the extension of "man" is identical to that of "rational animal."

Is "God is man" best understood, for Luther, in a nominalistic, extensional sense (DI) or in an intensionalist way (NM)? If "God is man" is construed intensionally, then the property of being God does not exclude the property of being a man. But this is impossible in philosophy. Here specification of the properties of God includes that of being infinite. But since human beings are not infinite, specification of

---

[177] Ibid., 252.

[178] See ibid., 241–306. Twentieth-century logic and mathematics also seek to ground the truth conditions of statements extensionally. For instance, property F is identified with $\{x \mid x \text{ is } F\}$, relation R with $\{<x, y> \mid x \text{ stands in R to } y\}$, and functions are constructable from relations. See John Pollock, *Technical Methods in Philosophy* (Boulder: Westview, 1990), 15–36.

[179] See Pinborg, *Logik und Semantik*. See also Jan Pinborg, "Speculative Grammar."

the God-making properties must include the property of not being a human being. Thus, the conceptual rules by which theology proceeds must differ from philosophy, for terms such as *God* and *mother* do not exclude predication by *man* and *virgin* respectively. One might even say that the terms *God* and *mother* have different *significations* in theology and philosophy respectively.[180] Do they not thus make the mind think about different things in the two discourses?

If we grant, however, "God is man" an extensional construal, then, in theology, the extension of "God" must be a member of the satisfaction set of "man." While this is surprising, it is nonetheless unproblematically true for theology. While philosophy regards "God is not man" as analytically true, it is not so in theology. Here there is simply a non-empty intersection of the extensions of "God" and "man." While the non-empty intersection of these sets demonstrates that "God is not man" is false, it is nonetheless true in philosophy. In the *region* of philosophy, "God is not man" is *true*, even though, as it turns out, it is not ultimately true. Conceptual truths like "God is not man" vary from region to region. Because revelation gives the deepest approach to what is, theological entailments differ from their philosophical counterparts. In the *nova lingua* of theology, "God is infinite" does not entail "God is not man," for the new tongue pre-supposes an epistemic access to regions that natural reason cannot apprehend. However, from the epistemically limited standpoint of philosophy, the entailment does hold. For DI, theology differs from philosophy in its entailment relations. White argues that while the "primary signification" of a term remains the same across the two languages, its "assertive signification" (or entailing relations) none-theless changes.[181]

On NM's intensionalist construal, theology forms a "new tongue" that is basically semantically discontinuous with the old language of philosophy. This irreducibility of theological discourse nicely parallels the irreducibility of the gospel to the law. With Christ, something new has emerged. Just as old legalisms have been taken up in the grace of Christ's free justification, so too the old language of philosophy has been interrupted by the presence of something new. Just as the gospel is a new ingredient in the old mix of the law, so does the language that talks about the gospel possess a new ingre-

[180]Luther claims that "mother" too becomes new in theology. See LW 38:253; WA 39 II, 19:7–12.
[181]See White, *Luther as Nominalist*, 326.

dient in the old mix of philosophy. Just as the law cannot contain the gospel, so too does philosophical language not contain the good news about which theology speaks. The law, reason, and philosophy belong to God's left hand, while the gospel, faith, and theology concern His right. This intensionalist alternative fits well with the Lutheran notion of the infinite being available in the finite, for just as there is a real presence of Christ in the Lord's Supper, so too is there a "real presence" of the deepest theological truths in human philosophical language. Just as God's presence is mediated through the earthly elements of the sacraments, so too is the presence of the *nova lingua* of theology mediated through the "old language" of philosophy. Just as everyday earthly elements are retained yet transformed sacramentally, so too is the everyday language of philosophy retained yet transformed in theology.

If the extensionalism of DI holds, however, then it seems there is a disconnect between Luther's thinking on semantics and the rest of his theology, for Luther's semantics loses its "both/and" character. Theological truth reduces to that which can be said philosophically. Accordingly, there is one vast tree of Porphyry, but only theology has access to some of the branches. Gone is the Lutheran dialectic between law and gospel, between the left and right hand of God, between the world and the in-breaking kingdom of God. Now, it appears, theological language is figured more along the lines of grace perfecting nature. There is nothing *intrinsic* to philosophical language that makes it incapable of stating theological truth.

Consider this syllogism:

(1) Every human being (*homo*) is a creature.
(2) Christ is a human being.
(3) Therefore, Christ is a creature.

Obviously, no non-Arian would subscribe to (3), yet (1) and (2) are true and the syllogism is formally valid. Luther points out that in their attempt to demonstrate that truths are consonant across theology and philosophy, the Sorbonne theologians attack the middle term *homo*, claiming that it equivocates between (1) and (2). But Luther argues that *homo* cannot equivocate between (1) and (2) without destroying the syllogism.[182] The syllogism is *valid*, even in theology.

---

[182]LW 38:246; WA 39 II, 11:8–20.

NM must hold that while the term *homo* means something different in theology than in philosophy, yet since *homo* does not equivocate between the two discourses, there must be a common signification of the term in the old and new discourse. A natural way to understand this is to claim a kind of metaphorical extension that accounts for the "semantic shift" from philosophy to theology. The advantage of the metaphor theory is that it captures the change in meaning while, paradoxically, holding to its constancy. (There is thus a "both/and" character to theological language itself.) Is there textual evidence for this?

There is textual evidence from Luther's controversy with Zwingli on the Lord's Supper and his tract *Against Latomus*. Luther here quotes Horace and praises the value of metaphor.[183] It is also here that we find him reflecting upon "is" in "this is my body," claiming that there is a statement of essence. The bread really is the body; it does not merely represent or signify it. Bread that cannot be Christ's body and Christ's body that cannot be bread are nonetheless identified. Such identification involves a collision of meaning and real semantic newness.[184] Based on these texts, I previously suggested that a "theological interaction metaphor" models the semantic situation in which the meaning of the term *homo* in (1) and (2) changes without equivocating.[185] Hinlicky too acknowledges Luther's "unavoidable equivocation" on the term *creatura* as one moves from a philosophical to a theological context, and rightly points out that "new meaning" arising in expressions such as "Christ is sin" or "the Word is flesh" is due "to the [soteriological] personal action of the Son."[186] NM claims that new signification arises from the salvific mission of the trinitarian God, a signification that is "new" because

---

[183]LW 37:173ff.; WA 26, 272:23ff. ("Confession Concerning Christ's Supper").

[184]See also Luther's 1521 "Against Latomus," LW 32:200–01; WA 8, 87:6–40. For an interesting exchange concerning the metaphorical attribution of sin to Christ, see Gerhard Ebeling, "Christus . . . factus est peccatum metaphorice," in *Tragende Tradition: Festschrift für Martin Seils zum 65. Geburtstag*, ed. Annegret Freund, 49–73 (Frankfurt am Main: Peter Lang, 1992); and Wilfried Härle, " 'Christus factus est peccatum metaphorice'. Zur Heilsbedeutung des Kreuzestodes Jesu Christi," *Neue Zeitschrift für Systematische Theologie und Religionphilosophie* 36 (1994): 302–15.

[185]For a sketch of a theological interaction metaphor, see Bielfeldt, "Luther, Metaphor, and Theological Language," 126–30.

[186]See Paul Hinlicky, "Martin Luther's Anti-Docetism," in *Creator est creatura, Luthers Chrstologie als Lehre von der Idiomen kommunikation.* Oswald Bayer & Benjamin Gleede (Berlin: Walter de Gruyter, 2007): 139–185.

of the presence of the eschatological kingdom of God within history. The "yet" of new theological meaning is, however, "not yet" shorn of the mundane semantics of philosophy. Attribution of sophisticated metaphorical accounts to Luther, however, is open to a charge of anachronism, for they are certainly not found in the immediate scholastic sources with which Luther was familiar.

Proponents of the extensionalist DI construal hold that because the signification of the term *homo* remains constant across the two languages, there is no equivocation. Because of nonstandard supposition, theology and philosophy countenance different entailment relations. But how do human beings come to know and learn the different, nonstandard inference patterns of theology? White suggests that a believer might have, for Luther, some kind of privileged access to divine truths by virtue of Christ's indwelling.[187] This idea has the advantage of not needing to invoke a theory of metaphor that may be anachronistic.[188] Another advantage is that it situates Luther nicely into the late-medieval nominalistic context and consequently does not demand that he has come to some startling semantic discovery. But there are also disadvantages. The theory must appeal to a distinction between the primary and assertive significance of terms; it must claim some kind of epistemic access to divine truths through *theosis*; and it seems to be in theological tension with the dialects of law and gospel, left and right hand, finite and infinite, world and coming kingdom of God, and with the notion of the real presence.[189]

---

[187]See White, *Luther as Nominalist*, 343. Deification in Luther is argued by Simo Peura, *Mehr als ein Mensch? Die Vergöttlichung als Thema der Theologie Martin Luther von 1513 bis 1519* (Mainz: Verlag Philipp von Zabern, 1994). See also Oswald Bayer, "The Being of Christ in Faith," *Lutheran Quarterly* 10, no. 2 (1996): 135–50. Paul Hinlicky suggests a variant of this view in his chapter in this volume.

[188]Modern interactionist theories of metaphor seem out of place in the late medieval discussion in which metaphor is understood as improper supposition. Both Ockham and Burley list three kinds of metaphor: *autonomasitic*, when a term signifying several things is appropriated to supposit for one of them; *synechdochical*, when a term signifying part of something is used to supposit for the whole; and *mytonymical*, when a term signifying the container supposits for what is contained. See Spade, *Thoughts, Words and Things*, 248ff.

[189]I worry that although the distinction between primary and assertive significance does apply to propositions, it does not concern terms, for to say that a term itself has different inferential capabilities (assertive signification) seems to entail it having different primary signification as well. The other problem concerns deification's providing an epistemic access to the *nova lingua* of theology. While White appeals to the ontic presence of the Word in the believer as efficiently causing a difference in her inferential capabilities, he does not explain how such causation is possi-

In summary, to conceive "this bread is Christ's body" as parallel to "God is man" is to adopt some kind of metaphorical predication in which the very meanings of "God," "man," "bread," and "body" are stretched. Accordingly, the jarring nature of both utterances is retained, for that which seemingly *cannot be* nonetheless *is*. On the other hand, to understand "God is man" extensionally mollifies that jarring nature. There are no semantic difficulties to the claim that a being named by "God" is a member of the set of all things having a human nature. "God is man" is true because both "God" and "man" supposit for the same individual.[190] The individual named by "God" has humanity in much the same way an individual named by "Peter" has white. But now the human nature itself seems in danger of becoming accidental to the thing named by "God." But one must ask whether this view has the semantic resources to articulate a *communicatio idiomatum* that is more than merely verbal predication.

On the Nature of "Nature"

I believe that NM's broadly intensionalist account is more faithful to Luther than DI's purely extensionalist one. While Luther could chop logic and draw semantic distinctions like any good nominalist, I do not think he was so committed to a nominalism that he denied the ontology of Christ's divine and human natures. We must remember that for a pure nominalist, all that ultimately exists are individual substances and qualities. According to Aristotle, a substance is that which neither can be said of another nor is present in another. Thus, the nominalist ascribes ontological status only to those things that cannot be said of another and those things that can be present in another. For Aristotle, while the essence of a thing is that bundle of properties that makes the thing what it is, its "nature" concerns the essence insofar as it is a source of activities. Aristotle declares, "Nature properly speaking is the essence (or substance) of

---

ble, for on Peura's analysis, Christ is always hidden to the believer in this life (White, *Luther as Nominalist*, 328ff.). Somehow White wants "direct epistemic access" to the presence of Christ causally to change the believer's inferential structure despite the fact that the hiddenness of the Word seems wholly to cloud such an access.

[190]Since the Ockhamist tradition understands the term *homo* to supposit for the divine suppositum carrying both the divine and human natures, the assertion "God is man" is unproblematic, meaning nothing more than God is the divine suppositum. See Reinhard Schwarz, "Gott ist Mensch. Zur Lehre von der Person Christ bei den Ockhamisten und bei Luther," *Zeitschrift für Theologie und Kirche* 63 (1966): 288–351.

things which have in themselves as such a principle of activity."[191] Accordingly, the nature of something is what makes it what it is. To say that my nature is sinful is to say that sin makes me what I am. To say that Christ has a divine nature and a human nature is to say that being divine is what makes Christ who he is and being human is what makes Christ who he is.

A pure nominalist understanding construes a nature more or less "adverbially"—for example, my "nature" is to be sinful; thus, I am *in a sinning way*. Accordingly, Christ's having both a divine and human nature means that Christ is both in a human and in a divine way. Christ has no bundle of human properties (or divine properties) that has ontological status beyond that of any qualities present in him. White points out that phrases such as "according to the human nature" and "according to the divine nature" must be understood adverbially—that is, "they do not stand for second or third entities [but for] the way in which this one entity makes itself manifest."[192] Adverbial theory reduces talk of a nature entity to talk of an entity in a "natured" manner or way. Just as an adverbial theory of perception replaces talk of the sense-datum red by talk of the object in a red way, so too does a christological adverbial theory replace talk of two independent natures of the entity Christ by talk of the entity Christ in two ways of being "natured."

But such a view of things cannot easily be squared with the genera of *communicatio* articulated in article 8 of the *Solid Declaration* in the *Formula of Concord*, genera found in Luther himself. There is a *communicatio idiomatum* from both natures to the person of Christ, and a *genus maiesticum* whereby the properties of the divine nature are attributed to the human nature of Christ. Luther himself seems even to have claimed on occasion that the properties of the human nature can be attributed to the divine nature,[193] though I don't find this a consistent theme in Luther. While it may be metaphysically possible to claim that one entity is divinely and humanly mannered, there is no metaphysical way in which the human manner itself can become divinely mannered without ascribing ontological status to the human nature. While we might claim that the transference

---

[191]Aristotle, *Metaphysics,* 1015a, 13.

[192]White, *Luther as Nominalist,* 249.

[193]See Dennis Ngien, "Trinity and Divine Passibility," *Scottish Journal of Theology* 19, no. 1: 31–64; and also Marc Lienhard, *Luther: Witness to Jesus Christ,* trans. Edwin Robertson (Minneapolis: Augsburg, 1982), 326ff.

of human properties to the divine nature and the transference of divine properties to the human nature are only a way of speaking about the unity of the two mannered ways in which the Christ is, it is logically impossible to claim any asymmetry in such a transference of properties. However, this asymmetry has always been part of the dogmatic orthodox Lutheran position. Believing itself to be in the spirit of Luther, it embraced the *genus maiestaticum* yet denied that the human properties are given to the divine nature. But such a view is logically and metaphysically impossible on an adverbial theory of natures.

The question of the ontological status of a "nature" becomes very important as we examine Luther's trinitarian thinking. If the three persons have one divine nature, and if "nature" is given an adverbial analysis, then it seems that the unity of God is constituted merely in the common manner in which three distinct persons are. Accordingly, a strongly social trinitarian position becomes more plausible for Luther. But while Luther emphasized the personal processions, he displayed no proclivities toward tritheism, a position strongly suggested if the divine nature is given an adverbial construal.

While I cannot adequately argue it here, I believe that when it comes to the semantics of incarnation, Trinity, and sacramental presence, Luther is not a philosophical nominalist. Rather, while he employs philosophical elements and insights from the tradition of Ockham, Gabriel Biel, and Pierre d'Ailley, he also uses some of the semantic resources of the earlier *via antiqua* tradition for specifically theological purposes.[194] These semantic resources allow for a metaphorical stretching of meaning of terms between philosophical and theological contexts. That new signification arises within theological contexts does not change the fact that Luther remains a semantic realist: theological language is made true by the existence of divine states of affairs, some of which remain in the future.

Summary

While Luther does presuppose semantic realism, his assertions about the *nova lingua* of theology suggest that *signification* and *intension-*

---

[194]See Reijo Työrinoja, "*Nova vocabula et nova lingua.* Luther's Conception of Doctrinal Formulas," in *Thesaurus Lutheri. Auf der Suche nach neuen Paradigmen der luther-Forschung. Referate des Luther-Symposiums in Finnland 11–12. November 1986*, ed. Tuomo Mannermaa, Anja Ghiselli, and Simo Peura (Helsinki: Luther-Agricola-Gesellschaft, 1987).

ality continue to play an important role in his theological semantics. Theologically, this is to be expected. While much of the proceeding theological tradition talked of "grace perfecting nature" and could thus speak of a "transubstantiation" of the finite into the infinite, Luther knew that grace is dialectically related to nature and that there is a "real presence" of the infinite in the finite. Accordingly, the *nova lingua* cannot be due to a "transubstantiation" of human language in which all things are now new and humans can thus speak the infinite language of the Spirit. Instead, there is a "real presence" of this language "in, with, under and beyond" the language of philosophy, as the old wineskins are stretched so new wine can be put inside. Because of the "majesty of the subject matter," language itself must become new.

6. Luther's Contribution to Catholic Trinitarianism

The Regnon thesis claims that while the East assumes the distinctiveness of the persons and tries to account for divine unity despite this difference, the West assumes the unity of the divine essence and tries to account for the distinctiveness of the persons despite this unity.[195] The East thus begins with the processions, understands the persons as individuated by the processions, and concludes with the relations among the persons. The West, on the other hand, begins with the relations among the persons, understands the persons as individuated by those relations, and concludes with the personal processions. The nature of the Trinity itself seems to be at stake. If the processions individuate the persons, then it seems a type of social trinitarianism can be maintained. If the subsistent relations individuate the persons, then social trinitarianism becomes more difficult, for the persons become merely the way the unity of God is constituted.

I believe that a careful reading of Luther's disputations shows that his interest was not to explore the ontological situation with respect to the Trinity, but rather to correctly name the trinitarian situation he already confessed: God is both one and three. This emphasis actually makes him neutral on the Regnon problematic. (This is so even though this "neutrality" actually made him more sympathetic than many of his contemporaries to thinking and speaking in terms of the procession of persons.) That he is neutral on the question of the metaphysical priority of relations or processions is perhaps

---

[195]Regnon, *Etudes de Theologie Positive.*

theologically appropriate, for it may ultimately be the case that the East and West do not divide in the way that Regnon has suggested. If they do not so divide, then perhaps one of Luther's greatest contributions to Catholic trinitarian thought may be that he refused to privilege the processions over the relations, or the relations over the processions, but held both accounts as theologically equivalent.

East/West Confusions?

Richard Cross argues that the East and West do not really "adopt radically divergent accounts of the Trinity."[196] The difference between the two traditions has little to do with theology but everything to do with differing philosophical assumptions: "The Eastern view does, and the Western view does not, generally accept a sense in which the divine essence is a shared *universal*."[197] Gregory of Nyssa claims that the divine essence is a singular multiply instantiatable universal; Augustine denies it.

Cross first distinguishes the substrate/property view of substance from the congeries of properties account, which employs the notion of *compresence*. He then discriminates properties as particulars from properties as universals. If properties are particulars, then the indiscernible properties of numerically distinct substances are themselves numerically distinct. However, if properties are universals, then the indiscernible properties of numerically distinct substances are identical and thus (by Leibniz's law) the *same* property. While a universal is a property that can be a constituent in more than one substance, particular properties *cannot* be. Accordingly, the only metaphysical possibility for overlapping substances on the bundle theory is that they possess *universal* properties ingredient in each and every compresence.

This insight is crucial for understanding the putative divergence between the East and West. For purposes of analysis, regard the terms *substance*, *hypostasis*, and *person* as coreferential and suppose the divine essence to be an overlapping property of the three persons that is a *universal*. Gregory of Nyssa holds that the divine essence (*ousia*) is a numerically singular universal that is multiply instantiated in the three divine persons: "But the nature is one, united to itself and a precisely undivided unit [*monas*], not increased through

[196]Richard Cross, "Two Models of the Trinity," *Heythrop Journal* 43 (2002): 275–94.
[197]Cross, "Two Models of the Trinity," 275.

addition, not decreased through subtraction, but being and remaining one (even if it were to appear in a multitude), undivided, continuous, perfect, and not divided by the individuals who participate in it."[198] The divine essence does not exist uninstantiated but rather is *immanent* in the persons; it is that "of which" the persons are.[199] While the divine essence is shared by the persons, the divine persons, constituted as overlapping bundles of properties, do not share their properties.

According to Cross, the Western theologians implicitly accept that the divine essence can be shared by the persons even though they explicitly criticize this view. They deny that the divine essence is a universal "in the sense of 'universal' accepted by the West, not the sense accepted by the East."[200] Though they deny that the divine essence is a universal, they accept that the essence is shared by the persons. Augustine writes, "In the simple Trinity one is as much as three are together, and two are not more than one, and in themselves they are infinite. So they are each in each and all in each, and each in all and all in all, and all are one."[201] More than eight centuries later, Aquinas echoes Augustine: "In God, the essence is really identical with a [viz., each] person, even though the persons are really distinct from each other."[202]

The Western theologians explicitly reject Nyssa's view of universals. Augustine supposes that if the divine essence is a species, and if a species is divisible, then the divine essence is divisible. But since this cannot be, he concludes that the divine essence is not a species. But if it is not a species, then it is not a universal at all. For Cross, Augustine must hold that a universal (species) is divisible because he assumes the Neoplatonic notion of an *in re* universal. Neoplatonists are nominalists on this point; they claim that universals (species) are merely aggregates of particulars.[203] Although Aquinas is no Neoplatonic nominalist, his Aristotelian realism agrees on this point:

---

[198]Gregory, *Abl. GNO*, III/I, 40.24—41.7.
[199]Cross, "Two Models of the Trinity," 281.
[200]Ibid.
[201]*Trin.* 6.10.12, CCSL, L, 243.
[202]*ST* 1.39.1, c.
[203]Quoting Augustine again: "If essence is species, like man, and those which we call substances or persons are three, then they have the same species in common, as Abraham, Isaac, and Jacob have in common the species which is called 'man'; and if while man can be subdivided into Abraham, Isaac, and Jacob, it does not mean that one man can be subdivided into several single men—obviously he cannot, because one man is already a single man—then how can one essence be subdivided into three

"No universal is numerically the same in the things beneath it."[204] Cross concludes, "Unlike the Eastern tradition, . . . the Western tradition accepts—as a matter of philosophical fact—that universals, even *in re* universals, are not such that they are *numerically* identical in each exemplification."[205] Thus, while the Cappadocians assume that all universals, not just the divine essence, "are numerically singular, and . . . the particulars are collections of such universals," the Western tradition rejects the claim of the numerical singularity of universals and the constitution of particulars from universals. While both traditions claim that the divine essence is a singular property formed by the intersection of the properties of the persons, the West disagrees with the East in claiming that this intersection can be accounted for by claiming the existence of a numerically identical universal. The divine essence as a universal *in re* is not logically or metaphysically prior to the persons, but dependent and posterior to them. Yet this essence is something more than its instantiations in the persons, for this essence is what makes possible the identity of these persons.

To the objection that Eastern and Western views must be theologically distinct because social trinitarian views can be grounded in the former and not via the latter, Cross claims that such views actually *cannot* be grounded in one tradition more properly than the other. It is neither the case that the Western view adopts a Trinity of subsistent relations between persons, disallowing a social trinitarian approach, nor that the East adopts a theory of personal processions completely compatible with robust social trinitarianism. Furthermore, according to Cross, the Western notion of subsistent relations claims that the persons are individuated with respect to dyadic relations holding *between* particular persons. These dyadic relations are *not* constitutive of the persons themselves because they do not inhere in things; rather, they "hang between" their *relata*.[206] Cross points to Augustine as the source of this view, for it was he who

---

substances or persons? For if essence, like man, is a species, then one essence is like one man" (*Trin.* 7.6.11, CCSL, L, 236).

[204]*Scriptum super Libros Sententiarum* 1.19.4.2.

[205]Cross, "Two Models of the Trinity," 284.

[206]*ST* 1.28.1, c: "Distinction in God arises only through relations of origin. . . . But a relation in God is not like an accident inherent in a subject, but is the divine essence itself. So it is subsistent just as the divine essence is subsistent. Just as, therefore, the Godhead is God, so the divine paternity is God the Father, who is a divine person. Therefore 'divine persons' signifies a relation as subsistent."

denied that God can be a subject for accidents, and by thus rejecting accidents, he identified *relations* as the noninherent "things" whose distinction does not entail a distinction in substance.[207] Because accidents require a substrate, and because the presence of a substrate is incompatible with simplicity, the assertion of simplicity requires a denial of accidental personal properties. So it is that "a divine person can include a relation without that relation thereby entailing composition."[208] Thus, for the West, the divine persons *cannot* be psychological subjects, for psychological subjects are necessarily individuated by their nonrelational properties.

Cross believes that Gregory of Nyssa effectively embraces the category of subsistent relations as well. In the following passage, the distinguishing features of the persons are clearly the causal relations they possess with respect to each other: "While confessing that the nature is undifferentiated, we do not deny a distinction in causality, by which alone we seize the distinction of the one from the other: that is, by believing that one is the cause and the other is from the cause. There is the one which depends on the first, and there is that one which is through that which depends on the first."[209] So as it turns out, the East is close to a doctrine of subsistent relations, and the West assumes that the divine essence is shareable among the three persons. Accordingly, both traditions deny social trinitarian accounts that hold the three persons as distinct psychological subjects. Both reject those accounts because of the need to individuate persons on the basis of something other than the accidental (nonrelational) properties of the persons.[210]

What is to be said of this analysis? Cross has clarified matters greatly. That God is one and three does seem to entail that the divine essence can be shared by persons. The Western view that this essence is a numerically singular property shared by the persons is not at all incompatible with the Eastern view that this essence is a universal that, while immanent in the persons, is nonetheless numerically one and multiply instantiatable in them. If this is so, then the unity from which the West begins is just the shareable property/universal. While

---

[207]*Trin.* 5.5.6, CCSL, I, 210: "What is stated relationally does not designate substance. So although begotten differs from unbegotten, it does not indicate a different substance."

[208]Cross, "Two Models of the Trinity," 287.

[209]*Abl.* GNO, III/I, 55.24—56.6.

[210]Cross, "Two Models of the Trinity," 288.

the West might ground its talk of personal diversity upon the divine unity, the shareable property of divine unity is nonetheless dependent upon the bundled properties constituting the persons. Alternately, while the East might ground its talk of divine unity upon the grounds of personal distinctiveness, this unity clearly, like the West, remains dependent on the existence of the persons. Cross's analysis, if true, suggests that while the Eastern and Western views have their own metaphysical models, each satisfies the same set of theological propositions. If this is so, then there is no theological difference between the two. (For a rather technical argument showing how Luther himself may be committed to East/West equivalency, see the appendix to this chapter, "Applying Logical Tools.")

7. Conclusion

I have argued that Luther assumes *semantic realism*, a view affording robust truth conditions to dogmatic theological language. On the basis of Luther's disputations, I have suggested a distinction between theology and philosophy whereby theology is figured as a *nova lingua* that allows for the statement of "incomprehensible" trinitarian truth. The new language is related to the old dialectically in the same way that the gospel is related to law, grace to nature, and the infinite to the finite. A semantic "real presence" makes the earthly language of philosophy into the heavenly language of theology. I have claimed that while Luther privileges neither the personal relations over the processions nor the processions over the relations, he does emphasize the processional account of persons perhaps more emphatically than many of his contemporaries. Finally, I suggest that the theological equivalency Luther finds between the two accounts may itself mirror the theological equivalency of Eastern and Western views generally— at least if Richard Cross is correct.

Appendix to Chapter 2:
Applying Logical Tools

It is important to be clear on any claims about the logical priority of the processions over the relations, or vice versa. Since I believe that Luther is making definite ontological and semantic assertions, I think it is justifiable to use contemporary logical machinery to make perspicuous those assertions. Let f, s, and h designate respectively the persons of the Trinity. Let us further assume that "Pxy" means "y proceeds from x" and "Bxy" means "x begets y." If we were to say that the relations have logically priority over the procession of the persons, we might use the following to pick out persons when "$\exists x$" means "there exists some x" and "$\forall x$" stands for "for all x":

(1) $\exists x \exists y(\{[(Bxy\ \&\ \exists zPxz)\ \&\ y \neq z]\ \&\ \forall w[(Bwy\ \&\ \exists zPwz) \to w = x]\}\ \&\ x = f)$

State (1) indicates there is one and only one thing that is the Father of some thing and from which some thing processes (and those two things are not the same thing), and that this thing is the Father. The formula effectively picks out an individual under a description. The claim is that there is something that instantiates certain relational properties and that this thing is the Father. Since there is one and only one individual satisfying the description, the relation picks out the person.

To make apparent that it is truly the relation that individuates, and to make clear the fact that anything satisfying this relation is the Father, we might give the following sufficiency condition:

(2) $\forall x \exists y\{[(Bxy\ \&\ \exists zPxz)\ \&\ y \neq z] \to x = f\}$

This formula claims that any individual having the appropriate relational properties is the Father. Just as three-sidedness is sufficient for triangularity, so is the possession of these relational properties sufficient for being the Father. One might even say that this relational individuation is the very *definition* of the person. Accordingly, the following biconditionals obtain for each trinitarian person:

(3) $\forall x \exists y\{[(Bxy\ \&\ \exists zPxz)\ \&\ y \neq z] \leftrightarrow x = f\}$

(3*) $\forall y \exists x\{[(Bxy\ \&\ \exists zPyz)\ \&\ x \neq z] \leftrightarrow y = s\}$

(3**) $\forall x \exists y\{[(Pyx\ \&\ \exists zPzx)\ \&\ y \neq z] \leftrightarrow y = h\}$

The first states that the Father is that which generates the Son and from which the Spirit proceeds; the second says that the Son is generated by the Father and is that from which the Spirit obtains; and the third says that the Spirit proceeds from the other two persons.

On the other hand, (4) below assumes that the person of the Father already exists, and it asserts a relationship between that person and the other trinitarian persons. Accordingly, the person is already constituted, and the relationships between persons obtain because of the nature of those persons.

(4) Bfs & Pfh

The relation of the Father to the Son is logically distinct from the Father and Son themselves. This differs from the relational account that says that the persons of the Father and the Son are individuated by the relationships holding between them.

Notice that in (4), if f and s designate at all, they designate *rigidly*.[211] Since there are no identities among persons, there are no identities in any possible worlds. Whereas descriptions merely pick out individuals contingently, rigid designators do so necessarily. If a relation constitutes the being of the person, then whoever the x is that satisfies the relation in one possible world may not satisfy it in another. Moreover, there may be no individuals satisfying it in some other possible world. This cannot happen, however, if names designate rigidly, that is, if the identity conditions of the person do not involve relations.

Statement (4) needs improvement, because it fails to specify the essential properties of the persons. I have tried to do this below by using I, W, and L for the personal properties of Father, Son, and Holy Spirit respectively. (One could think of I as innascibility, W as wisdom, and L as love.) D refers to the divine nature. For the processional account, we might write:

(5) $\exists x \exists y \exists z (\{[(Dx \,\&\, Ix) \,\&\, (Dy \,\&\, Wy) \,\&\, (Dz \,\&\, Lz)] \,\&\, [(Bxy \,\&\, Pxz) \,\&\, Pyz]\} [(x \neq y) (x \neq z) (y \neq z)])$

This is a statement claiming that there is a bundle of monadic prop-

---

[211]It is to Saul Kripke that we owe this notion of rigid designation. Since a name has the same bearer in all possible worlds, any identities between objects become necessary identities. See Saul Kripke, *Meaning and Necessity* (Cambridge: Harvard University Press, 1972).

erties each person has and that the relations among persons obtain as well. To say that the personal processions are logically prior is to claim the following of the *Father*:

(6) ∀x{[(Dx & Ix) → ∃y∃z(Dy & Wy) & (Dz & Lz) & (Bxy & Pxz)]

This formula says that any being with the essential property of divinity and the personal property of innascibility will sustain the dyadic relations of generating some being with the essential property of divinity and the personal property of wisdom, and the relation of producing the procession of some being with the essential property of divinity and the personal property of love. Correspondingly, the *Son* is:

(7) ∀x{[(Dx & Wx) → ∃y∃z(Dy & Iy) & (Dz & Lz) & (Byx & Pxz)]

This statement claims that any being having the divine essence and the personal property of wisdom will sustain the relation of being generated by some being with the divine essence with the personal property of innascibility and the relation of producing the procession of some being with the essential property of divinity and the personal property of love. Finally, we sketch the logical situation of the Holy Spirit:

(8) ∀x{[(Dx & Lx) → ∃y∃z(Dy & Iy) & (Dz & Wz) & (Pyx & Pzx)]

This formula states that any being having the divine essence and the personal property of love will sustain the relation of proceeding from some being with the divine essence and the personal property of innascibility, and the relation of proceeding from some being possessing the divine essence and having the personal property of wisdom.

Each of these shows how the personal processions are sufficient for the relations. Of course, if this is true, then, equivalently, the relations are necessary for the processions. The question, of course, is whether the relations are also *sufficient* for the processions. If they are, then logically the processional account and the relational account collapse. So are the relations *sufficient* for the processions?

Logically, the relations are sufficient for the processions if the processions are necessary for the relations. So are the processions necessary for the relations? The processions are necessary for the relations if and only if there are no worlds where there are relations without processions. Are there such worlds? Can the Father bear a dyadic relation of generating with respect to the Son without the Father and Son having particular personal properties? Simply put, are there worlds having relational individuation but no nonrelational property differences?

In thesis 13 of the Hegemon disputation, Luther claims that the relations and the hypostases are the same: "In divine matters a relation is a thing, that is, a hypostasis and subsistence, truly, the same as divinity itself; there are three persons, three hypostases and three subsistences."[212] He would do this if it were true that he did embrace the processional account of the persons and did hold, nonetheless, that there were no possible worlds in which the relations between persons held but where there were no differentiating personal properties. If the hypostases and the relations are the same, then it would seem that Luther is claiming that the trinitarian formulations must be *biconditionals*. Only if they are biconditionals can it be true that the relations and the hypostases are the same. But if this is so, if these are biconditionals, then it seems that logically there is no significant difference between the processional and the relational views: the nonrelational personal properties ground the dyadic relations among the persons, and the dyadic relations among the persons are themselves logically sufficient for the instantiation of the nonrelational personal properties. Perhaps Luther grasped that dyadic relations among eternal persons hold if and only if these persons have a particular set of properties. Perhaps he sensed a semantic equivalency between the processional and relational accounts.

---

[212]WA 39 II, 340:3–5.

CHAPTER THREE

Luther's New Language of the Spirit

Trinitarian Theology as Critical Dogmatics

Paul R. Hinlicky

Nonetheless it is certain that in Christ all words receive a new signification, though the thing signified is the same. For "creature" in the old usage of language and in other subjects signifies a thing separated from divinity by infinite modes. In the new use of language it signifies a thing inseparably joined with divinity in the same person in an ineffable mode. Thus it must be that the words man, humanity, suffered, *etc., and everything that is said of Christ, are new words. Not that it signifies a new or different thing, but that it signifies in a new and different way, unless you want to call this too a new thing.*[1]

---

[1]Theses 20–24 of the 1540 *Disputation concerning the Divinity and Humanity of Christ*, translated from the Latin text of WA 39 II, 92–121, by Christopher B.

How by the lights of the old Martin Luther may we today understand critically, affirm joyfully, and communicate and defend publicly
the substance of Christian faith—*res scripturae, doctrina evangelii?*
Can we do so in tandem with reverence for today's acknowledged
plurality of human experience, religious and secular? How do we
judge between deviation from the gospel ruinous of the church and
destructive of salvation in Christ, on the one side, and the proper
diversity that the Creator wills and pronounces very good, on the
other? Such are the questions explored in this final chapter, which
builds on the preceding, historically oriented probes by Mickey
Mattox and Dennis Bielfeldt but now takes into view implications of
the old Luther's theology for today.

Issues involved for contemporary theology in the tradition of
Luther are discussed in the first section below. The thesis formulated
here is that the later Luther's notion of theology as "new language"
given by the Spirit[2] contributes to this contemporary task both by
accounting for the disciplinary autonomy of theology and by specifying broadly its relation to other forms of human reason. This thesis
is demonstrated in the second section below by *theological* exposition[3] of a passage from a 1540 disputation of Luther (given above
as the epigraph to this chapter), informed by the insights of scholars
Graham White, Christine Helmer, Bruce Marshall, Reinhard Hütter,

---

Brown for *Project Wittenberg*. The translation may be found at http:// http://www.
iclnet.org/pub/resources/text/wittenberg/luther/luther-divinity.txt (accessed October
29, 2007). For a fuller account of the disputation and justification of the claims
about it made in this chapter, see Paul R. Hinlicky, "Luther's Anti-Docetism in the
Disputatio de divinitate et humanitate Christi (1540)," in *Creator est creatura:
Luthers Christologie als Lehre von der Idiomenkommunikation*, ed. O. Bayer and
Benjamin Gleede (Berlin: Walter de Gruyter, 2007), 139–85.

[2]The 1540 disputation's thesis 15 is *inclusive*: "It is rightly taught that in this
matter the manner of speaking [*usum loquendi*] preserved *in the scriptures and in
the orthodox fathers* should prevail" (my emphasis). Thus the problem of how the
catholic fathers (and also the canonical Scriptures) are to be "fittingly" (*commode*)
interpreted so that the Spirit-intended sense provided in the *usum loquendi* can be
distinguished from the many well-intended but inept expressions found in the Fathers
(and the Scriptures). Our guide is Spirit-given *usum seu formulas loquendi*. As Luther
puts it in the *praefatio* of the disputation: "*Ideo ut capere aliquomodo possimus,
dedit Deus nobis* formulas loquendi, *quod Christus sit Deus et homo in una persona,
etc.*" ("Therefore in order that we might somehow understand, God has given us
formulations of speech, that Christ is God and man in one person, *etc.*) (WA 39 II,
98:15; emphasis mine). In argument 7, we are told, "*Spiritus sanctus habet suam
grammaticam*" (ibid., 104, 24).

[3]That is to say, I am developing ideas latent in Luther's text in light of the concern I share with Luther to speak truthfully of the triune God. I am not restricting
myself to repeating what Luther said.

and others. The suggestive notion of a new language of the Spirit, however, may be misunderstood to license enthusiastic construction in theology and/or moral-philosophical readings of the Bible—procedures that Luther in fact adamantly opposed, as we shall see in the third section below. Here Luther's proposal is anchored firmly in the classical Christian narrative of "Trinitarian advent" (Helmer) with *its* dialectic of Word and Spirit in the understanding of Scripture and of Christian experience.

I will then argue that the foregoing insight suggests for us today a shift from the traditional regard for Paul's epistle to the Romans as the hermeneutical basis for dogmatic theology in favor of the narrative theology pioneered canonically in the Gospel we call Mark. Nothing against Paul is intended by this, but rather attention to what Paul himself also presupposed![4] The proposed shift reflects a better understanding of the proper relation of "rhetoric" and "dialectic" in the language of Luther's time or, as these are often tagged in contemporary theology, between first- and second-order discourse. This move may seem perplexing after lengthy arguments on behalf of paying heed to the old Luther's disputational procedure in theology—surely closer to Pauline diatribe than Marcan parable![5] But that perception would be misleading. With Luther, as with Paul, dialectic presupposes rhetoric, just as more generally logical analysis is put to work on some subject matter to be analyzed. Theological argumentation presupposes the "good story and report about a true Son of David" (Luther). Historically, the achievements of post-Reformation theology were possible insofar as this presupposition was not taken for granted; orthodoxy, in turn, descended to arid polemic when it was.[6] In the course of time, Romantic revolt against the now-empty shell of logical rigor and argumentative method finally followed on "the eclipse of biblical narrative" (Hans Frei). Now the biblical narrative of the redeeming God and the sinful, perishing creature gave way to anthropological interpretation, just as the logically careful analysis of the canonical story in dogmatics gave way to theology as construction.

[4]1 Corinthians 15:1-8. See Martin Hengel, *Between Jesus and Paul: Studies in the Earliest History of Christianity*, trans. J. Bowden (Philadelphia: Fortress Press, 1983), especially ch. 5, "Hymns and Christology."

[5]My thanks to Sarah Hinlicky Wilson for this clarification, as well as numerous other editorial queries and suggestions.

[6]Richard A. Muller, *Post-Reformation Reformed Dogmatics: The Rise and Development of Reformed Orthodoxy, ca. 1520 to ca. 1725*, vol. 1, *Prolegomena to Theology*, 2nd ed. (Grand Rapids: Baker Academic, 2003), 178–79.

If we are to take up Luther's new language of the Spirit, the real issue before us today will be how to separate it logically and substantively from Luther's lamentable penchant for demonizing opponents. This can be done, since the revolting invective in which Luther indulged is related to circumstances and a corresponding complex of thought, separable from his fundamental theological conviction and method. Even if this separation can be accomplished, however, we will still be left with a puzzle about the rhetorically indispensable figure of the Spirit's *antipode*, that is, with Luther's *demonology*. In view of the events of the twentieth century, the puzzle could prove surprisingly pertinent: "Are there in Christian faith understandings of God, self, and the world that can help one recognize the demonic *before* it shows itself boldly . . . ? Does Christian faith provide the courage publicly to name the demonic and to say, 'No'?"[7] In any contemporary retrieval of Luther's approach to dogmatics as a critical discipline of testing the spirits,[8] some approach to the solution of this difficulty must be indicated. With that a vision for theological work today is sketched and our book concludes.

1. The Problem of Theology
in Luther's Tradition Today
What's Wrong with "One God by Many Names"?

Graham White has written that the old Luther "was interested in the believer's knowledge of, and talk about, this absolutely unique individual, i.e. God."[9] This discourse about the Trinity, he says, comes in distinction from "philosophy." White speaks in this passage of "philosophy" as a priori essentialism. This is the medieval conception of a science concerned with general truths, which proceeds deductively from first principles on the assumption of the necessity of the cosmos, terminating in *theoria*, the contemplative intellectual gaze at

---

[7]Jack Forstman, *Christian Faith in Dark Times: Theological Conflicts in the Shadow of Hitler* (Louisville: Westminster John Knox, 1992), 20.

[8]I am indebted to Christopher Morse for the conception of theology as a critical discipline, which he has worked out in his highly commendable *Not Every Spirit: A Dogmatics of Christian Disbelief* (Valley Forge, Penn.: Trinity Press International, 1994). Morse, in turn, is significantly influenced by the apocalyptic interpretation of Paul, as appropriated by Martin Luther and Karl Barth.

[9]Graham White, *Luther as Nominalist: A Study of the Logical Methods Used in Martin Luther's Disputations in the Light of Their Medieval Background* (Helsinki: Luther-Agricola Society, 1994), 87; cf. 325. Luther participated in the general nominalist skepticism toward any necessity of the order of the world.

what truly is. Luther took aim at this. The eschatological critique of onto-theological metaphysics (as it is called today) was articulated already in his early commentary on Romans 8.[10]

This critique is surely an important aspect of Luther's legacy that critical dogmatics in his tradition will carry on. Yet it is not all that Luther means positively or negatively by "philosophy," as we shall see. In any event, Luther coupled this doctrinal-theological interest— so differentiated from metaphysics in the medieval appropriation of Aristotle[11]—with an Augustinian "emphasis on the publicly accessible nature of language, including religious language." To this end, Luther introduced a "technical concept, i.e. the idea of a new language, the mastery of which distinguishes believers from nonbelievers, theologians from philosophers."[12] This new language, taking rise in the world adventitiously with the coming of the gospel promise, proceeds inductively in the core belief that the world itself exists contingently as the free creation of God. The gospel being a promise about the world's destiny, this new discourse comes to eschatological rest in worship and adoration.

White's allusion to Augustine is important here. From student days onward, Luther had carefully studied Augustine. He absorbed the great theological lesson of *The Confessions*, book 13: "You created, not because you had need, but out of the abundance of your own goodness."[13] He carefully noted *De Trinitate* and from it drew lessons about divine eternity, simplicity, and the equality of the persons as anchorage for the "economic" doctrine of the Trinity.[14]

---

[10]LW 25:360ff. The source of the contemporary critique of onto-theology is Heidegger in his encounter with Luther during the 1920s. See Benjamin D. Crowe, *Heidegger's Religious Origins: Destruction and Authenticity* (Bloomington: Indiana University Press, 2006), 41–43. I would want to differentiate this stage of Heidegger's work very much from what developed in the turn to Nietzsche during the rise of Nazism. See also Merold Westphal, *Overcoming Onto-theology: Toward a Postmodern Christian Faith* (New York: Fordham University Press, 2001).

[11]Dependence on Aristotle should not be exclusively associated with Thomas Aquinas. New research reveals a Thomas who is stimulated by Aristotle and admiring of his intellectual achievement but not uncritically dependent on him at the expense of Christian theological commitments. See the revealing Fergus Kerr, *After Aquinas: Versions of Thomism* (Malden, Mass.: Blackwell, 2002). On the other hand, the nominalist *via moderna* is as deeply engaged with Aristotle as the *via antiqua*.

[12]White, *Luther as Nominalist*, 16.

[13]Augustine, *Confessions*, XIII:4, trans. R. S. Pine-Coffin (New York: Dorset), 313.

[14]Edmund Hill, O.P., introduction to Augustine, *The Trinity* (Brooklyn: New City Press, 1996), 45ff.

As Mattox showed in chapter 1, this trinitarianism frames his own reformatory teaching of the righteousness of Christ, which comes from God and counts before God in faith.[15] Helmer has similarly argued that Luther "achieves a conceptual privileging of the inner-Trinity as the site to which the concept of infinity can be assigned. Only on the 'inside' are located the eternal trinitarian relations that are beyond finite reason."[16] This move determines "the inner-Trinity as the starting-point for the stories told in the other genres."[17] I will discuss this important idea of Helmer's in detail later. What is at stake in the claim for present purposes is that we read Luther in continuity with the great tradition (as the first thesis of the 1540 disputation claims: "*Fides catholica haec est . . .*," that is, "This is the catholic faith . . ."), on the one hand, and so also read Luther theologically, as partner in contemporary discourse about God, on the other hand.

But that is not easy for us today in a spiritual situation in which pluralist perspectivalism has made us like the denizens of ancient Hellenism, worshiping one (unknown) God by many names, cults, idols (Acts 17). To understand at its root the difficulty theology in Luther's tradition faces today in finding its public voice in this pluralistic society,[18] we might go back to the notorious case of early Protestant intolerance to which Bielfeldt made reference. In 1532, Martin Luther made mention at table of the ideas of the Spaniard Michael Servetus,[19] who would later be burned at the stake in Protestant Geneva for denying the doctrine of the Trinity. Servetus's book *On the Errors of the Trinity* had been published the year before. Its attack on the binding dogma of Christendom did not, however, arise out of the blue; it had a background in medieval theology. Centuries before, Peter Lombard had lifted up what scholars after

---

[15]Indeed, Luther's famous evangelical breakthrough in understanding the Pauline righteousness of God may be no more than a *recollection* of something he had read in *De Trinitate* years before. See XIV:4 in Augustine, *Trinity*, 383.

[16]Christine Helmer, *The Trinity and Martin Luther: A Study on the Relationship between Genre, Language and the Trinity in Luther's Works (1523–1546)* (Mainz: Verlag Philipp von Zabern, 1999), 69.

[17]Ibid.

[18]Ronald F. Thiemann, *Constructing a Public Theology: The Church in a Pluralistic Culture* (Louisville: Westminster John Knox, 1991), 18–19.

[19]Roland H. Bainton, *Hunted Heretic: The Life and Death of Michael Servetus 1511–1553* (Boston: Beacon, 1953), supplies the reference as *Tischreden*, WA 50:475, and reports that Melanchthon read Servetus's book (67).

Jaroslav Pelikan have come to call the "axiom of impassibility,"[20] to insist that the "the [divine] substance neither generates nor is generated." Against this uncritical expansion of the metaphysics of being into the church's understanding of God as Trinity, "Joachim of Fiore in the late 12th century pointed out that if the Lombard were right, and the substance was aloof from the process, then the substance would constitute a fourth entity and there would be a quaternity." It was this implication—for Joachim clearly heretical—that four centuries later Servetus publicly owned: "Precisely!"[21]

The danger for Christian theology in this turn of thought is that a master conception of deity as timeless impassibility is independently established (by "philosophy," by "natural" human "reason") as an epistemic fundament over against the knowledge of God given by the Father in the gospel processions/missions of the Word and the Spirit. The aloof "quaternity" would then represent the real operative conception of God; a Trinity erected on this foundation in turn would appear as mere decoration, a surface "representation"— perhaps God as God "appears" to us, but surely *not* God as God is to God: "The [divine] substance neither generates nor is generated." According to Roland Bainton, Martin Luther took precise exception to this kind of division between divine nature and person that Servetus so eagerly appropriated from Lombard. Luther stated that it "does not please me that Servetus does not make Christ truly a natural Son of God. That is the gist of the controversy."[22] Christ's demotion in being would undermine the new unity of reconciled God and believing sinner, which for Luther is the *res*, the thing itself.

The controversy stayed with Luther and was important to him. As Bielfeldt shows in the preceding chapter, to resolve it Luther reverted by way of logical analysis to Augustine's absolute-relative distinction. This allowed him to retain—but also to focus sharply— the axiom of impassibility. In the absolute sense, it is a predicate of

---

[20]Jaroslav Pelikan, *The Christian Tradition: A History of the Development of Doctrine*, vol. 1, *The Emergence of the Catholic Tradition (100–600)* (Chicago: University of Chicago Press, 1971), 52.

[21]Bainton, *Hunted Heretic*, 25. "To obviate this conclusion Joachim reduced the one substance to such a wraith that nothing remained to hold the three persons in unity and, in consequence, they became three gods. This conclusion also appeared to Servetus to be inescapable." Ibid. Luther engaged this issue. Helmer offers an extended analysis of Luther's objection to Lombard on the quaternity question (*Trinity*, 71–90), as does White (*Luther as Nominalist*, 98–118).

[22]Bainton, *Hunted Heretic*, 68.

the one divine essence and, as such, is consistent with each person of the Trinity having one and the same divine nature. Generation, in turn, is properly predicated of the Father as a relative, personal property. Shifting to Christology, Luther had already worked out in his 1540 disputation the logic of the proposition that "Christ is truly a natural Son of God," for here too the same enigma of eternity relating itself in time occurs. In the process, Luther made a number of remarkable claims about theology as the discipline of the church's mind, a *logically* rigorous way of *referring* to and *explicating*[23] this *unique* creature in the world (since he is also one of the divine Trinity)[24] that he may be *known* aright and so *yielded free course* in the church's speech.[25] If there is a christological problem with Unitarianism, then, it is because somehow it hinders or even blocks hearing the voice of Jesus in the church as the saving voice of God. Hearing the voice of Jesus as the voice of God, however, requires meeting the daunting difficulties that Jesus also speaks *to* the divine Father and is spoken *about* by the divine Spirit. The resolution to this difficulty gives reason why "one God with many names" is not a Christian theological possibility.

A Thesis

Our need, then, of Luther's new language of theology in distinction from the old is that *what* the old language indicates as *deity* (think, for example, of Aristotle's Prime Mover) is something that never attains to the free transcendence or commitment or engagement of the Creator of all that is other.[26] *This* infinity antecedently consists

---

[23]In general, see Ignacio Angelelli, "The Techniques of Disputation in the History of Logic," *Journal of Philosophy* 67, no. 20 (Oct. 22, 1970): 800–815. See also White, *Luther as Nominalist*, 208–12. For a social analysis of the role played by the disputation in emergent Lutheran Orthodoxy, see Kenneth G. Appold, *Orthodoxie als Konsensbildung: Das theologische Disputationswesen an der Universitaet Wittenberg zwischen 1570 und 1710* (Tübingen: Mohr Siebeck, 2004).

[24]*Hic est unus homo, cui nullus est similes* (WA 39 II, 116a:2).

[25]White, *Luther as Nominalist*, 30.

[26]*Creatio ex nihilo* is the virtual signature of the one true God for Luther. In his second Galatians commentary, Luther captured this pattern that characterizes the God of biblical narrative as he reasoned from the justification of the ungodly to the "nature" of God as the almighty Creator: "All hypocrites and idolaters try to do the works that properly pertain to the Deity and belong completely and solely to Christ. . . . ["Hypocrisy," i.e., works-righteousness] refuses to be merely passive matter but wants actively to accomplish the things that it should patiently permit God to accomplish in it and should accept from him" (LW 26:259). But in truth, "God is the God of the humble, the miserable, the afflicted, the oppressed, the desperate, and

in the Father's love for the Son in the Spirit and in the same Spirit the Son's love for the Father. So the new language of theology, I am arguing, is the Spirit's *own* hearing, confessing, rejoicing in us of the infinite inner-trinitarian love of the Father for the Son and the Son for the Father. In the Spirit, the Son hears the Father: "You are My beloved." In the Spirit, the Father hears the Son: "Your will be done." In the Spirit, this discourse is heard—in us, by the new state of faith with its new language that speaks after (*confessio*) and thinks after (*nachdenken*). Our personal inclusion in the divine life of these divine persons becomes effective as we entrust ourselves to it—not some wordless emotion—but in the act of faithfully speaking this very language, that is, by the "authority of instituted liturgy."[27] In the Spirit, the Trinity's own discourse here and now freely turns outward to the creation, including creatures *in spite of sinfulness* in eternally loving discourse of divine life.[28] Divine baptism is the rite of entrance into the life of the Son in his earthly body, the church, and so a personal (not natural) participation by grace in divine trinitarian discourse. "Christians dare address God, however others may do it, only because Jesus permits them to join his prayer, appropriating his unique filial term of address and relying on his fellowship in the prayer. We pray *to* 'our Father.' We pray *with* the one who, by uniquely addressing God as 'my Father,' makes himself the Son, and

---

of those who have been brought down to nothing at all. And it is the nature of God to exalt the humble, to feed the hungry, to enlighten the blind, to comfort the miserable and afflicted, to justify sinners, to give life to the dead, and to save those who are desperate and damned. For He is the almighty Creator, who makes everything out of nothing. In the performance of this, His natural and proper work, He does not allow Himself to be interfered with by that dangerous pest, the presumption of righteousness, which refuses to be sinful, impure, miserable and damned but wants to be pure and holy" (LW 26:314).

[27]Robert W. Jenson, *Systematic Theology*, vol. 1, *The Triune God* (New York: Oxford University Press, 1997), 34.

[28]Helmer follows Oswald Bayer: "Theology as a science of language analyzes the performance of this statement ['I am the Lord your God'], and explicates the actual competence in it" (*Trinity*, 27 n. 99). Theology as a discipline consequently is the study of "words that communicate the God who comes to creation as a story to be told" (36), since, if *promissio* "privileges the present tense as the time of its coming, then there must be a narrative that assigns the past tense to plot the 'where from,' and the future tense to plot the 'where to'" (36). "Through its narrative extension, the *promissio* reveals the 'ontic plus' of God" (36). Helmer accordingly criticizes theories that devaluate the trinitarian witness of both testaments and relocate the inner trinity to a transcendental status behind the narrative (37). The "immanent Trinity is the condition for the possibility of its economy; the economy is the 'noetic' revelation of God as three persons in salvation history, and on the basis of this revelation, the triune essence of God is known to be a necessity of the divine nature" (24).

us as his adoptive siblings children, of his Father. Just so, we enter into the living personal community between them, that is, we pray *to* the Father, *with* the Son, *in* the Spirit"[29]—just because the Father has first spoken to us through the Son in the Spirit: "You are all sons of God through faith in Christ Jesus" (Galatians 3:26). Theology as new language of the Spirit repeats and extends on earth—in ever new amplifications through time—this language of heaven. Expanded to its full narrative depth and breadth, this is the first-order discourse of theology.

If this thesis can be sustained, theology in the tradition of Luther may be understood to conceive of the discipline itself as *nova lingua Spiritus Sancti*. This bold thesis, which identifies certain human words with the divine Word, to be sure, requires the working distinction between rhetoric and dialectic or, in more modern formulation, between first- and second-order discourse in theology. It thus grants a necessary space of freedom and exploration in theology, as Reinhard Hütter has insisted.[30] Yet at the same time it militates

---

[29]Jenson, *Systematic Theology*, 37. My great debts to Jenson are hereby indicated. Writing of the Council of Constantinople's decision on the divine personhood of the Spirit, Jenson states his elusive causal notion as implied by his strong doctrine participation in the life of the Trinity: "The true God blesses and the gospel agitates no religious dynamism not identical with God's own active presence, no religious seeking or journeying that only leads to him. . . . Any pattern of thought that in any way abstracts God 'himself' from the actual historical dynamism of the church's life has no place in Christianity" (107). Causality for Jenson is not a way of sanctifying an effect in the world as, unlike others, specially, "miraculously," hence authoritatively produced. Rather, Jenson understands divine causality as an implication of trinitarian identification. Certain effects in the world, all of which are "caused" by God the Creator, have theological significance as they are parsed by the trinitarian relations. With the further Augustinian qualification that "God is the cause of all causes but not the maker of all choices," I follow Jenson here. On the other hand, I am not inclined to follow him in what to my mind appears too often as unrestricted polemic against the axiom of impassibility, which is essential not only for Luther (think only of the *Bondage of the Will*'s chief concept of the "necessity of immutability"!), but in any serious doctrine of God as Creator, even though this leads to the kind of logically "paradoxical" discourse that Bielfeldt defends in this volume.

[30]Hütter acknowledges the difficulty of this claim today: "Only if theology participates in its object such that the latter authoritatively qualifies it as a distinct practice is argumentative theological discourse possible at all. Within the context of modernity, this can easily appear to be 'fundamentalism . . .'" (Reinhard Hütter, *Suffering Divine Things: Theology as Church Practice*, trans. D. Stott (Grand Rapids: Eerdmans, 2000), 183. Yet a living tradition has to argue its way through to understanding in new context and challenges (184). In this framework, "theology is essentially qualified by and distinguished from *doctrina*. It is shaped by it and yet is not identical with it, and thus in and of itself . . . it does *not* possess any definite validity" (185).

against any kind of strong separation between them. Indeed, for Luther (and historical Lutheranism), second- order discourse may in the course of the church's Spirit-led history become the decisive, precedent-establishing first-order word of confession,[31] for example, the *homoousios* of the Nicene Creed. The Nicene Creed passed from the drafting tables of professional theologians to the liturgy of the church, where it went to work as faith-forming doxology.

The example of the *homoousios* is illuminating for Luther's own theological development. From early critical remarks in the debate with Eck, Luther matured to a consistent lifelong anti-Arianism, just as he increasingly grasped that the old philosophical language about a Prime Mover never attains to the free transcendence or commitment or engagement of the Creator of all that is other—all of which by contrast are indicated in the confession of the Father and Jesus as "of one being." Pondering the Nicene dogma of the Son's eternal, not temporal, generation, Helmer writes that the old Luther opposed the "imposition of temporal categories onto the theological region . . . as the demonic and heretical challenges driving apart the Father from the Son,"[32] as in Arianism, which maintains that there was a time when the Son did not exist. Rather, with Athanasius, Luther figured the Creator/creature distinction spatially, as the posit of something "outside" the Trinity: "The Trinity has an 'outer' side at which the Creator is situated in relation to the creature. By implication, the Trinity has an 'inner' side, a side 'outside' the creature's grasp."[33] Just this kind of reflection led Luther, as we shall see, to "the 'new language' of theological discourse [which] must account for the way in which terms refer to a subject matter in an eternity lying beyond creaturely grasp."[34]

This thesis thus raises important questions about divine substance and causality, as Bielfeldt has indicated. Some interpreters of Luther today seem positively allergic to the very helpful notion of

[31]The Formula of Concord can call the Augsburg Confession the "symbol for this time." *The Book of Concord*, ed. R. Kolb and T. J. Wengert (Minneapolis: Fortress Press, 2000), 487; cf. 524–25. Hütter notes this point with regard to Luther's own "chief doctrine": "Luther rethought the *theological* doctrine of justification and pushed it to a new formulation (sola gratia and sola fide) that precisely maintained the *doctrina* of Scripture in light of a specific nominalist heterodoxy (facere quod in se est)." Huetter, *Suffering*, 142.
[32]Helmer, *Trinity*, 56–57.
[33]Ibid., 68.
[34]Ibid., 71–72.

"participation";[35] they fear some kind of confusion of natures that obfuscates abiding sinfulness where a communion of persons based on grace is intended. Prima facie, the importance of the motif of the *joyful exchange* throughout Luther's career speaks against imputing this allergy to Luther himself. Already in a letter to George Spenlein dated April 8, 1516, Luther articulates the consistent pattern of thought, or model, of the life of faith that stands behind Luther's development of the Reformation doctrine of justification:

> . . . learn Christ and him crucified. Learn to praise him and, despairing of yourself, say, "Lord Jesus, you are my righteousness, just as I am your sin. You have taken upon yourself what you were not and have given to me what I was not." Beware of aspiring to such purity that you will not wish to be looked upon as a sinner, or to be one. For Christ dwells only in sinners. On this account he descended from heaven, where he dwelt among the righteous, to dwell among sinners. Meditate on this love of his and you will see his sweet consolation. For why was it necessary for him to die if we can obtain a good conscience by our works and afflictions? Accordingly you will find peace only in him and only when you despair of yourself and your own works. Besides, you will learn from him that just as he received you, so he has made your sins his own and has made his righteousness yours.[36]

The *joyful exchange*[37] of our sin and Christ's righteousness provides the operative model in Luther's mind of how the event of justification transpires in uniting the believer with Christ in His death and resurrection. According to this model, forgiveness and the new birth are double-sided aspects of the one saving event of encounter and union with Christ in divine faith through the gospel, such that the sinner dies and a believer is born. I have argued elsewhere that the notion of "participation" here is compatible with the Eastern Orthodox doctrine of theosis, when the latter is not misunderstood as some kind of fusion or confusion of natures.[38] Indeed, I think

---

[35]Ibid., 71–72 n. 24.
[36]LW 48:12–13; cf. LW 31:343ff.; LW 35:49ff. On revelation as incorporation, Helmer writes, "As the hearers are gathered into the Spirit's view, they learn to speak about what they have been shown" (*Trinity*, 230; cf. also 266).
[37]See the classic articulation of it in "The Freedom of a Christian" (LW 31:343ff.).
[38]Paul R. Hinlicky, "Theological Anthropology: Towards Integrating Theosis and Justification by Faith," *Journal of Ecumenical Studies* 34, no. 1 (Winter

this argument for the compatibility of justification and theosis quite parallels Bielfeldt's important challenge to the Regnon thesis at the end of chapter 2.

We can and should in any event see Luther's teaching of justification by faith (modeled in the joyful exchange) as drawing deeply on trinitarian dynamics. Faith is not a speechless, isolated attitude but is temporal participation in the Spirit's own speech-acts of love, of the Father for the Son and the Son for the Father. These eternal words of love now spoken in time on human lips are the Spirit's own, who in incorporating us by faith makes our language new. In more familiar language from Luther's tradition: A creature apprehends in faith through the preaching of the gospel her inclusion by the Son who gave himself for her. She understands in faith this divine love as sufficient for her inclusion in the Father's reign. She is justified by this faith *as such* and *in spite of* abiding unbelief, hopelessness, and lovelessness against which she now struggles. Becoming the temporal object of the Father's eternal love for the Son, she therewith becomes a new subject in the Spirit of its trusting apprehension.[39] When she in this trusting apprehension of the Spirit arises with the Son to glorify the Father in a new life of confession of faith, works of love, and hope for her world, she likewise participates in the Son's love for the Father, by the very same Spirit that led Jesus once and for all through the cross to the crown. The *sequence* reflected here is decisive, and it is *all* that "justification by faith," taken as *rule* for preaching Christ aright, *stipulates*. So preach Christ that anyone is included in God's reign for His sake *alone*.

What the rule *indicates* is the living, triune God in His coming to us. The Father's love for the sinful world initiates the Son's coming into the flesh and our inclusion in Him by the Spirit in a free act of grace. The Son's response to the Father's love in the Spirit works out the inclusion of the godless by His way to the God-forsaken death on Golgotha. Consequently, as the crucified but risen Lord, He bestows His own Spirit to bring the Father's love to fulfillment in the gathering of the church, the resurrection of the dead, and the life everlasting. The work of the Spirit in conforming us to Christ as the object

---

1997): 38–73. This argument has received surprising—to its author—confirmation from Pentecostal theology in Veli-Matti Karkkainen, *One with God: Salvation as Deification and Justification* (Collegeville, Minn.: Liturgical Press, 2004), 116ff.

[39]This is admittedly to side with Luther against the purely forensic doctrine of justification of the later Melanchthon.

of the Father's love and just so new subjects with the Son in love with the Father consists in teaching us to speak this new language of repentance and faith. Theology as the communal self-discipline of the baptized community subsists within this calling of Jesus by his Father at his baptism and the kingdom prayer which Jesus spoke with his words and his life in reply. Theology actually follows the motions of the triune life so indicated as *Nachdenken*, thoughtful speaking after God, *confessio*, same-saying the Word spoken by the Father to the Son and the Son to the Father in the power of the same Spirit (Mark 1:9-13).

The Pluralist Objection

Intriguing as we hope our thesis appears, we may now confront an apparently fatal objection from the side of contemporary pluralism. Does the proposed retrieval raise the specter of casting poor Servetus to the flames anew? Surely not, any more than it is a proposal politically to restore Christendom. It is all the same a political proposal. The politics of our proposal need to be put on the table.

In the same study of a half century ago, Bainton concluded with a sharp twist to the tale of Servetus, which has been used for centuries to decry the dangers of dogmatism, rallying the knights of the Enlightenment to particular scorn against the obscurantism of the doctrine of the Trinity: "Today any one of us would be the first to cast a stone against Calvin's intolerance; and seldom do we reflect that we who are aghast at the burning of one man to ashes for religion do not hesitate for the preservation of our culture to reduce whole cities to cinders."[40] These are the final words in Bainton's book, put to paper in living memory of the British-American firebombing of German cities and the atomic incineration of Nagasaki and Hiroshima. Bainton's precise indictment of the Reformers' intolerance of Servetus as product of their Constantinianism[41] was thus redeployed in the contemporary context: "What modern state

---

[40]Bainton, *Hunted Heretic*, 215.

[41]"If all of this rhetoric savors to the modern reader of hypocrisy, one does well to recall that these zealots—the best of them at any rate—were genuinely concerned to save souls from the eternal fires." Ibid., 80. Regarding Calvin's account of his pastoral visit to the condemned Servetus, Bainton comments: "Nowhere does Calvin more clearly disclose himself as one of the last great figures of the Middle Ages. To him it was all so perfectly clear that the majesty of God, the salvation of souls, and the stability of Christendom were at stake. Never for a moment did he suppose that he was acting simply on behalf of the laws of a single city" (210).

would hesitate to extinguish an individual who threatened its very existence?"[42] In other words, Bainton insinuated, the problem of "dogmatism" is not exclusively a religious one, nor is obscurantism an exclusively trinitarian one, in any case overcome by the privatization of religion in the progressively more secular republic. The pluralist objection to the strong claim of Christian theology to participate in time by its language of faith in the inner discourse of the eternal Trinity is not overcome with the new intolerance of Enlightenment Unitarianism, with its oppressive claim to know everyone's religion better than they themselves.[43] The pluralist objection is overcome in being reframed as a question about the difference between a legitimate diversity in the plenitude of divine creation and the demonic assault on the reconciliation of the sinner to the holy God in Christ.

Certainly, "the law under which Servetus had first been imprisoned was that of the Holy Roman Empire; the law by which he was in the end condemned was that of the Codex of Justinian, which prescribes the penalty of death for two ecclesiastical offenses—the denial of the Trinity and the repetition of baptism. Here again [in Calvin's Geneva] in variant form was a revival of the ecclesiastical state in the sense of an entire society operating under the law of God."[44] Today, that Holy Roman Empire—itself under Charlemagne a Western revival of Constantinianism[45]—is history, in part because of divine judgment on the church's sins in witch-hunting, heretic burning, and holy crusades. But *plus ca change, plus c'est la meme chose.* John Millbank has impressively argued that with the establishment of Hobbes's *Leviathan* in the place of Augustine's *Civitatis Dei*, the problematic of orthodoxy and heresy was not solved but merely transposed—all the more dangerously in not being recognized. It is *not* recognized insofar as the story of Servetus's cruel fate is told *only* to consign dogmatism and intolerance to the region of the antecedent religion, indeed to exempt ascendant secularism from this same scrutiny. It is *not* recognized until a Christianity that finds the Trinity obscure realizes how far it has drifted from the gospel narrative.

---

[42]Ibid., 172.

[43]Tomoko Masuzawa, *The Invention of World Religions* (Chicago: University of Chicago Press, 2005).

[44]Bainton, *Hunted Heretic*, 210.

[45]Derek Wilson, *Charlemagne* (New York: Doubleday, 2006).

Critical Dogmatics in Distinction from "Philosophy"

The way through this confusion is to conceive of dogmatics as a *critical* discipline, that is, as the "*new* language of the Spirit" that exists in the act of critically differentiating itself from a discourse that is *old*. To undertake that task today certainly requires that theology overcome the confessionalistic form of dogmatics that emerged after the Western schism (as ideological-political justification for the divided churches;[46] that is why in this volume we have spoken not of "Lutheran theology" but of theology in the tradition of Luther). Even more radically, it requires that dogmatics set aside the static dualism of spheres[47] that characterizes Cartesian and Kantian secularity: thinking things and extended things, mind and body, fact and value, nature and spirit, necessity and freedom, and so forth. "Theology purports," Millbank writes, "to give an ultimate narrative, to provide some ultimate depth of description, because the situation of being oneself within such a continuing narrative is what it means to belong to the Church, to be a Christian." The task here is extension of the biblical "world-absorbing narrative" (George Lindbeck), the "thick" redescription of secular reality (Ronald Thiemann) under the conviction of the "unrestricted epistemic primacy" (Bruce Marshall) of the church's faith in the "man Jesus, who created the heavens and the earth," as Luther put it in the 1540 disputation. Such an approach requires a differentiated discourse about "philosophy," which Luther in fact practices but often fails—causing considerable confusion—to articulate.[48]

This approach puts theology in *direct* conflict with the vari-

---

[46]"The Formula of Concord was not only a religious but also a political document. This was the source of a basic problem: The Formula of Concord was written on the basis of the problematic decision to consolidate the Lutheran confessional identity by finally and absolutely distinguishing Lutheranism from Calvinism." Friedrich Mildenberger, *Theology of the Lutheran Confessions*, trans. E. L. Lueker (Philadelphia: Fortress Press, 1986), 151. One might make precisely the same observation with respect to Roman Catholicism. Jenson's *Systematic Theology* is pioneering and exemplary in this regard. Theology in the tradition of Luther, as I have qualified it, is not "confessional Lutheranism."

[47]See Dietrich Bonhoeffer's now-classic analysis, "Thinking in Terms of Two Spheres," in *Ethics*, trans. N. H. Smith (New York: MacMillan, 1978), 196–207.

[48]Luther: "I make a distinction." Reason may be captive to the Devil or to the Spirit. "The same holds for all the *naturalia* (endowments of nature): though in the ungodly they may serve in the cause of ungodliness, yet in the godly they may serve in the cause of salvation. . . . Reason, in fact, must be transformed—slain, but raised to newness of life . . . Sometimes Luther oscillates between two kinds of statement: (1) that the old light (reason) is extinguished, and a new light (faith) is kindled; and

ants in modernity of totalizing theory stemming from the secular fundamentalisms of a Thomas Hobbes or a Benedict de Spinoza, in that, as Millbank adds, in theology "the claim is made by faith, not a reason which seeks foundations."[49] In distinction with epistemological foundationalism, however, "theology, as the theory of a new practice, the Church, can position itself as a gaze at once above, but also alongside (with or against) other, inherited human gazes."[50] Thus, theology, as argued above, can and should be able to endorse a definite pluralism as divinely commanded openness to the world's diversity as God's good, albeit oppressed, creation. Recall that Millbank's critical differentiation of theology from onto-theological metaphysics (whether in the predominant dualistic or the variant totalizing form) is that "the claim is made by faith, not a reason which seeks foundations." This criticism of modern thought coheres with Luther's thought about the antipode of his new language, that is, the "old language of philosophy," when Luther is thinking of what Ockhamists claimed for the "natural knowledge of God."[51] This was a process of reasoning based on the light of natural reason that led to radical notions of absolute divine volunteerism.

It is a disputed point among Luther scholars, because Luther thinks of "philosophy" and uses the term in a variety of ways and also because Luther too affirms strongly a notion of divine freedom. Yet I take the early disputations against scholastic theology and the philosophical theses of the Heidelberg Disputation as decisive[52] for

---

(2) that the old light is transformed into the new light." B. A. Gerrish, *Grace and Reason: A Study in the Theology of Luther* (Oxford: Clarendon, 1962), 23.

[49]John Milbank, *Theology and Social Theory: Beyond Secular Reason* (Malden, Mass.: Blackwell, 1997), 249.

[50]Ibid., 248. This is not, as we shall see, to accept without qualification Millbank's rhetoric of *theoria*, gaze.

[51]Gerrish's chief conclusion in the aforementioned study is "that the principal force of Luther's assault on reason, so far from being explicable in Nominalist terms, is directed precisely against the via moderna and its tendency toward Pelagianism" in spite of "some resemblance to Ockham's religious epistemology." "Luther struck out on a line of his own which eventually ranged him, not with, but against the champions of the via moderna" (*Grace and Reason*, 6). "For the problem of human reason, according to Luther, is that it cannot comprehend the Gospel's message of free forgiveness by grace alone" (9).

[52]LW 31:3–16 and 41–42 respectively. Burnell F. Eckhardt Jr., *Anselm and Luther on the Atonement: Was It 'Necessary'?* (San Francisco: Mellen Research University Press, 1992): "In his 'Disputation against Scholastic Theology' (1518), Luther contends against the view of William of Ockham who held that God could accept the sinner without justifying grace (WA I, 227:4–5; AE 31, 13)." Luther's position amounts to a rejection of the distinction between *potentia absoluta* and *potentia*

the claim that Luther strove against the metaphysics as well as the theology of the *via moderna* in which he was educated—with the aid of logical tools learned from these same masters. It is not only, as Heiko Oberman taught us, that Luther opposed the theological *facere in quod se* of nominalism,[53] but also that he opposed the prototypical metaphysics of secularism[54] with its dark vision of deity as *potentia absoluta*: willful, essentially incommunicable omnipotence whose relation to the world is arbitrary, whose *potentia ordinata* in covenants could therefore at any moment be revoked, all earnestly pastoral assurances to the contrary notwithstanding.[55] Bielfeldt, I judge, is quite right in chapter 2 to have argued in detail that Luther is the modern *Augustinian*, with the emphasis falling on the realism in language reflecting, in howsoever oppressed and distorted a way, a world created by the word of God. This means, moreover, that Luther's evident acknowledgment of divine volunteerism in terms such as *deus nudus, deus absconditus* is decisively qualified, indeed situated, by his trinitarian commitment: the hidden and revealed God are not two but one, and this one is, and will prove to be, the Trinity. For Helmer, indeed, Luther's achievement stands out in contrast to the volunteerist abyss. In understanding the infinity of the Trinity as the love in the Spirit of the Father for the Son and of the Son for the Father, she sees Luther discerning an infinity of *compassion*, of

ordinata, which is also found in Gabriel Biel. "Luther's contention here makes it clear that he, like Anselm, recognizes that there are certain things which not even God can do if he is to be true to himself" Eckhardt, *Anselm,* (29).

[53]See Heiko A. Oberman, *The Harvest of Medieval Theology: Gabriel Biel and Late Medieval Nominalism* (Grand Rapids: Baker Academic, 2000); and Heiko A. Oberman, *The Dawn of the Reformation: Essays in Late Medieval and Early Reformation Thought* (Edinburgh: T&T Clark, 1986).

[54]For what is at stake in this dispute, see Michael Allen Gillespie, *Nihilism before Nietzsche* (Chicago: University of Chicago Press, 1996).

[55]The question of nominalist content and its influence on Luther has been controversial. See White, *Luther as Nominalist,* 27–31. As heavily as I draw on Graham White's study of Luther's logical and semantical concerns, I do not agree with him that Luther in any simple sense can be designated a modernist, nominalist, or Ockhamist. Oberman established the background of Luther's theological struggle in the nominalist construal of the *facere quod in se*; I see Luther also breaking with the pure voluntarism of Ockhamist natural theology in the name of trinitarianism. "Luther's development can best be understood in terms of nominalism and humanism domesticated and put into the service of a new Augustinian theology which conditioned him." Lewis W. Spitz, *Luther and German Humanism* (Brookfield, Vt.: Variorum: 1996), 89.

boundless self-giving love: *esse deus dare*.[56] Dogmatics, which lacks epistemological grounding in the sense of modern foundationalism, would then seek to ground internally all statements of Christian belief in *this* infinity of the divine love. This is of course a work of *faith* in the revealed God; as such, it is undertaken in the state of *Anfechtung*, the acutely felt tension of a promise yet to be fulfilled. This is just how Luther concluded his *Bondage of the Will,* in which the problematic passages occur: "To think that we cannot for a little while *believe* that He is just, when He has actually promised us that when He reveals His glory we shall all clearly see that He both was and is just!"[57]

Hütter has in any case made a similar analysis of the contemporary situation, explicitly on behalf of theology in the tradition of Luther. Today, he argues, theology amounts to private opinionating, so-called constructive theology, freewheeling metaphysical speculation without the rigor or restraint that would be required in academic philosophy.[58] The dissolution of Constantinianism has not worked a re-Christianization of the churches but their evolution into soft institutions of civil religiosity.[59] He cites a letter of Bonhoeffer to Bethge from September 9, 1940: "It is the question whether, after separation from papal and worldly authority in the church, an authority can be established in the church and grounded solely on the word and on confession. If such an authority is not possible, then the last possibility for the Protestant church has passed by; then there really is only a return to Rome or to the state church or the path of isolation, to the 'protest' of genuine Protestantism against false authorities."[60] In Friedrich Schleiermacher, Protestant theology left

---

[56]Helmer, *Trinity*, 165–69, draws this primarily from her analysis of the Luther hymn *Nun freut euch, lieben Christen gmein* (1523).

[57]Martin Luther, *The Bondage of the Will*, trans. J. I. Packer and O. R. Johnston (Grand Rapids: Revell, 2000), 315.

[58]Hütter, *Suffering Divine Things*, 22.

[59]Ibid., 10–11.

[60]Ibid. One may note here Robert W. Jenson's frequently misunderstood diagnosis of the theological sickness of Protestantism: "There is an obvious problem here. It is the teaching office that speaks dogma, that speaks theologically for the church to its own members. Every proposal of dogma, like every proposal of theology generally, must be tested against Scripture and existing dogma. But we now see that it is, again, the teaching office by which Scripture and dogmatic texts can assert themselves. Here is a circle that obviously could set the teaching office adrift to define the gospel as whatever pleases its momentary holders. Sensitivity to this threat has notoriously made Protestantism uneasy with the posit of an authoritative magesterium. Yet

behind the dogmatic principle of authority and turned to an enthusiastic/ charismatic principle of religious virtuosity.[61]

But in reality, modern Protestantism hitches its wagon to collective nationalisms or, alternatively, to radical individualisms.[62] Church and theology become a helping profession in a secularized society. To Lindbeck's call for church that would be sociologically a "sect" but ecclesiologically "catholic," like the pre-Constantinian church, the objection from the side of American civil religion or the German *Volkskirche* runs thus: Can we so easily divide believers from nonbelievers? Peter Berger's "heretical imperative" militates against dogmatics as a discipline for the same reason.[63] A Habermasian general theory of communication acts like an updated Kantian tribunal of reason, muzzling the church, which is no longer permitted to be or to act as a genuine public under these conditions.[64] What is left of the church disintegrates under these pressures, since it cannot sustain even minimal unity when expressive-individualistic religiosity runs awry or peace and justice goals lead to contradictory strategies. Unity for the church as a genuine public, Hütter concludes, requires a "pathos external to itself . . . to be determined or defined through binding acts and through a *doctrina evangelii*, a teaching of the gospel, formulated explicitly in a confession."[65]

Dogmatics as a critical discipline today in Luther's tradition would then have this political edge: it cuts through the static dualistic boundaries internalized both in today's church and in society in favor of the eschatological conflict of the ages; it challenges directly totalizing aspirations of immanence in the name of the free transcendence of the triune God; it abandons the anachronistic battle lines drawn in the seventeenth century and reinforced in the nineteenth. Against regnant deist conceptions of absolute divine freedom, it will insist on the trinitarian harmony of freedom with wisdom and love that is committed to and engaged with the world in the missions of the Word and Spirit. From this definite perspective, it welcomes all perspectives as ones potentially to be recognized as good creatures of God, knowing that all perspectives (including its own) suffer the

---

now we see that a teaching office is necessary if Scripture or dogma are themselves to exercise authority" (*Systematic Theology*, I:40).

[61]Hütter, *Suffering Divine Things*, 14.
[62]Ibid., 15–16.
[63]Ibid., 18.
[64]Ibid., 20.
[65]Ibid., 21.

distortion of the fallen world. But it knows this simultaneously, indeed on account of, its own knowledge of the Trinity, which requires theology not only critically to examine its own discourse but likewise critically to incorporate other perspectives. The divine perspective is revealed and known in the Spirit's speaking love of the Father for the Son and the Son for the Father.

The Causal Claim

All this becomes possible and necessary when theology has a "pathos external to itself." Yet manifestly that entails some kind of *causal* claim. Building on such analyses of the contemporary situation, I will in the next section lay out a reading of Luther's new language of the Spirit, which conceives of theology as a discipline in *direct* consequence of the new creative word from God spoken in Christ (in the sense of participation in the Father's spoken love for the Son and the Son's spoken love for the Father previously sketched).[66] As indicated above, this new language of theology is nothing less than the Holy Spirit's *own*—in Hütter's provocative formulation of the causal claim, a "suffering of divine things."[67] As White explains, for Luther the "meaning [*significatio*] of a term, or a proposition, depends crucially on the context of its use," but "this dependence is a causal dependence, brought about by access to varying referents of the term."[68] Or again, "for Luther, the crucial difference between Christian and non-Christian contexts is that, in the former, one has access to the religious realities that one talks of."[69]

Abstractly, the claim to "found" theology on the *causal* word and Spirit of God could be mistaken as resort to a private miracle, exempting the theologian from critical scrutiny. It is, however, a claim of *faith*, not "reason seeking foundations," and as such cannot work epistemologically to justify theology outside the circle of shared faith, nor is it so intended. If anything, it casts doubts on the possibility of epistemology altogether as the misbegotten project of secular fundamentalism.

---

[66]Helmer, *Trinity*, 233.

[67]Hütter, *Suffering Divine Things*, 129–32, 145–51.

[68]White, *Luther as Nominalist*, 336–38.

[69]Ibid., 340. White thinks that Luther resorts to *deificatio* to provide causal mediation between "vision in heaven" and "hearing on earth" (342; cf. 345). This resort to *deificatio* is what seems most to trouble Bielfeldt, but it is not to be understood in the extrinsically causal and privatized way that is often imagined. It is participation by the Spirit in the Father's speaking love for the Son and the Son's for the Father.

Rather, the very existence of the theological circle—absurd within the modern system, perhaps any system—is the real bone of contention, while the theological task of testing the spirits consists for the most part in the adjudication of community-threatening claims that arise within it. In either case, the point of appealing to the Spirit to authorize the new language is never to claim private inspiration for the individual theologian and immunity from criticism for her doctrines, but rather to locate publicly access to the theological region in the field of the Spirit's proclamation of the Crucified One as risen, that is, the church. This directs theological discourse to the movements of the Father's love for the Son and the Son's love for the Father.

Such *direction* of theology goes to the heart of Luther's thought. White connects Luther's concern for "theologically correct language about God . . . the appropriate logic for talk of God . . . a theological grammar" with his famous distinction: "The law talks of our actions, and the gospel talks of Christ's action in making us righteous. This concept of subject, then, is a semantic concept," that is, a referential term. Accordingly, those who "understand Scripture morally and philosophically [that is, as anthropology, as talking in symbols about what we should think, do, or feel] . . . do not understand that its grammatical subject is God, and they replace this subject, God, by man. This false grammar does not any more allow it to be said who is God and who is man"—nor for that matter that these two others are nevertheless united in Christ, causing us by the Spirit to sing a new song, speak a new language. To accomplish that, we need clear conceptual distinctions between divine and human *nature* and a clear concept of what the *personal union* of these natures in Christ could be. To meet these needs, the aging Luther with his lifelong treasury of Scripture interpretation turned anew to the genre of the *disputatio*. That is to say, to succeed in speaking the primary discourse of faith as the Spirit intends, Luther realizes that we need to think logically and reflectively about what we are saying, not only how we say it. The movement to second-order discourse is entirely organic to sustaining gospel discourse through time as it extends through space.

2. What Is the New Language of the Spirit?
The Necessary Equivocation

It is in part, therefore, the language of disputation itself, the logically rigorous examination of dogmatic theses. Luther "loved" the medieval *disputatio*, according to Helmer; "study of the *disputatio* opens up a view of Luther's understanding of the activity of reason that is illuminated by faith."[70] Likewise White: "Luther himself was very fond of disputation, and saw the right to carry out disputation as an extremely important part of the role of a doctor of theology. Correspondingly, many of his own disputations are directed against particular heresies, or theological difficulties, which he saw as facing the church."[71] Helmer puts the resort to the disputation genre into the broader context of Luther's theological concerns: "Under the rubric of the Spirit, the church is incorporated into the divine defense of the trinitarian article against heresy. Throughout its history, the church is guided by the Spirit in clarifying its understanding of the trinitarian nature of God, and in articulating that understanding. On a personal level, each Christian grows in the knowledge of faith's object, and begins to speak rightly about divine matters."[72] Luther wants to learn how to express the affirmative, to resist the enemy, to care for the weak, to defend the borders against the adversary by articulating the truth at the center.[73] In the disputation, the ground of faith is uncovered in "the *promissio* that the benefits of Christ are true for eternity."[74] Thus, the *disputatio* genre worked above all for Luther to articulate or explicate the logic inhering the axial Christian proposition of Jesus Christ as the saving truth of God.[75]

Concretely, the problem Luther was addressing in the 1540 disputation had been created by Caspar Schwenckfeld's monophysite denial of the creature in Christ. The problem is this: "A creature, in the old use of language, is that which the Creator has created and distinguished from himself. But this meaning has no place in Christ the creature. There the creator and the creature are one and the same." Luther solved the problem by attending to the contexts in which the term *creature* is spoken and the logical inferences valid in these contexts respectively, along with the new connotations produced by these varying usages.

---

[70]Helmer, *Trinity*, 41–42.

[71]White, *Luther as Nominalist*, 23.

[72]Helmer, *Trinity*, 269.

[73]Ibid., 47.

[74]Ibid., 120.

[75]For this claim, see Oswald Bayer's instructive study "Das Wort ward Fleisch: Luthers Christologie als Lehre von der Idiomenkommunikation," in *Creator est creatura*, 5–34, which connects the late Luther's *Disputatio de senentia: Verbum caro factum est* with the breadth and depth of the Reformer's earlier christological teaching.

It was just such linguistic contexts with their "grammars," that is, rules of inference, that Luther named the old and new languages. Thus, argument 7 of the 1540 disputation announces: "For the Holy Spirit has his own grammar . . . and we must remain content with the pattern prescribed by the Holy Spirit." The discipline of critical dogmatics is launched with God's self-declaration. Christ, who sends His Spirit so that we hear and believe, is the access to the theological region. But Luther now associates the hard work of logical analysis with the Spirit who illuminates human reason to think after the Trinity. "The deployment of the disputation is connected with the appeal to the third person of the Trinity. . . . In times of defense, the Spirit's speech is the only source of knowledge concerning a subject matter that exists beyond the bounds of natural reason. Connected to the necessity of disputing against those who disobey the Son is the insistence on listening to the Spirit."[76] This is no appeal to inner experience, to the "still, small voice within" or anything like that. Listening to the Spirit is listening to the proclamation of the Son's resurrection, which involves us in thinking through a peculiar equivocation, logically speaking, that I shall designate a *rhetorical* paradox. The new language of the Spirit is the Spirit's own assertion of the rhetorical paradox of Christ crucified, dead, and buried and yet now risen. Somehow Schwenckfeld has missed this. He is speaking of Christ in a way not the Spirit's, that is, which turns out on rational examination to betray "old" modes of thought.

A clarification made here, then, is important: the "words *man, humanity, suffered*, etc., and everything that is said of Christ, are new words" (thesis 23), not in the sense of pointing out some "new or different thing" but by signifying the same entity "in a new and different way [*nove et aliter*]" (thesis 24). Luther's anti-Docetism turns on this point.[77] The new language continues to point at, designate, refer to the same object in the shared world as the old language: the man Jesus, the Jew born of Mary, crucified under Pontius Pilate, dead and buried. This Jesus is surely and abidingly one and the same creature: "The thing signified is the same." As Marshall puts the logical point: "The one thing we cannot do" in making sense of the Christian assertion "This man is God" is to agree to hold " 'Homo est Deus' true by taking 'homo' to mean something like 'Deus.' " We

[76]Helmer, *Trinity*, 69.
[77]White, *Luther as Nominalist*, 326.

cannot by a deft redefinition of "homo"[78] render the term equivocal (although, as Marshall notes, holding such sentences true "may
of course extend or otherwise alter the sense of their terms"[79]). As
Bielfeldt has argued, Luther is a semantic realist, a point that speaks
against extravagant extrapolations on Luther's new language of the
Spirit, as though it were intended to do the very thing Marshall rules
out, that is, generate new *conceptualizations* rather than stipulate
new *uses* of referential terms.

The point bears emphasis because of the massive influence in
modern theology of the content/scheme epistemology deriving from
Kant, according to which perception is blind until conceptualized by
the action of mind—a notion that evolves in some versions of idealism into the kind of pure constructivism that has now found congenial habitat in contemporary theology. Luther does not think that
the material of theology is infinitely malleable in such fashion.[80] We
are in all cases speaking about Jesus the man, the *object* in the world
that suffered along with everything else that is told *about* him.[81] This
objectivity abides. "Thus the Son of God died and was buried in the
dust like everyone else."[82] If this is not so, Jesus Christ ceases to be
truly human, truly creature. The gospel, on the other hand, resides in
the new use to which the Spirit puts this very "old" language about
the one born from Mary and executed under Pilate. The ordinary
or mundane reference (the *significata)* remains forever; the several
contexts of usage are consequently not somehow sealed off from one
another, but the new presupposes and indeed requires the old.

---

[78]Bruce D. Marshall, "Faith and Reason Reconsidered: Aquinas and Luther on
Deciding What Is True," *The Thomist* 63 (1999): 43.

[79]Ibid., 44.

[80]According to White, Luther held "a very standard, realist, semantics, which
was in many respects similar to the semantic theories of his scholastic sources. On the
other hand, his causal stories about the use of religious language are quite unusual,
and certainly innovative" (*Luther as Nominalist*, 145; cf. 148).

[81]Bielfeldt rightly commented on this: "It is important to preserve the original
meaning of a word even within a theological context if one is not to compromise
God's real incarnation in theological phrases like 'God is in Jesus,' or 'Christ's body
is in the bread.' . . . If the meaning of 'human being' [is changed to mean] 'uncreated
person that God becomes' [i.e., as in monophysitism], then 'God becomes a human
being' does not really assert the infinite becoming finite; it does not really assert
the communication of idioms so necessary for salvation. . . . The everyday meaning
of terms remains important. God really did become what God is not; God became
a flesh and blood human being." Bielfeldt, "Luther, Metaphor and Theological
Language," *Modern Theology* 6, no. 2 (January 1990): 125.

[82]WA 39 II, 98:19–20.

What is new is that the reference to the Jew crucified under Pilate is placed by the Spirit into a new framework and put to a new use as the act of this preaching brings access to the region of theology. In this, the reference acquires for us a new, extended sense or "meaning," as it must if the same man has been raised from death. Thus, in the Spirit's preaching of the crucified Jesus, he is revealed as the Eternal Son incarnate. Note that beliefs about Jesus—his resurrection from death in time, his birth from the Father in eternity—come as the resurrection to faith and new birth as a child of God is effected in the auditor. Faith therewith perceives this same crucified Jesus yet now, with the coming of these new beliefs, as the Christ, the Son of God, who lived and died but lives and reigns, also "for me."[83] As Marshall puts it, for Luther, "the believer is 'aroused to faith' (that is, trust) in Christ just because he has a different propositional attitude," holding to the eternal generation of the Son from the Father.[84] With this preaching by the Spirit, the context shifts from what natural reason can know to what God alone can know and share with us. Likewise, the use of the designated object shifts, from simple

---

[83]This is a fundamental result of Regin Prenter's seminal inquiry in *Spiritus Creator*, trans. John M. Jensen (Philadelphia: Muhlenberg Press, 1953): "In connection with Romans 1:1-4, Luther often points out that work of the Holy Spirit is to proclaim the divinity of Jesus Christ in the resurrection. By the incarnation the Son of God humbled himself and assumed the *forma servi*. He became *humiliatus* so that his divinity was emptied out and hidden in the flesh. . . . The public proclamation of the divinity and power of Christ is done *per spiritum sanctificationis*, which was not given before the resurrection of Jesus. . . . By the work of the Holy Spirit the resurrection is really taken from the hidden sphere of God into the message of the gospel, so *that the risen Christ lives his risen life in our midst in this message.* . . . The center in the Word of God is the risen Christ himself. . . . The outward Word does not become the Word of God until the Spirit causes the risen Christ to live his life in that Word" (111–12).

Lienhard likewise calls attention to Luther's theologically formative exegesis of Roman 1:2-4 in this connection: "Christ in the flesh is God hidden and not recognized as such. After the resurrection, his rule begins in the sense that the Holy Spirit glorifies him and makes him known for what he is, the Son of God in the flesh of the son of David. This rule is exercised through the apostolic Word. The real source of it is the Holy Spirit. By the public proclamation . . . Christ is instituted in his rule. Thus he becomes the Son of God with power . . . the work of the Holy Spirit, i.e., the glorification of Christ by preaching, the manifestation of what he has been since the incarnation, the proclamation of the divinity of this man who suffered. That is the true elevation of Christ . . .the distinction between what Christ is and the fact of being recognized for what he is, which fact is linked to preaching." Marc Lienhard, *Martin Luther: Witness to Jesus Christ; Stages and Themes of the Reformer's Christology*, trans. Edwin H. Robertson (Minneapolis: Augsburg, 1982), 55.

[84]Marshall, "Faith and Reason Reconsidered," 30.

indication to assertion of a promise inviting faith.[85] There is then *rhetorical* paradox, an unavoidable *equivocation*, as Luther puts it (*vocabula aequivoca*). The term *creature* acquires not a new reference but a new connotation. Yet, logically, no contradiction is involved, that is, no assertion of contrary notations of one and the same entity in one and the same sense.[86] The connotation shifts with the frame of reference and the use.[87] What is at stake in this shift?

The Gospel Narrative and Its Dogmatic Interpretation

Really, the theological validity of the *gospel narrative* itself, the Pauline motif of the *obedience* of Christ in Romans 5—as opposed to a punctilinear preaching of the cross as the sheer negation of all immanent meaning. How can the man dying forsaken on the cross connote creature separated from God by an infinite mode and the same dying man connote union with divinity in an ineffable mode?[88] The question is as exegetically well founded as the juxtaposition of Mark 15:34 and 15:39. Is this meant as a logical paradox, a genuine and irresoluble contradiction that by some kind of explosion creates a transcendent signification? Or is it a rhetorical paradox, contravening our usual ways of thinking, inviting a story to be told whose inner sense is disclosed in the obedience of the Christ forsaken by God in Gethsemane?[89]

In the old language, as understood from within the philosophical perspective, the context is the vast and inscrutable cosmos and the awakening of the human mind to wonder; here the word *creature*

---

[85]Reinhard Hütter has made this point in his critique of Oswald Bayer's overlooking of Austin's distinction between reference (locution) and performance (illocution). *Suffering Divine Things*, 82–84.

[86]As Marshall concludes about Luther: "Theology and philosophy each has its own 'sphere'; neither provides the content for the other's discourse, and each has its own rules for forming true sentences. But this distinction turns out to be a way of insisting that theology has to keep its epistemic priorities straight. Theology's 'sphere' ends up being the whole; theology puts philosophy in its place" ("Faith and Reason Reconsidered," 46). See also the criticism of the "robustly paradoxical view" of a dualism of spheres, 35–36.

[87]White, *Luther as Nominalist*, 338.

[88]Bruce D. Marshall, *Trinity and Truth* (New York: Cambridge University Press, 2000), argues this point incisively, 246–56.

[89]See Luther's commentary on Psalm 8, WA 45:205–50; trans. LW 12:95–136. One could also reference here the sermons for Wednesday after St. Elizabeth on November 21, 1537, titled "Jesus Christ, True God and Man" and "On His Office and Kingdom Which He Conducts in Christendom," and Thursday, November 22, 1537, "On the Humanity of Christ and Its Office," WA 45:265–324; no English translation.

signifies "a thing separated from divinity by an infinite mode" (thesis 21). In argument 20, this old language is called a "philosophical argument," which holds that "there is no *proportio* between the creature and the Creator, between the finite and the infinite." And in philosophy, Luther seems to agree, this is so—*finitum non capax infinitum*—even though, crucially, the accounts of this ignorance of God by philosophy and theology differ.[90] Luther, of course, wants to offer a *theological* account of philosophical ignorance of God, which will be based finally not on the finite perception of its own incapacity for the infinite but on the moral discordance between the Creator and the creature revealed by the cross of the Incarnate Word. Because of sin, no image of God is available to us in the creature as we know it now after the fall, in what *seems* natural and philosophically reasonable to us.

"Creature," as we know creature, is that which passes in and out of existence, so with the "natural" connotation of suffering and imperfection, yielding no clue to the mind (assuming It has one) of the Transcendent Causality, the cause of all causes.[91] Is It also the maker of all choices? Or only of good ones? How could we ever tell? How do we ever get from *potentia absoluta* to *potentia ordinata*? The problem of "natural theology" arises here—which for Luther is not a philosophical riddle but an urgent matter of knowing whom to trust and obey in life and in death. There are many creatures. Which of them, if any, is or could be the image of God? Emperor Nero? Comrade Stalin? Mother Teresa? All of them, perhaps, the totality in splendid diversity and final harmony—including then also Nero and Stalin? But the totality of the creature is not available to us until the end of history. Perhaps the "person," in the sense of that primeval couple called in Genesis 1: 27 to live before God as partners in dominion over the creation, might have been the image of God, if that status had not, according to Luther, been forfeited in the fall.

But now God has provided the image in the gospel narrative. In

---

[90]Remember that the metaphysical First Cause that some claim as knowledge of God is for Luther an idol, that is, ignorance of the true infinite, the Creator God, the Trinity who creates ex nihilo!

[91]Gerrish highlights Luther's view that philosophical reason "concludes either that there is no God, or that He is disinterested in human affairs. It is only the Holy Scriptures that give us a true understanding of the efficient and final causes of creation; reason can go no further than the material and formal causes." Gerrish, *Grace and Reason*, 19, commenting on Genesis 2:21. "Philosophia est quasi theologia gentium et rationis," cited from Tischreden 1, no. 4 (30).

the creature narrated in the gospel story, we see humanity as God wills it to be, the one analogue in our midst that makes certain and responsible speech about God possible. One creature among all the creatures *corresponds* to God, and so reveals God, being God incarnate in the person of His Son, one of the divine Trinity. "Jesus Christ, the Son of God" is the new language of the Spirit. In him, a *proportio* or *analogia* between Creator and the creation is constructed by the Spirit, who anointed the man at his baptism. We see it in the faith and obedience of the assumed humanity made visible to us in the narrative portrayal, culminating in Gethsemane.[92] God Whom reason cannot declare from below thus declares Himself from above in intelligible words of human language about a human object in the world: Jesus *qua* creature, the New Adam who corresponds to God because God in the person of the Son has made this human nature His very own and given it in turn to the Spirit's leading.

As Luther put it in the preface to the 1540 disputation:

> It is an incomprehensible thing, such as not even the angels can grasp and comprehend, that two natures should be united in one person. Therefore, so that we may grasp this in some small measure, God has given us formulations of speech: that Christ is God and man in one person, and there are not two persons, but two natures are united in one person, so that what is done by the human nature is said also to be done by the divine nature, and vice versa. Thus the Son of God died and was buried in the dust like everyone else, and the son of Mary ascended into heaven, is seated at the right hand of the Father, etc. We are content with these formulations.[93]

Luther's *new* language of the Spirit turns out to be the old language of the dogmas of the church about Christ as the Incarnate Word and the New Adam.

Interestingly—given the long tradition of Protestant biblicism in his name—Luther expressly notes that Scripture taken by itself, abstractly, as sheer paradoxical assertion of divine Word in some human script, can fail us. Even Scripture taken dumbly, that is, without proper appreciation of the rhetorical paradox of the Spirit who challenges accustomed ways of thinking about divinity by making the Crucified One the image of God, can fail us. He provocatively

---

[92]See Paul R. Hinlicky, "The Deity Has Withdrawn: Luther's Preaching of Christ Forsaken by God in Psalm 8" (forthcoming).

[93]WA 39 II, 98:15–20, Brown's translation, altered.

illustrates the point with the weighty text of John 1:14: "The Word was made flesh." This statement can be taken to suggest a substantial metamorphosis of the divine Logos into a creature of flesh. In thesis 14, Luther claims the evangelist would have better expressed the matter by saying, "The Word is incarnate or made fleshly." Does Luther here correct the *verba* of Scripture in the light of the later *fides catholica*? Luther corrects inept expressions of *both* Scripture *and* tradition for the sake of *the* Word, that is, the "one Lord Jesus Christ, true God and man."[94] As the creature who corresponds to God, he is the truth, and as this person he is therefore the Spirit-intended sense of Scripture and catholic doctrinal tradition, which together form for Luther a hermeneutical whole. Thus, the final thesis, thesis 64, reads: "This is what it means to be a heretic: one who understands the Scriptures otherwise than the Holy Spirit demands." In strict trinitarian construal, what the Holy Spirit demands that we see and understand in Scripture is Christ crucified. In this life-act of obedience to the Father, he is the sense intended by the Spirit in every word and all the words—no matter what human authors might have thought!

Perhaps here as nowhere else it is manifest that to take up Luther's new language, rightly understood, is to call for dismantling of the current regime in which "moral and philosophical," that is, anthropological, reading of Scripture effectively neutralizes the evangelical claim of biblical text, leaving as a consequence contem-

---

[94]Thesis 15 is *inclusive*: "It is rightly taught that in this matter the manner of speaking [*usum loquendi*] preserved *in the scriptures and in the orthodox fathers* should prevail" (my emphasis). Thus the problem of how the catholic fathers (and also the canonical Scriptures) are to be "fittingly" (*commode*) interpreted arises. Kevin J. Vanhoozer fails to grasp this decisive point in his effort to restore a strong doctrine of *sola scriptura* for a "post-conservative" theology in *The Drama of Doctrine: A Canonical Linguistic Approach to Christian Theology* (Louisville: Westminster John Knox, 2005). He cites my precise words, "The principle of 'Scripture alone' has self-destructed, because it has set aside the relation of Scripture to the Holy Spirit and the church," and then criticizes me for "too hasty" a "dismissal of *sola scriptura* as a beneficial church practice—indeed, as a work of the Spirit" (232), as if somehow this were not precisely my point. By *sola scriptura*, he claims only to mean "scripture as prior norm, potentially set in judgment over the tradition" (233). Then the correct designation would be *prima scriptura*, the very terminology that I had proposed in the cited article, "The Lutheran Dilemma," *Pro Ecclesia* 8 (1998). Luther, in the 1540 disputation, makes clear that real error, that is, false teaching about Christ that gives the victory to Satan, does not lie in the commission of verbal mistakes of expression, with which the Bible is filled, as Luther points out regarding the two versions of the Decalogue. See also Helmer, *Trinity*, 269, 273. The point is to break fundamentally and in principle from the idle proof-texting of *sola scriptura* dogmatics in the interest of sustaining the Schism.

porary talk of God to constructive fancy, if not fantasy. Theology for Luther is about the redeeming God incarnate in Christ crucified, seeking, finding, and restoring the lost and dying creature. The saving unity of humanity and deity confessed in the doctrine concerning this person is the one essential truth claim articulated in a variety of ways,[95] but primarily by the work of the *doctrinal exegesis* of Scripture, as Mattox has shown in the first chapter: "We miss the point of [Luther's] continuing appeal to Scripture 'alone' as a theological court of last resort if we hear it as an appeal to the Scriptures as understood apart from the traditions of living Christian faith or, for that matter, outside the *mater ecclesia* within which faith itself is imparted through Word and Sacrament."[96] Likewise, White has made the point that while Luther, along with other humanists, indeed asserted the primacy of *grammatica* over *logica*, what *grammatica* is for Luther is "semantic analysis, which is making clear to *logica* what the various terms in the sentence . . . stand for. . . . And *logica*, by contrast, has the role of explaining what the nature of things is, of saying what identity statements they are able to figure in and which not."[97]

Mattox's claim about the *verba* known in light of the *res* is thus valid.[98] To be sure, there is a dialectic here of the letter and the Spirit, the *verba* and the *res*, as Paul and Augustine taught Luther. More broadly, every theology that does not flatly equate God with the world (or the Word with the words) requires some dialectic, just as we might succinctly define the demonic temptation (the *sic eritis deus* of Genesis 3:5) as that undialectical doctrine that confuses divine and human possibilities, that violates the distinction between the natures (as descriptive sets of possibilities) befitting Creator and creature. Melanchthonian Lutheranism works with a hermeneutical dialectic of God's word as demand and promise, law and gospel; Zwinglian Calvinism works with a dialectic of the divine and human natures in Christ.

In distinction from these as hermeneutical approaches to the doctrinal exegesis of Scripture, I want to suggest along with Mattox

---

[95]See Marshall on Luther's "relative insouciance about what the chief article is" ("Faith and Reason Reconsidered," 32).

[96]Mickey L. Mattox, "From Faith to the Text and Back Again: Martin Luther on the Trinity in the Old Testament," *Pro Ecclesia* 15, no. 3 (Summer 2006): 281–303.

[97]White, *Luther as Nominalist*, 41–42.

[98]Ibid., 44, 317.

that theology in the tradition of Luther, the modern Augustinian, might better grasp the dialectic as one of understanding the Word in the words and the letters in the Spirit, concretely, Jesus in the gospel narrative and the gospel narrative in the Spirit's beloved community: "Jesus was having dinner at Levi's house, many tax collectors and sinners were eating with him and his disciples, for there were many who followed him" (Mark 2:15). Here the issue of critical understanding and appropriation is one of grasping by faith the figured Jesus Christ in his saving solidarity with captives under the thrall of the unholy spirit, who cannot by their own reason or strength believe that they are sought, found, claimed, won, and restored to God's reign. They cannot believe because the unholy spirit works in all directions to render this faith in Jesus, the friend of sinners, incredible. In this approach to hermeneutics, an overarching war for human allegiance is under way between powers of life and of death. Knowledge of the Word in the words is not leisured *theoria*. Knowledge emerges in Spirit-led experience in the form of well-tested rules for engaging in battle, enduring to the end (Mark 13:13).

Theological Pragmatics

The preceding argument requires that historical-critical research take place as an operation *within* the critical dogmatic task of theology, which is to know Christ *aright*, as the Holy Spirit *intends*. To make the point another way: the very existence of the Scripture as a canonical collection organized into the Genesis to Revelation narrative represents the first dogmatic decision of early Christianity. It is a decision *for* the unity of God in creation, redemption, and fulfillment, indeed, at the point where dualism threatens most, in the act of judgment and mercy once and for all in the cross of Christ. It is a decision therefore *against* dualism in theology and Docetism in Christology. One cannot read the Bible as the Spirit intends except in dependence on this dogmatic decision. Of course, we are arguing that dogmatic decisions *are* the work of the Spirit. That can be articulated by a nonmechanistic doctrine of the inspiration of the Scriptures, which in turn is fully compatible with, indeed demands, the most rigorous historical criticism, provided only that the criticism—as Barth famously contended—is as critical as the new language of the Spirit in differentiation from the old.

The ontology involved when historical criticism is undertaken as an operation within critical dogmatics amounts to little more than the noncontroversial claim that there are objects to which words refer (without the further claim that words, or sentences, in every aspect *represent* like miniatures or replicas the objects they name, and further, that our justification for using names or sentences consists in such mirroring). Moreover, and somewhat more controversially, these objects as named or as formulated in truth-claims are human linguistic artifacts, which belong to various worlds/regions/systems/language games/forms of life/contexts.[99] This contextual qualification means that the aspects of objects that appear to us are those noticed by interested human beings, who as such attend to them. Moreover, what they take note of is shaped by the linguistic traditions, conventions, and imaginations of human communities of interpretation, of which there are and can be many in the shared world. Contemporary forms of pluralist perspectivalism rightly grasp this important qualification of objective knowledge against naïve realism, which imagines that by simply staring at something undistracted, it apprehends the *Ding-an-sich*. If the foregoing is right, then historical criticism is and can be little more than an operation for getting the names right—an important but limited task that can hardly be the alternative to classical theology some have imagined.

Far more important in this connection is the fact that Luther does not think of knowledge of God in theology as "theory," as intellectual "gaze" upon a perfect, simply self-identical substance, the being that abides through the ever-becoming of the cosmos. Luther rejects *theoria* as the ideal of theological knowledge (though he does not at all reject the ideal of theological knowledge).[100] To name God is to call on God truly, not to comprehend God in a concept of timeless impassivity; it is to pray to One who hears and answers, not to gaze in the eye of the mind at Perfect Being, whose power is the worship it inspires. There is, we have to note, a fundamental ambiguity involved in the language of being that requires attention here. In the metaphysical tradition, "being" bears the stamp of Plato's and also

---

[99]On Luther's *regionalism*, see Helmer, *Trinity*, 55, and White, *Luther as Nominalist*, 127, 138–41.

[100]As Luther had already put it in his early *Commentary on Romans*: "For the philosophers so direct their gaze at the present state of things that they speculate only about what things are and what quality they have, but the apostle calls our attention away from a consideration of the present and from the essence and accidents of things and directs us to future state." Seeing what is forces the spectator/speculator to derive "a happy science out of a sad creation," when the creatures themselves groan over their "essences." LW 25:360–62.

Aristotle's valuation of that which endures over that which changes. Being is that which abides amid all the becoming, which the mind can contemplate in *theoria*. If we set aside this metaphysical construal, as do critical realists like Bielfeldt, and concern ourselves with logical and semantical issues, "being" becomes a designator of that which is the case, independently of my knowledge of it, which therefore determines finally the truthfulness of my claims about it. Given these differing notions of ontology, one must be alert to the sense in which the rhetoric of being is employed. Luther's criticism of *theoria* is a form of his criticism of onto-theological metaphysics: if we judge only according to appearances (even the intellectualized abstractions from experience that appear as pure forms before the eye of the mind), we go badly wrong, not least in thinking that "being" is divine, not that aspect of the creation that abides in becoming. But such "being" is in principle what Hegel exposed as a "false infinite." Hegel learned this from Luther. The immanent being of the cosmos— its substances or natural laws or mathematical axioms—does not rise to the true God, almighty Creator of all that is not God, being as well as becoming. That precisely is Luther's problem with Aristotle's account of deity. It falsely divinizes the perfect form of being within the eternal cosmos of becoming, without grasping that "being" too is a contingent creature of God.

Nevertheless, there is for Luther *notitia*, based upon direct access of faith to the object of knowledge, which is named but not (ever, in all eternity) comprehended. This access is based on *hearing* promises— when and if the Speaker wills—of the reign of God that *will* come, not on seeing what *is*, which is actually the sad and oppressed creation groaning in travail.[101] In this way, Luther thinks that dogmatic beliefs can be true or false: not because we can see how they correspond with their objects, but because we can understand what God the Holy Spirit intends by bestowing to faith the persona of Christ attested in Scripture, when Scripture itself is read

---

[101]As White puts the distinction: "Luther is talking about things which are perfectly real—and indeed, present—but not *apparent*: so, even though Luther will reject the metaphor of vision, he will gladly embrace that of hearing. . . . This access may not be like vision, but nevertheless, the fundamental problem is whether one gets through to the things themselves, or only deals with their outer appearance. . . . The way in which we reason about theological matters will be affected by our access to God, i.e., the presence or absence of the Spirit, or Christ, in us" (*Luther as Nominalist*, 331).

critically, that is, as "inspired," in accord with the intention of the Spirit.[102]

A circle of course occurs here. If we are right, it is the circle of the triune life, in which the Spirit is given through the Word and the Word is borne witness by the Spirit. In this dialectic, theology participates. Bielfeldt, on the other hand, is certainly right to insist against tendentious modernizers that Luther is realist in his semantics. He is right to stress the abiding theological significance of this realist stance: God does not exist on account of our language. I agree with this. Yet I have added that our language, if truly theological, subsists in, speaks with, and thinks after the Trinity. Bielfeldt would, I believe, bow enough in the direction of critiques of empiricism (I would deploy the *New Essays* of the nonepistemological[103] Gottfried Leibniz, not Immanuel Kant's *Critiques*) to qualify his own position as one of *critical*, not *naïve*, realism, since he expressly eschews foundationalism, presumably also John Locke's. How in any case does one reconcile Luther's realism with his penetrating insights into context and usage as well as his critique of *theoria*? I suggest a notion of theological pragmatism.

The rational task of theology for Luther is not an individualistic, theoretic *credo ut intelligam* but a churchly and pragmatic *credamus ut confiteamur* in spiritual battle with that world that refuses the promise of God's reign.[104] In the latter case, theology attains a genuine *cognitio Dei*—"*in order that we might somehow understand*, God has given us formulations of speech"—but in, and only as, the incarnate Son (not *through* him as an earthly *symbol* on the way to *gazing* upon a heavenly substance) sent by his Father to the cross and raised by the Spirit from death as harbinger of the redeemed creation. What we are to *understand* in Christ is the promise of reconciliation

---

[102]This is nicely captured by Eeva Martikainen, "Der Doctrina-Begriff in Luthers Theologie," in *Thesaurus Lutheri* (Helsinki, 1987), 214. See Hütter's discussion of Martikainen's contribution in a series of endnotes, in *Suffering Divine Things*, 250–51, which is notable for its succinct and decisive analysis of how doctrine is disabled when drawn through the sieve of Kantianism.

[103]"Of the great early modern philosophers, however, Leibniz was probably the least preoccupied with epistemology. . . . The Leibnizian approach to metaphysics might seem embarrassingly uncritical, and perhaps it would be, if strong constraints on metaphysics could be derived from an epistemology that deserved our full confidence." Robert Merrihew Adams, *Leibniz: Determinist, Theist, Idealist* (New York: Oxford University Press, 1994), 3.

[104]Kenneth Hagen, "Luther on Atonement—Reconfigured," *Concordia Theological Quarterly* 61, no. 4 (October 1997): 254.

of humanity to God and redemption of creation from corruption by God, that is, God in the processions/missions of the Word and Spirit. There is here no tacit assumption that faith represents some lower order of representational knowledge, dumbly accepted on account of ecclesiastical authority but now seeking in theological speculation the certainty of intellectual comprehension—as tendencies in Anselmian theology taken up in Hegelian philosophy might suggest. It would be too much an anachronism, of course, to claim that Luther's critique of *theoria* makes his own claim to *knowledge* of God in theology *pragmatist,* but the affinity is real, just as Lutheran orthodoxy afterward consistently described theology as a *practical,* not *theoretical,* discipline.[105]

Pragmatism avoids the untenable claim to possess adequate representation of objects of knowledge even in our justified beliefs, since they are still in the process of formation and will be until the hypothetical final consensus when all true beliefs are reconciled to one another. That eschaton of inquiry will be the truth that corresponds to reality. In the interim, the truthfulness of our beliefs is critically tested by the double criterion of utility in experience and coherence with other beliefs we hold true. The lineage of this pragmatist line of thought can be traced via German idealism to Reformation theology and its critique of onto-theological gazing at passive, self-absorbed being in preference to the realm of becoming. Theologically adapted, a pragmatist approach today would have the advantages of respecting the ineffability or hiddenness of God in revelation on which Luther so stringently insists, of pointing to the eschatological verification of beliefs that only God can provide by the coming of the reign, and in the interim of putting us to work on the coherence of these beliefs, both internally in the body of church doctrine and externally with respect to all the creation, beloved in Christ and destined for fulfillment in the Spirit.

Needless to reiterate, this is a comprehensive project, quite incompatible with the current regime of theological studies. Under the current regime of theological education stemming from Schleiermacher's

---

[105]*The Doctrinal Theology of the Evangelical Lutheran Church*, ed. Heinrich Schmid, 3rd ed., rev. H. E. Jacobs and C. E. Hay (Philadelphia: Lutheran Publication Society, 1899), 17. Pragmatism regards beliefs as rules for action that are provisionally validated by their utility and coherence with other beliefs we regard as true. Lindbeck's rule-theory of doctrine is a version of pragmatism, drawing deeply however on Luther's *Verbum externum* and the ancient church's notion of doctrine as *regula fidei.* Lindbeck's account accords with the 1540 disputation. Argument 17 of the *Disputatio* contains the statement "In theology we have our own rules."

Brief Outline, it is impossible.[106] To be clear, unlike anything imagined in philosophical pragmatism, theological pragmatics derives from the supervening agency of the God manifest in the divine processions/ missions of Christ and the Spirit, in whose projects theology participates as *confessio* and *Nachdenken*.

Theses 61 and 62 of the 1540 disputation read: "Such is the simplicity and the goodness of the Holy Spirit, that his people, when they speak falsely according to grammar, speak the truth according to the sense. Such is the craftiness and the wickedness of Satan, that his people, while they speak truly according to grammar, that is, as to the words, speak lies according to theology, that is, according to the sense." In the context of divine mission and apocalyptic struggle, it is not timeless correspondence with fixed objects in an eternal cosmos that renders speech-acts true or false to the Spirit's intention, who is Christ crucified, the New Adam, the truth in person, the man who corresponds to God because he is the man who is God the Son's own. In the context of faith as churchly practice, the truth of *doctrinal-theological statements* does not reside in their literal correspondence to fixed realities. The living, moving Jesus Christ is their truth, as will be revealed and fully understood when he comes again in power and great glory. In the interim, the truth of doctrinal-theological statements resides in their regulative service as attesting this saving person of Christ, the person who unites God and humanity in a new covenant of mercy, against the deceptions of Satan, who would tear asunder this saving unity of God and humanity by attacking Christ's person through deviant teaching. This pragmatism is, of course, not for Luther license to speak ineptly or inaccurately. In battle, life itself depends on hitting the target. Thesis 16 of the 1540 disputation reads: "Many things are allowed even to the fathers who

---

[106]The distinction between historical theology, to which dogmatics as a discipline is now subordinated, and practical theology is decisive in Schleiermacher's reorganization of the study of theology. This very distinction unfolds from this "point of departure of philosophical theology . . . [which] can only be taken 'above' Christianity, in the logical sense of the term, i.e., in the general concept of a religious community or fellowship." Friedrich Schleiermacher, *Brief Outline on the Study of Theology: Philosophical, Historical, Practical*, trans. T. N. Tice (Atlanta: John Knox, 1977), 29. Under Luther's "epistemology of access," one could never get to dogmatics as a critical discipline from this point of departure. This no doubt was Schleiermacher's purpose. Lindbeck's theory of the nature of doctrine could be read in conformity with Schleiermacher; but see Hütter's critique, *Suffering Divine Things*, 59ff.

are agreed to be orthodox, which we should not imitate." The same might be said of much modern Luther interpretation.

3. Idealist and Existentialist Misinterpretation of Luther's New Language

Disdain for Logic

We have now to set out in contrast to the understanding of critical dogmatics that we have gained from Luther's new language of the Spirit an influential modern misappropriation of Luther's theology. The argument about this is now commonplace, stemming from the Finnish school of Luther interpretation.[107] We wish to trace the fate of *Luthers Lehre* in the modern history, which proceeded from Kant's consignment of theological statements to noumenal status, through the existentialist reduction of theology to symbolic expressions of states of consciousness, to contemporary constructivism. As Bielfeldt pointed out, White complains of "descriptive foundationalism: one tries to find some concept which is fundamental for the description of Luther, or scholasticism, or the difference between the two,"[108] or even worse, according to White, one tries "to associate the mere *use* of logical methods with some root idea or other,"[109] that is, the Kantian picture of logic as part of a structure imposed on a world that is, in itself, structureless.[110] White provides a scathing series of samples of what he here has in mind.

He cites Ebeling's famous claim that "the scholastics are trying to set up a theologically neutral anthropology," while Luther "only talks of people in their situation vis-à-vis God."[111] As a result of this, Ebeling's Luther "had discarded the armour of scholastic logic and moved in a freer style of thought. And certainly Luther, as far as his relationship to logic is concerned, can certainly not be placed on the side of scholasticism and distinguished from the renaissance and humanism. The break with the rule of scholastic logic in theol-

---

[107]Risto Saarinen, *Gottes Wirken auf Uns: Die Transzendentale Deutung des Gegenwart-Christi-Motivs in der Luther Forschung* (Stuttgart: Franz Steiner, 1989). Saarinen's recounting of Prenter's critique of the dialectic of divine and human natures in Barth's theology as "idealistically colored," and in any case conceived not in the categories of being but as event and act, is particularly relevant to the present proposal to articulate a trinitarian dialectic of Word and Spirit. Cf. 180ff.

[108]White, *Luther as Nominalist*, 37, 69, 75.

[109]Ibid., 39, 18.

[110]Ibid., 46.

[111]Ibid., 75.

ogy could not have occurred more decisively and sharply as it did with him."[112] In so arguing, Ebeling "does not have any clear idea of the difference between logic and other forms of inquiry." Ebeling "imposes his own philosophical background on the thought of Luther's time. . . . It is certainly true, as Ebeling remarks, that Luther saw himself as being radically different from the scholastics. The only question is, in which respect?"[113] But Ebeling takes scholasticism as a monolith, overlooking the differences between the *via antiqua* and *via moderna*, and consequently misidentifies the supposed Novum in Luther's thought.[114]

A similar critique is made of Bernhard Lohse, who ignores *ratio* as analytic practice and regards it idealistically as constructivism, the imposition of order on the world, the synthesizing of the manifold with some categorical scheme. Yet, White asks, "suppose that this is all true, and that, when non-Christians are involved in acts of knowledge, they are motivated by nothing else than egotism and self-assertion, and that, conversely, when Christians go about it, they are purely motivated by love of Christ, then what *difference* does it make to the sort of logic they do?" Answer: "Logical rules of inference seem to be peculiarly unresponsive to such influences as the human will."[115] Jorg Baur likewise thinks that "some metaphysical principle . . . is supposed to lie behind all logic."[116] Thus, there is "language of being and identity, or a logic of identity, which is also the Aristotelian logic" in contrast to "language of becoming and communication and with it a logic of becoming."[117]

But this simply is not how Luther takes up and logically uses terms such as *nature, person, essence,* and *identity,* for example, in Luther's proverbial statement "Whatever is an ass cannot be an ox." The concern in speaking of natures here is neither epistemological nor metaphysical in the sense of a priori essentialism, but logical and ontological in the semantic sense: "We have some sort of idea of what it is possible for [an ass or ox] to be, and what it is not possible for it to be. This sort of information—this set of descriptions—is what has been called the nature, or essence, of a thing."[118] As Bielfeldt

---

[112]Cited from *Lutherstudien*, 1982, vol. 2, 2, p. 4.
[113]White, 71–72.
[114]For example, ibid., 73–74.
[115]Ibid., 51–52.
[116]Ibid., 55.
[117]Ibid., 56–57.
[118]Ibid., 57–58.

documented in the preceding chapter, Luther holds to a "valid use of logical deduction in theology. . . . [His] approach to reason was quite differentiated" since "logic is, basically, concerned with inferences between propositions."[119] In short, modern Protestant polemics against arid Scholastic logic-chopping in order to extract the alleged Novum of Luther in existentialist bathos immune from logical scruples "is like seeing a group of blind men busily writing polemics against Rembrandt."[120]

Nonfoundationalism in Theology

The decisive issue is the autonomy of theology—for Luther, as also for any contemporary alternative in theology to the still-dominant Kantian proscription of the very possibility of true human language about God. One might say *philosophically* that the region of theology is the types of infinity, the posits of eternity, the possibilities of ultimacy. "Life is enabled not by a posit that life means, but by a posit of what it means. The plot and energy of life are determined by which eternity we rely upon, and the truth of any mode of life is determined by the reality of the eternity it posits. If we speak of 'God,' a life's substance is given by which God we worship, and a life's truth is given by whether this is the God that really is."[121] In this region of possible deities, "the importance of academic formulation as a theological necessity of disputing [is] not the event of revelation buts its [putative] truth."[122]

Apart from some event of revelation, in other words, we *know* nothing about the theological region and so we have nothing about which even to *argue*. We can only *speculate*. Philosophically, we are in a place like Plato's *Timaeus*, where engaging myths can be told and examined only to conclude that God remains beyond declaration. So if we allow that there is a region of possible eternities, the question arises how we would dare to speak of one, true eternal life for us to know and trust, even modestly and descriptively as Luther intends. Luther's answer to this question is draconian. There is no *epistemological* justification for the sovereign gift of faith with the epistemic access it provides. "I believe that by my own understanding or strength I cannot believe in Jesus Christ my Lord or come to

---

[119]Ibid., 83.
[120]Ibid., 347. See also Helmer, *Trinity*, 52.
[121]Robert W. Jenson, *The Triune Identity* (Philadelphia: Fortress Press, 1982), 2.
[122]Helmer, *Trinity*, 45.

him," the Small Catechism has pupils repeat, "but instead the Holy Spirit has called me through the gospel, enlightened me with his gifts, made me holy and kept me in the true faith, just as he calls, gathers, enlightens, and makes holy the whole Christian church on earth and keeps it with Jesus Christ in the one common, true faith."[123] This rigorous refusal of epistemology (i.e., the justification of a claim to knowledge by grounding it on universal foundations accessible to all rational beings as such) is meant not to exempt theology from critical scrutiny but to protect the ineffability of God from profanation. Properly understood, it has the strength of sustaining particularity in a pluralist world by leaving the truth of this revelatory claim and stance of faith to divine eschatological verification.

Only God knows God as God; this is the truth of the inner region, the region of theology. If human beings are to think after God and "somehow understand" the One in Whom they believe, God must share with believers His own self-knowledge. Access is at God's initiative and so available "when and where it pleases God," as article 5 of the Augsburg Confession puts it. To understand Jesus as the Christ "for me" is a Damascus Road/By the Sea of Tiberius encounter with Jesus in his sovereign self-presentation. As Marshall has argued, Christ, the living person, not even logically necessary sentences of true belief about him, is the Truth, the one as person who corresponds to God (as will the reconciled creation, at last, conform to Christ). In distinction, doctrinal statements like "Jesus is risen" are true if and only if Jesus is risen. To know Jesus as a person at all is impossible without such true beliefs.[124] Knowing Jesus at all requires having true beliefs sufficient to identify him—as alive and no longer dead, as eternal Word of his Father, not a passing thought.[125] Such beliefs are necessary but not sufficient, since as the risen and living one, this person is and ever remains the free *agent* of our knowing him and thus also of the truth of the belief, Jesus is risen, which cannot then be treated as a worldly fact, a given, a self-interpreting objectivity, on "automatic" as it were. These, rather, become our conviction in faith only by virtue of Jesus' own self-presentation.[126]

The circle here is not vicious. This is in fact to treat the matter of

[123]Cited from Kolb and Wengert, *Book of Concord*, 355–56.
[124]Marshall, *Trinity and Truth*, 244.
[125]Ibid., 246.
[126]Ibid., 247; cf. also 336.

Christian belief as really depending, causally, on the risen Lord who is ours by *faith*, faith *alone*, *divine* faith, *the Spirit's* efficacious calling by the gospel. As befits the object, the knowledge of God is appropriate only to God. The resurrection, properly speaking, is an event between the Father and the Son, which permits as such no human witnesses, who hear and see only its consequences in the vacated tomb and in Jesus' greeting of victory peace. Even these are granted not to all, but only to chosen witnesses by the Spirit's effective calling. Our access to this knowledge of God, mediated by the apostolic witness through the preaching of the gospel, can likewise only be by sovereign grace, apart from any merit, at the Spirit's beck and call. The provision of this access in the auditor's resurrection to faith and new birth as a child of God is no grounds for boasting but requires in him the profoundest humiliation of repentance and faith. It provides no basis for systematic apologetics, but rather demands a rigorous, communal self-discipline in the critical dogmatics of testing the spirits to see whether they correspond to the one who corresponds to God. The disputation procedure in theology is restricted to this latter matter, the putative (intersystemic) truth of the event of revelation, which as event is and must be presupposed within the theological circle. Citing Matthew 17:5 in the Major disputation, Luther argued that God wishes to limit disputing in *theology* when He says to Peter, James, and John concerning His Son, *Hunc audite*.[127] At this command, there is nothing but a fork in the road: faith or scandal, obedience or disbelief. The *disputatio* genre in this way acknowledges its access to the region in Christ, the figure of the gospel narrative, which access it now explicates in the act of faith. This limitation is the basis of the disciplinary autonomy of theology.

Such clarifications also bear intellectually and pastorally important fruit for those today who struggle with the truthfulness of dogmatic beliefs, particularly when these are ripped from context in the new language and held up to scrutiny in philosophical frames of reference. Clearly such doctrinal beliefs are taken as true in theology and so as necessary for identifying Jesus as the Christ, that is, as the one object in the world who is also one of the Trinity and thus always subject, even in the objectivity of the Word incarnate. The truth of these doctrinal statements may be said then to be semantic in the sense that such statements identify an aspect of that objectivity

---

[127]Helmer, *Trinity*, 46.

in the world without these statements therewith claiming replication or comprehensive correspondence as epistemological justification. "Born of the virgin Mary" is doctrinally true for pointing to the Jew born from Mary "in a new and different way" as God's act of new creation in our midst, without claiming wholly to represent that ineffable event. "The vacated tomb" is doctrinally true for pointing to the crucified, dead, and buried Jesus "in a new and different way" as the one and only not to suffer corruption but rather divine recognition, vindication, exaltation—again without claiming exhaustively to represent what is and only can be an event between the Son and the Father, that is, within God (of course, biblically, "within God" does not exclude but includes events in space-time). The statement "The bread of the Eucharist is the body of Christ" is true in locating the time and place on the earth of the promised self-giving of the risen Lord—yet again without claiming to possess the glorified Lord in some kind of manipulative grasp or gaze.

"Luther definitely seems to prefer semantic analysis," White writes.[128] He "was extremely reticent about saying 'what goes on,'"[129] and he cites Luther: "As for what goes on, here one simply has to remain silent and believe God, who put himself on show in his Word to be known by us." Further "inquiry in 'what goes on' is prohibited," if by that one would go after "some sort of ontological theory, or theory of the composition of the persons, which would explain the identities and non-identities."[130] Luther has no interest in *theoria* penetrating the ineffable mystery of God, and such inquiry is no part of the theological task of critical dogmatics. This much the existentialists have right in rebellion against Hegel. Granted. But Hegel was even more right, for his part, to maintain that those who abandon the claim to knowledge of God no longer have the right to call themselves theologians—a critique that also strikes today's constructivists, who, for all luxuriant God-talk, never claim to know God.[131] Because existentialists construe Luther's

[128]White, *Luther as Nominalist*, 223.
[129]Ibid., 225–26.
[130]Ibid., 228–29.
[131]See G. W. F. Hegel, *Lectures on the Philosophy of Religion*, One-Volume Edition, The Lectures of 1827, ed. P. C. Hodgson (Berkeley: University of California Press, 1988), 400–402. My differences with Hegel should be clear. I do not subscribe to the philosophical conceit of comprehending in theory what religion naïvely represents (even though I would grant that despite Luther's rejection of *theoria*, an evangelical interpretation of *theoria* and the *ut intelligam* is possible). Having

proscription of *theoria* in Kantian fashion as a stricture on the reach of reason, they miss what matters most to Luther: the *knowledge* of God given by God in God's *self-objectification* in the world as the crucified Son, which for Luther is the *axial proposition* of Christian theology and the test of the spirits. *Ergo in Christo crucifixo est vera theologia et cognitia Dei.*[132] If that is so, a final question arises in this miniature prologomena: What would be false theology and knowledge of God?

4. Demonology
Dangerous Ground

"Beloved, do not believe every spirit, but test the spirits to see whether they are from God; for many false prophets have gone out into the world. By this you know the Spirit of God: every spirit that confesses that Jesus Christ has come in the flesh is from God, and every spirit that does not confess Jesus is not from God. And this is the spirit of the antichrist, of which you have heard that it is coming; and now it is already in the world" (1 John 4:1-3). In distinction from Hegel's claim finally to comprehend all, theology as critical dogmatics in the tradition of Luther has to reckon most seriously with the *surd* of positive evil: the existence of that which knowingly, willfully, pleasurably contradicts God, as the citation from 1 John contends. This too involves the claim to know God. One can hardly reckon with that which contradicts God apart from knowledge of God's word. But once again, it is not theoretical knowledge, gazing at a timeless form above the fray. It is knowledge of the crucified and risen Lord, sent by His Father's love for those in thrall of alien powers, sending with His Father His own Spirit to these set free, reigning until He subdues the contra-divine powers. This is the practical knowledge of those engaged in battle; here doctrinal statements are rules for the action that is speaking the gospel with authority to expose and put the demons to flight.

Luther was accordingly wont to advise students to "discern the

---

said that, I do subscribe to Hegel's claim to orthodoxy in his philosophy as opposed to arbitrary and enthusiastic procedures arising under the name of theology: "The fundamental doctrines of Christianity have for the most part disappeared from dogmatics." Undoubtedly, he is thinking of the consignment by his rival at Berlin, Friedrich Schleiermacher, of the Trinity to the appendix of his *Glaubenslehre*. "Philosophy is preeminently, though not exclusively, what is at present essentially orthodox; the propositions that have always been valid, the basic truths of Christianity, are maintained and preserved by it." Hegel, *Lectures*, 403–4.
    [132]WA 1:362.

antithesis" in any attempt to understand a doctrinal statement. That means to grasp what is being denied in any affirmation. If we follow Luther's counsel, we fully understand Luther's *new* language of the Spirit not merely when we oppose it to natural or philosophical theology or distinguish it from other forms of human reason. We grasp it concretely in antithesis to the language of the unholy spirit(s); (see Mark 1:27).[133] In thinking this out, we will in point of gospel narrative be taking our cue from the inauguratory account of the descent of the Spirit on Jesus at his baptism, who, as Mark tells it, immediately "drove" Jesus into contest with Satan (Mark 1:10, 12). With this orientation, we will also be sustaining exegetically the critical break with nineteenth-century progressivism, for example, when Johannes Weiss realized to the dismay of his Kantian convictions that Jesus' preaching of the reign of God was an "antithetic, not a thetic notion."[134] As respected a Luther scholar as Heiko Oberman has argued that, in general, this is the correct way to read Luther's theological legacy today,[135] and Obermann was accordingly careful to distinguish Luther's contribution, as he wanted to appropriate it, from "the origins of anti-Semitism."[136] Yet there is little doubt that we are here treading on dangerous ground.

Mark U. Edwards Jr. has located Luther's notorious verbal violence against Peasant, Pope, Turk, and Jew in apocalyptic convictions, which took on a life of their own after his excommunication by Leo X and the disaster of the Peasants' War—signs to Luther of

---

[133]Paul R. Hinlicky, "The Spirit of Christ amid the Spirits of the Post-modern World: The Crumley Lecture," *Lutheran Quarterly* 14, no. 4 (Winter 2000): 433–58, although today I would allow that my effort here relied too much on Kojeve.

[134]*The Kingdom of God*, ed. B. Chilton (Philadelphia: Fortress Press, 1984), 7–8.

[135]Heiko Oberman, *Luther: Man between God and the Devil*, trans. E. Walliser-Schwarzbart (New Haven: Yale University Press, 1989): "Holding fast to the Gospel was indeed much, but it did not constitute a 'success'. For Luther reformation was the beginning not of modern times but of the Last Days. . . . The only progress he expected from the reformation was the Devil's rage, provoked by the rediscovery of the Gospel. . . . God himself would bring about reformation through consummation; it would be preceded by the Devil's counterreformation" (266–67).

[136]Heiko Oberman, *The Roots of Anti-Semitism in the Age of Renaissance and Reformation*, trans. J. I. Porter (Philadelphia: Fortress Press, 1984), which demonstrates in the manner of *Sachkritik* the material, theological contradiction between Luther's venomous statements of 1543 and his own gospel: "Our heinous crime and weighty sin nailed Jesus to the cross, God's true Son. Therefore, we should not in bitterness scold you, poor Judas, or the Jewish host. The guilt is our own" (124). See also Paul R. Hinlicky, "A Lutheran Contribution to the Theology of Judaism," *Journal of Ecumenical Studies* 31, nos. 1–2 (Winter-Spring 1994): 123–52.

the imminent end of days. "Luther understood his disagreement with
[opponents] in the context of this struggle between God and Satan.
Behind them all loomed the figure of the devil, the father of lies.
Often Luther directed his attacks not at his human opponents but at
the devil whom he saw as their master, and, of course, no language
was too harsh when attacking the devil."[137] Certainly, Luther spewed
those noxious tirades from within a *religious* frame of reference; he
does not single out Jews, moreover, as opposed to other theological
enemies for exclusively targeted invective. He was an equal opportunity demonizer. But in practice, the distinction between Satan and
his various human minions collapses, and in the process of spiritual-
ized warfare, as Edwards notes, all ethical restraint collapses. Verbal
violence slides imperceptibly into sanction of physical violence, as in
the disgraceful *On the Jews and Their Lies*.

Public theology in the tradition of Luther today cannot but confront the difficulty here head-on. The issue is unavoidable. Holocaust
historian Martin Gilbert, for example, began his harrowing account
drawn from the oral testimonies and written memoirs of survivors
citing the "first steps to iniquity" as Martin Luther's " 'honest advice'
as to how Jews should be treated. 'First,' he wrote, 'their synagogues
should be set on fire.' . . . Jewish homes, he said, should likewise
be 'broken down or destroyed.' Jews should then be 'put under one
roof, or in a stable, like Gypsies, in order that they may realize that
they are not masters in our land.' "[138]

This xenophobic venom actualized the worst possibilities in traditional Christianity: the recourse to demonization in John 8:42-47.
It was a source of embarrassment to Luther's friends already in his
lifetime and was quickly buried on library shelves, forgotten from
living memory, as Nazi sympathizers complained.[139] In any case,

---

[137]"Luther's Polemical Controversies," in *The Cambridge Companion to Martin
Luther*, ed. D. K. McKim (Cambridge: Cambridge University Press, 2003), 194–95.
See also "Supermus: Luther's Own Fanatics," in *Seven-Headed Luther: Essays
in Commemoration of a Quincentenary 1483–1983*, ed. P. N. Brooks (Oxford:
Clarendon, 1983), 123–46; *Luther's Last Battles: Politics and Polemics 1531–46*
(Ithaca: Cornell University Press, 1983).

[138]Martin Gilbert, *The Holocaust: A History of the Jews in Europe during
the Second World War* (New York: Holt, Rinehart, and Winston, 1986), 19. The
excerpts are drawn from Luther's late tract "On the Jews and Their Lies" (1543).

[139]This now-notorious 1543 tract has a peculiar reception history. Johannes
Wallman has shown that "practically all the writers of Hitler's time who, by making
references to Luther's opinions about the Jews attempted to legitimate the national
socialist enmity against them, voiced the complaint that Luther's struggle against the

even in reliance on John 8, Luther's frame of reference remains religious, not racial. It is the devil, not genetics, that lies at the basis of his vicious stereotyping and unrestrained rage. Nevertheless, we cannot fail to see how religious demonization formed the slippery slope to racialism, as is evident in the use of Luther's tract against the Jews made by German Christians in 1941: "Dr. Martin Luther, after harsh experiences, demands the most severe measures against the Jews and their expulsion from German lands. Since the crucifixion of Christ and up to the present day the Jews have fought against Christianity or have misused and falsified it for the attainment of their selfish ends. Baptism in no way changes the racial traits of a Jew, his nationality or his biological characteristics."[140] In the long march of history to the Holocaust, theological demonization stemming from John 8 provided the bridge to racial theory's reification in the picture of the incorrigibly malicious and hardened Jew. In light of this *Wirkungsgeschichte*, one may well be inclined to ditch devil-talk altogether—indeed, to hesitate *only* with the thought that forfeiture of talk about the devil might be yet one more victory for the devil.

God's Devil

If the "polemical" task of theology as a "conflict discipline" is to be preserved at all today, it must be methodically subordinated to the irenic ideal of achieving disagreement, exemplified by the ecumenical dialogues (which have been the one congenial habitat nowadays for traditional dogmatics—unless and until the current regime is overthrown). As Marshall has argued in this precise regard: "The epistemic priority of the church's central beliefs does not depend on the apparently hopeless suggestion that the gospel is opposed to most or all of the beliefs which the rest of humanity holds true, but only on the contrast between the gospel and the epistemic *priorities* human beings are otherwise inclined to have."[141] This is surely right—not least as interpretation of Luther's primary meaning in

---

Jews was unknown, that it had been concealed by the Lutheran Church for centuries, and that Luther's writings on the Jews had completely fallen into obscurity." "The Reception of Luther's Writings on the Jews from the Reformation to the End of the 19th Century," *Lutheran Quarterly* 1 (Spring 1987): 73–74.

[140]Cited by Ernst Ludwig Ehrlich, "Luther and the Jews," in *Luther, Lutheranism and the Jews*, ed. J. Halperin and A. Sovik (Geneva: Lutheran World Federation, 1984), 46.

[141]Marshall, *Trinity and Truth*, 157–58.

affirming what Marshall calls the universal scope of Jesus' reign.[142] In Luther's words, which we have previously cited from the 1540 disputation: *This man created the world.* As icon of the Father, there is no higher court of appeal;[143] Jesus is the highest truth there can be.[144] If such a belief about the unrestricted scope of Jesus' agency holds in the community speaking the new language of the Spirit, then other beliefs in the world must be found compatible, or at least consistent, with it.[145] If that were not so, then there would not be anyone in the world who is the Jesus narrated in the gospel, or there would be other worlds than this world in which Jesus so exists. Unrestricted scope requires that all other beliefs be subject to correction and inclusion theologically in a "comprehensive view of the world."[146] That requires in turn that theology grows in understanding along with the gospel's progress through space and time, reforming beliefs that prove inadequate in the light of new knowledge (while not on the way ever presuming to have attained adequation).

But even with this helpful clarification of the actual sense of the christological conviction of Luther as representative of the great tradition of *fides catholica*, the present problem is not solved for us but is actually exacerbated. Granted the unrestricted scope of Jesus' agency, what can this mean for the persistence of sin in the life of the redeemed, the scandalous failures of the church, the world's continuing unbelief, or to sum all these up: the incorrigible malice of the biblical figure of the Evil One who wills not to do but rather to undo the will of God? Marshall argues for eschatological correspondence as the theological possibility of the rectification of all true beliefs in Christ, with the notable exception of evil. Marshall turns here to the time-honored privative account: evil is the nothing that does not correspond to God's will and as such cannot be rectified, only exposed as illusion and error and as such left behind, forgotten, annihilated.[147] Yet, somehow, like the privative doctrine of evil itself, this does not satisfy our sense from the gospel narrative—certainly Luther's very vivid sense—of evil as the positive reality of a transindividual, perhaps transhuman, supremely active (albeit creaturely)

[142]Ibid., 108–12.
[143]Ibid., 124.
[144]Ibid., 120.
[145]Ibid., 116 n. 15.
[146]Ibid., 117–18.
[147]Ibid., 267–74.

contradiction (not just failure to correspond). The problem with this sense, however, is that it implies that God, in willing this very world in which His Son would be crucified, permits this positive evil actually to exist. In that case, it is God's devil after all.

If that spells out a daunting theological perplexity in the narrower sense, certainly there is an equally burning rhetorical problem. Luther's preaching of the apocalyptic conflict of the ages requires a "devil," just as it did of its apostolic author. J. Louis Martyn, who before all others in our times has contended for an "apocalyptic" interpretation of Paul, notes the problem of receiving Luther's Paul interpretation today at the outset of his insightful commentary on Galatians. Even though we have to repudiate "Luther's pejorative and indefensible references to 'Jews, Turks, papists, and sectarians'" and register "notable reservations related to Luther's portrait of Judaism," nevertheless Luther's captivation "by the message of God's free and powerful grace" produced an "interpretation that has happily influenced—to one degree or another—most readings of the letter since his time."[148] Are these two aspects of Luther's legacy so separable? Is the proclamation of the free and powerful grace of God *separable* from the reduction of all who do not believe it (or believe it rightly) to the status of hardened reprobates, instruments of the devil? If not, is Paul's apocalyptic theology, however happily appropriated by Luther, guilty of "historicizing the eschatological?"[149] Is the very notion that in Christ the ages have turned, the new creation begun, inherently demeaning to outsiders? Does not this affirmation of the presence of the new creation in our midst necessarily always mean: here and not there, for Paul, in the *ecclesia* and not the world?

Yes, some such differentiation *is* required, even when the Pauline gospel is rightly understood as potentially universalistic. The difficulty is not wiped away by attributing it to Paul's or Luther's personal limitations. The "apocalyptic antinomies" (Martyn) of the greatly appreciated Galatians 3:27-28 are engendered by the in-breaking of new creation in the field of the *ecclesia*. This Pauline eschatology provided Luther, as we have seen, the basis upon which he refused and sharply criticized the traditional metaphysical dualisms as merely

[148]J. Louis Martyn, *Galatians*, Anchor Bible, vol. 33A (Garden City: Doubleday, 1997), 35. See particularly comment #51, "The Apocalyptic Antinomies and the New Creation," 570–74.
[149]Rosemary Radford Ruether, *Faith and Fratricide: The Theological Roots of Anti-Semitism* (New York: Seabury, 1979), 246ff.

immanent. Apocalypse as promise of inclusion in the coming reign by the grace of Christ provides the reason why Luther can conceive of the doctrinal beliefs brought with the gospel not theoretically but pragmatically, with all the advantages that hold over untenable claims to objective representation in the world as it stands. But can this new language of the Spirit be retrieved without hauling along with it the theological potential for invective, which Luther learns also from Paul (cf. Galatians 5:12; Philippians 3:2)?

Refiguring the Evil One

The question is huge, and in conclusion it must be fittingly narrowed to the scope of the present inquiry into the possibility for today of dogmatics as a critical discipline in the tradition of Luther. We can here recall the Lindbeckian arguments above, that the truth of theological statements for the most part resides not in their literal correspondence to fixed realities but in their regulative service as attesting the saving person of Christ, the person who unites God and humanity in a new covenant of mercy, against the deceptions of Satan, who would divide anew this saving unity of God and human-ity by attacking Christ's person through deviant teaching. With this antithesis in mind, perhaps the problem of figuring "Satan" can be reframed by resort to the source of creedal-catechetical theology in the gospel narrative (that is, in distinction from the argumenta-tive course of Paul's Letter to the Romans, as became traditional in Protestant dogmatics). That would indicate a revision in manner of presentation, if not a more fundamental hermeneutical revision at the basis of dogmatics, bringing it closer to Luther's Great Catechism than Melanchthon's *Loci Communes*.

In the gospel narrative, it is the coming of Jesus that exposes hitherto hidden demonic powers in the very act of showing mercy on weak and strong, godless and pious, insider and outsider alike, as the opening chapters of the Gospel of Mark indicate (Mark 1:23-24). The demons in turn want to expose Jesus. In the 1540 dis-putation, Luther expressly mentioned this Markan motif of Christ's silencing the demons who wanted prematurely to expose his identity as the divine Son. Theses 59–60 read: "On the other hand, anyone with a wicked meaning, even if he shall speak aptly and brandish the Scripture itself, is not to be tolerated. For Christ did not permit the demons to speak when they testified that he was the Son of God, as if they were transfiguring themselves into angels of light."[150] Can the narrative outcome of this contention between Christ and the demonic powers disclose for us the intention of the Spirit, and so provide the hermeneutical basis for dogmatic theology? In recent years, notable theologians have experimented with such a shift in the scriptural basis of dogmatics. Thiemann employed the first canonical Gospel, Matthew, in a work with which I am broadly sympathetic,[151] although for many reasons shortly to be adumbrated I find the Gospel of Mark more amenable to the task. Frei worked with this Gospel, which most historians regard as first.[152] In some distinction from Frei's interpretation, I attempt the same.

In chapter 13 of the Gospel, we learn that Mark is writing to churches that are being overrun with miracle workers, messianic pretenders, false prophets trying to read the signs of the times and claiming to speak in the name of the risen Lord. They are saying that they have the mind of Christ, that they speak in the voice of the Spirit. They preach an attractive but false message that somehow evades the necessity of confessing the name of Jesus with the

---

[150]WA 39 II, 96:27–30.

[151]Ronald Thiemann, *Revelation and Theology: The Gospel as Narrated Promise* (South Bend: University of Notre Dame Press, 1987), 112ff.

[152]Hans W. Frei, *The Identity of Jesus Christ: The Hermeneutical Bases of Dogmatic Theology* (Philadelphia: Fortress Press, 1975). But see the acute objections raised by James F. Kay, *Christus Praesens: A Reconsideration of Rudolf Bultmann's Christology* (Grand Rapids: Eerdmans, 1994): "The more one reads Frei's account of the identity of Jesus Christ as depicted by 'the Gospel narrative,' the more apparent it becomes that this term refers to no work of literature whatsoever but only to a literary-critical construct imposed onto the synoptic Gospels by Frei's imagination. What he presents us with is a postmodern 'harmony of the Gospels,' which, like its older liberal siblings, still picks and chooses from the three synoptic accounts whatever it needs to construct, in Frei's words, 'Jesus' inner life,' albeit 'within the story'" (133). I hope to have avoided these difficulties in the present account strictly drawn from the Gospel of Mark; I eschew as well the liberal doctrine of *Personlichkeit*, that is, "Jesus' inner life," by speaking instead of the *persona*, which for me, as for Luther, is the Eternal Son incarnate in public not private obedience. Kay himself concludes that for Bultmann, "the historical Jesus and empirical church can occasion but never condition, or causally effect, the saving presence of Christ" (174), which would be the same "dialectic" position held by (at least) the early Barth—a dialectic that, I am arguing, should be replaced by the trinitarian dialectic of Spirit and Word. This comports with Kay's conclusion: "Bultmann's doctrine of the Christus praesens can be legitimately criticized as relatively indifferent to the narrative identity of the Savior (Hans Frei), the social location of the scriptures and their hearers (Dorothee Soelle), and the still-outstanding promise of redemption setting Christians in solidarity with the present sufferings and longings of creation (Jürgen Moltmann)" (175).

willingness to suffer for that confession. This enthusiastic preaching raises acutely the christological question: Who really is Jesus Christ? Which spirit is his Spirit? Which story of deliverance really is *Jesus'* story? Imagine if someone were to tell the following story of deliverance in one of our tired and worn-out churches of Europe or America some Sunday: "Someone has risen from the dead. Death has been defeated. He's on the march and he's coming to establish his justice. And his name is Josef Stalin."[153] Should Christians be able to detect here a perversion of the gospel, even though the world is still filled with admiring Stalinists for whom his return in glory would be welcomed with joy? What difference does the *name* of Jesus make, that it cannot be substituted—that "no other name under heaven [is] given among mortals by which we must be saved" (Acts 4:12)—with another name? What does the name of Jesus name?

Names have references; they are words that work ostensibly, by pointing to something other than themselves (in that words as such are arbitrary sounds). Apart from this work of pointing to an object in the world, a name can become a clanging gong, a magical incantation, as if chanting "Jesus, Jesus" in itself effected His promised liberation (Matthew 7:21). But the truth of the name of Jesus is the personal identity rendered in the gospel narrative to which it points; accordingly, the truthful *use* of the name of Jesus is that which accords with Jesus' personal *intention*, as Lindbeck famously showed when he asked, *"Christus est dominus!"*—is it true when the Crusader cries it out in a war whoop, cleaving the infidel's head?

Lindbeck's attention to rules for usage seems to suggest that it is not true in this case. Any possible ontological correspondence depends on a usage that is "intersystemically coherent." This latter is a necessary though not sufficient condition for ontological truth. In other words, *Christus est dominus* acquires propositional validity as part of a performance in language, which performance itself helps to create the very correspondence—an insight Lindbeck particularly credits to Luther and Paul.[154] Lindbeck thus acknowledges that there is a place for correspondence in his model, when a lived religion "as a whole" corresponds to the being and will of God.[155] This view may be taken to imply the eschatological place of correspondence; if

---

[153]I am indebted to Robert Jenson for this illustration.
[154]George A. Lindbeck, *The Nature of Doctrine: Religion and Theology in a Postliberal Age* (Philadelphia: Westminster, 1984), 66.
[155]Ibid., 51.

so, it has the merit of protesting realized eschatology and Christian triumphalism, since it bears witness to the being of Christians qua individuals as *simul iustus et peccator*,[156] no matter the purity of their doctrine or the profundity of their feelings. It underscores that they are elected to faith for service.[157] Long discussion of Lindbeck's parable brings the clarification that it is the Crusader's speech-act that is false to the propositional content the sentence bears, since the content points to the Gospels' Man of Sorrows who was nevertheless vindicated by God.[158] The letter must be used in conformity with the Spirit. Following Lindbeck, critical dogmatics gives attention to the *usus*, to what we are doing with the language of belief. But that task redoubles the problem. How shall we know Jesus in his personal intention, according to the Spirit of his personal identity?

Mark takes the decisive early step in answering this question. He commits to writing a definite plot[159] on which early Christianity builds in order to give narrative content to the name of Jesus as a personal identity. Matthew and Luke, for all their important differences from Mark in emphasis, material, and even criticism and correction of him (Luke 1:3!), are nevertheless his theological children.[160] Essentially, they only expand on what he has done, and this especially in the central matter of Christology. The profound reason

---

[156]Ibid., 60.

[157]Ibid., 61.

[158]See Hütter, *Suffering Divine Things*, 53–57. This leads to the right kind of dialectic, the trinitarian dialectic of Word and Spirit. The Spiritless, binitarian tendency of modern Protestantism, which assimilates either Word to Spirit or Spirit to Word, "makes it impossible for any genuine salvific-historic work of the Spiritus Creator to be related to or even distinguished from the salvific-economic mission of the Son" (112). The task is to see the Spirit's work objectively in church doctrine (113).

[159]Has Mark constructed the plot out of apologetic needs (Wrede) or out of a sinister "illusion of innocence" (Burton L. Mack, *A Myth of Innocence: Mark and Christian Origins* [Philadelphia: Fortress Press, 1988])? This seems to me doubtful, though it is a much cultivated suspicion that keeps the shameless "Jesus of history" industry in business. The matter of history reduces to the unquestioned facts: Jesus told parables of the reign of God and acted on them. Jesus was crucified. To their own astonishment, his followers reported his tomb vacant and subsequently recognized him as risen. What seems suspicious to me is to deny historically that there is any connection between these remarkable and irreducible facts. Moreover, C. H. Dodd, *The Apostolic Preaching and Its Developments* (New York: Harper, 1960), still seems to me essentially correct in detecting within the speeches attributed to Peter in the book of Acts primitive recitation of the evangelical plot.

[160]I would hold that John too is rightly understood as theological commentary on the Synoptic tradition, which the Fourth Evangelist knew in a form related to the Lukan tradition, though arguing this claim would take us far afield. I would

for this is that they owe to Mark the narrative framework of their own Gospels. Recall again that plotline. The Synoptic story begins with the baptismal calling of Jesus, in which Jesus is identified by God as His Son upon whom the Spirit descends and remains. The narrative proceeds with Jesus' proclamation of the nearness of the reign of God in Galilee, which he manifests in healings, exorcisms, parables, and calling of disciples. This activity, however, comes into conflict with the law of God, and this conflict provokes the christological questions—by what authority does Jesus heal on the Sabbath, overrule Moses, forgive sins? At the turning point of the story, Jesus himself poses the question to his disciples: "Who do you say that I am?" In rapid succession then, Peter confesses Jesus to be Christ, and Jesus responds by disclosing his way to the cross to incomprehension and disbelief.

Nevertheless, the transfiguration story divinely validates both Jesus' messianic status and his unheard-of destination of suffering, rejection, death, and resurrection in Jerusalem. Now everything turns toward Jerusalem. The crowds led on by the still-uncomprehending disciples welcome Jesus as a political Messiah, but Jesus immediately heads to the temple. His business is with the temple. In a prophetic action, he cleanses it of profiteering, demanding that the temple resign from its lucrative trade in the religion business and, rather, become fruitful for the reign of God, that is, to acquire the praise and prayer of the Gentiles for the Lord. Disappointed at this turn away from expected revolutionary violence, one of Jesus' own betrays him to secret arrest. The temple authorities try him by night, find him a blasphemer for making himself out as the Son of God, and denounce him to the Roman governor as a political rebel. Roman justice bows to the demands of the mob. Jesus dies in the place of Barabbas, a condemned terrorist whom the mob preferred to him. Jesus dies alone, forsaken, taunted, disgraced. He is buried without ceremony on the eve of the Sabbath. Nevertheless, on the third day, his tomb is discovered empty by grieving women followers. What can this mean? A divine messenger declares: "Do not be alarmed; you are looking for Jesus of Nazareth, who was crucified. He has been raised; he is not here. Look, there is the place they laid him. But go, tell his disciples and Peter that he is going ahead of you to Galilee; there you will see him, just as he told you" (Mark 16:6-7).

---

deny then that John represents some kind of special, independent early Christian tradition.

In tersest outline, this is the plot of the Synoptic Gospels, really of Mark's Gospel, which Matthew and Luke have adopted from him. The plot is what is christologically decisive in rendering the persona. The motif of the secrecy of Jesus' identity indicates that, as Jack Dean Kingsbury has shown, "hearing aright the Gospel-story of the divinely wrought destiny of Jesus, which has its center in the cross, is indispensable for understanding aright his identity."[161] The narrative's purpose is to establish that the name of Jesus refers to the one who in obedience to his Father went to the cross as a testimony and as a ransom. This historical event of the Spirit-led fidelity of the man Jesus to his Father's will is the touchstone of true Christology. Hengel is therefore half right to assert that Mark the Evangelist, in a completely unproblematic way, so far as he is concerned, brings together "narrative historical and biographical account and the proclamation of salvation as address." Hengel is half right in that this joining together of Word and Spirit, this "historicizing of the eschatological," is precisely Mark's purpose: in speaking to urgent present circumstances, hearers "are invited to turn aside, to spend some time with the preacher and miracle worker Jesus in distant foreign Galilee, to stand beside him in the last battle in Jerusalem and take part in his passion, like the women, from afar. At that time, when the Son of God was delivered over to be ultimately forsaken by God, God himself founded the new covenant in his blood and sealed it though the resurrection of the dead."[162] Yet it is misleading to call this "unproblematic," so far as Mark is concerned, particularly if the Gospel ends deliberately at 16:8. That ending leaves the auditor/reader with no human, historical transition for the communication of the Easter message, but only recourse to the apocalypse that had occurred at the cross and to the summons, spiritually, to meet Jesus in Galilee again, to continue what had there begun, the Spirit-led confrontation with Satan and his hosts. Thus, we have the nonfoundationalist foundation of revelation and faith—a causal claim that eludes objective grasp and gaze yet effectively calls.

The narrative renders this reality[163] and draws the hearer into it,

---

[161]Jack Dean Kingsbury, *The Christology of Mark's Gospel* (Philadelphia: Fortress Press, 1983), 174.

[162]Martin Hengel, *Studies in the Gospel of Mark*, trans. J. Bowden (Philadelphia: Fortress Press, 1985), 39.

[163]To "construct" reality is *not* to create it out of nothing but to fashion it out of definite materials that themselves admit only of limited uses.

not to evade the present circumstance but drastically to alter perception of it and so to engage it in a different way. A human being in Mark's church finally knows what it means to call Jesus the Son of God in his or her present circumstance, when with the executioner he or she sees Jesus die on the cross his God-forsaken death in solidarity with all who are in the thrall of the unholy spirit. Only then are the sufferings of the present time comprehended and understood in their true significance. Or to make the same point from the opposite direction: human beings come to think about Jesus as God thinks about Jesus, not as humans would nor as Satan tempts. The confrontation between Jesus and Peter in Mark 8 illustrates this. After Jesus informs that he will exercise the messianic office by way of the cross, Peter "rebukes" Jesus (Mark 8:32)—a technical term in Mark for silencing a demon (e.g., Mark 3:12). And Jesus in turn "rebukes" Peter in a verse that should be translated "Get behind me, Satan, because you are not thinking the things of God but those of humans" (Mark 8:33). Disciples, then, are to think of Jesus as God thinks of Jesus. That knowledge is given in revelation, received in faith, rebuking not merely human philosophy but Satanic opposition; it is articulated in "confession" or "dogma": "Truly this was Son of God!" The executioner is thus made the confessor. There is no merely immanent, historical mediation. To believe at all is the sovereign work and gift of the Spirit. The apocalypse has us signify the God-forsaken "in a new and different way"—or not at all.

As is well known, all sorts of problems and objections arise for us here. It is typical in idealist or existentialist theology, for example, to object that any demand to affirm doctrinal teachings is an intellectual form of works-righteousness, which makes faith conditional on something other than God's "unconditional acceptance" (Paul Tillich). It is also customary to object that the gospel story as told cannot be true: mental illness is not caused by demons, the forgiveness of sins is an imaginary solution to an imaginary problem, God does not "act" within the closed system of the universe, people do not come back from death, and so forth. In order then to speak gospel as a word of emancipation for people today, it is said, we have to "demythologize" the gospel story (Rudolf Bultmann) and/or radically extend the doctrine of justification by faith to include in faith the movement of critical doubt modern Christians experience vis-à-vis the antiquated story and traditional dogmas (Tillich). Dietrich Bonhoeffer, in the opening salvo of *The Cost of*

Discipleship, however, posed a counterquestion from the side of the gospel narrative to the reduction of theology to value judgments and existential trust:

> Cheap grace means grace as a doctrine, a principle, a system. It means the forgiveness of sins proclaimed as a general truth, the love of God taught as the Christian "conception" of God. An intellectual assent to that idea is held to be itself sufficient to secure remission of sins. The Church which upholds the correct doctrine of grace has, it is supposed, ipso facto a part in that grace. In such a Church the world finds a cheap covering for its sins; no contrition is required, still less any real desire to be delivered from sin. Cheap grace therefore amounts to a denial of the living Word of God, in fact, a denial of the Incarnation of the Word of God.[164]

Important as the objections of a Tillich or Bultmann are for understanding our intellectual situation, it is important here to emphasize that these are *not* the problems that were being addressed in the formation of the gospel's narrative genre in primitive Christianity, and which, according to the present argument, ought to reframe our questions today along Bonhoeffer's lines. Neither Mark nor his opponents, of course, had objections to miracles. Indeed, Mark's opponents performed them (or claimed to perform them) "to lead astray, if possible, the elect" (Mark 13:22b). This was a plausible temptation among early Christians, including Mark's community, since Mark's Jesus also works wonders ("Who then is this, that even the wind and the sea obey him?" Mark 4:41). The problem Mark is dealing with is that opponents are, rather, *mythologizing* the gospel, so to say. By this freighted term, I do not refer either to the widespread belief in miracles or particularly to the fact that under the inspiration of the Spirit early Christian prophets of the post-Easter church spoke "in the name of the Lord" and in this way put words in Jesus' mouth.[165] Mark himself is willing to contemporize Jesus in this way and does so dramatically in making Jesus speak directly to his own community's dire situation in the Gospel's thirteenth chapter (Mark 13:37). Indeed, belief in the contemporaneity of Jesus as the

---

[164]Dietrich Bonhoeffer, *The Cost of Discipleship*, trans. R. H. Fuller (New York: Simon & Schuster, Touchstone Edition, 1995), 43.

[165]See Ernst Käsemann, "Sentences of Holy Law," in *New Testament Questions of Today*, trans. W. J. Montague (Philadelphia: Fortress Press, 1979), 66–81.

active, communicating agent of salvation was an implication of the universal scope of his agency, as we have heard, given with faith in his resurrection (Mark 14:28). He is, after all, in some most significant sense for early Christians alive and no longer dead, the living subject, not merely the object of their faith (Mark 16:7). Consequently, all true preaching was for them prophecy in "the name of the Lord" to and for the community of faith. The critical question is how to discern that the contemporary message is really *his*.

The problem is that within the circle of resurrection faith, there have arisen some *false* prophets speaking in the name of the Lord Jesus who have detached and indeed must detach their message of salvation from the public persona of the one crucified *sub Pontio Pilato*. They are *mythologizing* Jesus in the sense that they are using his name magically, that is, as an incantation no longer referred to the narrative content of Jesus' life demarcated by his earthly coming and earthly fate, which Mark narrates as the "beginning of the gospel" (Mark 1:1). We can see this concretely in the words that Mark's Jesus addresses to the urgent situation of war and persecution (Mark 13:5-8) in which Mark's suffering community looked for the coming of the Lord Jesus in the clouds of heaven to rescue them: "And if anyone says to you at that time, 'Look! Here is the Messiah!' or 'Look! There he is!'—do not believe it. False messiahs and false prophets will appear and produce signs and omens" (Mark 13:21-22a). For Mark, faith knows its object; it must be able to distinguish true and false prophets, the true Messiah from false messiahs. The simple demonstration of wonder-working power does not suffice for this task. The problem runs far deeper. The false prophets indeed have a "gospel," a contemporaneous message of liberation; in working wonders, it even resembles in part Jesus' own beginnings. But decisively the false prophets are now promising escape from the tribulations surrounding the community.

This message of liberation *as escape*, tested against Mark's story of Jesus' obedient way to the cross, is what the gospel judges theologically false and spiritually ruinous. For the same reason, the Holy Spirit is not presented as a source of new and independent revelations, heralded by "signs and omens," but as the very same Spirit who now leads disciples, as He had led Jesus, into conflict with Satan and his unclean spirits (Mark 1:8, 12, 23-27). This Spirit gives courage and words of truth to suffering disciples so that they testify truly in the time of trial (Mark 13:11). Against the deep-seated human prejudice to which the false prophets' message of escape appeals, the counterintuitive truth that God's salvation comes not in escaping from sufferings but through bearing the cross had to be articulated and expressly taught: "You will be hated by all because of my name. But the one who endures to the end will be saved" (Mark 13:13). "But be alert; I have already told you everything" (Mark 13:23). The gospel narrative thus requires express teaching about the "name" of Jesus, if the "I" of Jesus is to be understood truly and followed faithfully. The Word is mediated by the Spirit. The Spirit is given by the Word. The circle cannot be avoided, only entered—or missed altogether.

So in a world of contending stories that promise liberation, the Spirit implicates all true users of the name of Jesus in his same destiny, freeing them in the process from their own willful and persistent incomprehension (Mark 8:33). The name of Jesus is not magical incantation but a real object in the Spirit of theological knowledge, whom disciples are to know as God knows. In turn, the person of Jesus (not in the sense of inner psychological processes but in the sense of the public persona as rendered in the gospel narrative) displays the leadership of the Spirit (Mark 1:12). The action of Jesus in establishing the new covenant reveals the Spirit's aim. The call of the Spirit reveals Jesus as the agent of God's new community. This dialectic comes to living synthesis in the act of the church's confession of faith: "Crucified Jesus is the Son of God." The centurion's confession in the apocalypse of the Son's God-forsaken death is the narrative formulation of Christian doctrine. The demonic attempt prematurely to identify Jesus as the Son of God, that is, *apart from this history, apart from his people, apart from the Son's participation in their God-forsakenness*, is rebuked and silenced by confession. The narrative confession, in turn, is to be known and understood in theology, when theology itself is understood, also in its reasoning mode, as the new language of the Spirit.

Conclusion

We must draw to an end with many questions left hanging for future work. The new language of the Spirit is the Spirit's own telling of the Father's love for the Son and the Son's love for the Father in and among us in order that we may be freed from the "strong man's house" (Mark 3:27). This new language constitutes the first order of narrative theology. In the course of battle, insights extrapolated from second-order disputation can emerge under the Spirit's promised guidance and so be recognized as first-order confession, as it were, in a cumulative process. The distinction between the two modes of theological thought is real but fluid, yet the latter depends on the former, which it serves. The matrix of this critical dogmatic work is the doctrinal exegesis of Scripture, understood as the Spirit's construction of the Genesis to Revelation narrative of one God determined to create, redeem, and fulfill one world by the processions/missions of the Son and the Spirit. The habitat of this work is the community of those baptized into the triune name, designating this God of the gospel, for just this is the community where these canonical Scriptures are received and recognized as *holy*. The calling to this work from among the baptized is, as well, a free and sovereign work of the Spirit, who blows as He wills, making theology an autonomous discipline on the earth.

APPENDIX:
THREE DISPUTATIONS OF
THE LATE LUTHER WITH
EXPLANATORY NOTES

The *Promotionsdisputation* of Erasmus Alberus
(August 24, 1543)

This disputation *de unitate essentiae divinae* took place on August 24, 1543.[1] Consisting of thirty-eight theses, it treats a number of interesting topics, the first dealing with the trinitarian relations: God is one in three persons, each person is wholly God, and no one person alone is all of God. Luther declares that these claims are so rationally difficult that "reason, corrupted by original sin, must be taken captive; moreover, it must be extinguished, with its own light and wisdom, through the obedience of faith."[2]

Theses 2–17 explore the semantics of *totus* and *solus* in the trinitarian context. After arguing that Scotus's formal distinction can ultimately be understood only as real or essential, Luther concludes that neither the formal distinction nor reason and mathematics can

---

[1]The editor of the Weimar reports that Drews has (a. a. O. S. 748f.) demonstrated that the thirty-eight theses of the first series, "De unitate essentiae divinae," were collected together with a 1545 series of theses for the doctoral promotion of Petrus Hegemon entitled "De distinctione personarum fideliter explicatae" and was subsequently passed on as a single document in 1545 (WA 39 II, 252).

[2]WA 39 II, 253:9–10.

grasp how one thing can be three things. Indeed, when dialectic says that things do not play by her rules, this is the same as saying "a woman should be silent in church."[3]

At thesis 20, Luther begins treatment of the question of the semantics of eternity, specifically how the use of tenses differs in theological contexts: "Although it is certain in divinity, since he is eternity itself, there is no place in grammar or philosophy where past, present and future is the same."[4] After this, Luther moves into a discussion of the incomprehensibility of eternity, in the course of which he criticizes the use of Aristotle's actual or potential infinite in thinking the divine.

Finally, in theses 35–39, Luther speaks of the limited epistemic grasp human reason has on trinitarian truths. Knowledge of God by both reason and faith is obscure and partial. It is as a "line [that] touches the whole sphere but at a point, and thus does not comprehend the whole thing."[5] Luther concludes, "Whoever in searching wishes not to err, nor to be crushed by the glory of his majesty, let him by faith touch and lay hold of the Son of God manifest in the flesh."[6] Far from attaining the standpoint of the divine, limited human beings have access to God only by faith through the incarnate Son of God.

The Theses

1. Sacred Scripture teaches that God is most simply one and, as they say, most truly three distinct persons.[7]

2. Each of these persons is the whole God, beyond which there is no other God.[8]

---

[3]Ibid., 254:15–16.
[4]Ibid., 254:30–32.
[5]Ibid., 255:17–19.
[6]Ibid., 255:20–21.
[7]Luther believed that the doctrine of the Trinity can be derived from Scripture. He writes in the Hegemon disputation (WA 39 II, 382:6–7) that "there are many places in Scripture that clearly witness to the Trinity." Because "the article of the Trinity is grounded in Holy Scripture" (WA 39 II, 382:6–7), and because it agrees with the church's conciliar definitions, its material content is normative for belief.
[8]*Solus* and *totus* can be used either *categorematically* or *syncategorematically*. While categorematic subject and predicate terms signify completely, syncategorematic terms do not, but rather are used with categorematic terms in fixing the supposition (what the term stands for) of those terms, and thus ultimately the truth-values of the statements in which they appear. Quantificational terms include "all" or "every" (*omnis*), "except" (*praeter*), "all" or "whole" (*totus*), and "only" or "alone" (*solus*). Luther writes, "Harum personarum quaelibet totus est Deus, extra quam nullus est

3. Nevertheless, one cannot say that any one person alone is God.[9]

4. In fact, this would be the same as saying "God is nothing," since by excluding any person, all of God would be excluded, and the person would thus be excluded as well.[10]

5. Here, in fact, reason, corrupted by original sin, must be taken captive; moreover, it must be extinguished, with its own light and wisdom, through the obedience of faith.

6. It is a different thing to say, "one person is all of God" and "one person alone is the one God."[11]

7. In this way the person should be distinguished from the divine itself; it is not to be sought out by reason, nor is it comprehensible to the angels.

8. Moreover, it is most dangerous, and one must be cautious to suppose that any person is distinct, since any person himself is all of God.

9. The thinking of Scotus and the like, who imagine here a formal or other distinction, is vain and comes to nothing.[12]

---

alius Deus." Here *totus* is used syncategorematically; each and every person is wholly God, but no person alone is the Trinity. Allowing "P" to be person, "G" to be God, "F" to be Father, "S" to be Son, and "H" to be Holy Spirit, "$(x)(Px \rightarrow Gx)$" is true but "$\exists x[(Px)\ \&\ (Fx\ \&\ Sx\ \&\ Hx)]$" is not. (While each and every person is God, it is not true that there is some person is himself the triune God.)

[9]Luther says that this is false: ". . . quamlibet personam solam esse Deum." This is false because a particular person, *and no other* (e.g., "Father"), does not supposit for that which "God" supposits for. Allowing "F" to be Father, "P" to be person, and "G" to be God, "$\sim\exists x\{(Fx\ \&\ Gx)\ \&\ \forall y[(Py\ \&\ \sim Fy) \rightarrow \sim Gy]\}$."

[10]The reasoning seems to be this: If one person alone were God, then the triune God would not exist, for that God is, by definition, three persons. But if the triune God did not exist, and God is essentially triune, then no person could itself have "God" predicated of it.

[11]These two make different claims: (1) "una persona est totus Deus," and (2) "una persona sola est unus Deus." The true claim of the first is that the whole God is predicated of one person; the false claim of the second is that one person *and no other* is the one God. (Allowing "P" to be person and "G" to be God, we have for the first "$\exists x(Px\ \&\ Gx)$" and for the second "$\exists x\{(Px\ \&\ Gx)\ \&\ \sim\exists y[(Py\ \&\ \sim x = y)\ \&\ Gy]\}$." If *totus* is used syncategorematically in the first, it is true; however, if it used categorematically, it is false. (There is clearly a distinction between "$\exists x(Px\ \&\ Gx)$" and "$\exists x[Px\ \&\ (Fx\ \&\ Sx\ \&\ Hx)]$."

[12]Scotus's formal distinction is neither a real distinction nor a mere conceptual one, though it has characteristics of both. For Scotus, the essence of God is formally distinct from the persons. This means that there is an objective distinction between the essence and persons that is "more than" conceptual but "less than" real. Adams says of this formal distinction that "within what is really one and the same thing there is often a plurality of entities or property-bearers whose non-identity and distinction in no way depends upon the activity of any intellect, created or divine." See M. M. Adams, "Universals in the Early Fourteenth Century," 411–39 in *CHLMP*, 414.

10. They do not know what they say or affirm when they wish to aid reason by such a wizard of wisdom.

11. For no matter how subtly they seem to have said those things, nevertheless, reason does not lay hold of the formal distinction as anything other than real or essential.[13]

12. This is because reason does not grasp that one indistinct thing is three distinct things.[14]

13. Therefore, mathematics and every creaturely thought must be excluded when considering what ought to be believed about divinity.[15]

---

[13]Luther follows the *via moderna* generally in roundly criticizing the formal distinction of Scotus. What is the ontological status of an *objective* distinction that is not *real*? Where does this objectivity exist?

[14]Both this thesis and the one following speak of the unsuitability of mathematics for conceiving the Trinity. We see similar ideas expressed in the Major/Faber disputation (WA 39 II, 287:17f., 27f.) and the 1539 *Verbum caro factum est* disputation (WA 39 II, 22:29—23:21). In the latter, Luther writes, "Illa creata trinitas et unitas est alia trinitas, quam quae comprehendatur ab arithmetica." As Graham White points out, Luther surely said "*uncreata*" here (White, *Luther as Nominalist: A Study of the Logical Methods Used in Martin Luther's Disputations in the Light of Their Medieval Background* [Helsinki: Luther-Agricola Society, 1994], 389). Luther is saying that the "uncreated threeness and unity is *another* Trinity than which can be understood by arithmetic."

I believe that Luther's emphasis here and in the following theses on the contra-rationality of the "three being one" pushes him to assert the real existence of paradoxical states of affairs within the immanent Trinity. God literally is *one* thing and *three* things at the same time. This cannot be comprehended by philosophical categories that attempt to understand the unity of God through a common nature and the threeness of God as three individual instantiations of that common nature. Logically, the paradox can be expressed as follows, where "G" refers to God: "$\exists x[Gx \& \forall y(Gy \rightarrow x=y)] \leftrightarrow \exists x \exists y \exists z[(Gx \& Gy \& Gz) \& (x \neq y \& x \neq z \& y \neq z) \& \forall w(w=x \vee w=y \vee w=z)]$." This formula states that there is one and only one thing that is God if and only if there are three and only three things that are God. While this is a very problematic thing to assert, it seems, for Luther, that this paradox keeps one from falling into either modalism—the assertion that there is one and only one thing (that which is asserted on the left of the $\leftrightarrow$)—tritheism—the assertion that there are three and only three things (that which is asserted to the right of the $\leftrightarrow$).

[15]While mathematics could grasp that three things have a common nature, it clearly cannot grasp that one and only one God can be three persons where God is instantiated. Mathematics is oriented toward the temporal realm and so cannot grasp the eternal divine realm. Like mathematics, grammar too is oriented to the created, temporal order. In the Major and Faber disputation, Luther says that since grammar is concerned with the temporal, it cannot grasp the eternal. See WA 39 II, 293:18–26: "Doctores dicunt, Filium natum et semper nasci. Filius namque debet dici semper natus, non nasci in praesenti, nec semper nascendus in futuro. Grammaticum est de futuro et praesenti. Illae autem speculationes non habent locum in divinitate, Christus neque in praeterito neque in futuro neque in praesenti dicitur nasci. Ergo confundunt scriptores. Quare sive futurum sive praesens sive praeteritum accipias,

14. In any case, it seems no less impossible that from among these three things of one simple essence, one was made human without the other.

15. Nevertheless it is truly impossible that one indistinct thing is three most distinct things.

16. Therefore, to believe that the Son of God was made a human being is easier than to believe that he himself is consubstantial with the Father and Holy Spirit.[16]

17. Because the art of reasoning [*dialectica*] argues that these things do not square with her own rules, one should say that a woman [viz., *dialectica*] ought to be silent in church.[17]

18. It is no wonder that Arius, the Jew, Mohammed, and the whole world deny that Christ is God.

19. For just as a blind person judges regarding color, so also they judge that the creator subsisting in his own self is like the creature, who is made from nothing.

20. Some stir up a fuss over whether one ought to say: "The Father always 'generated' or 'generates' the Son; or, whether the Son 'always has been born' or 'always should be born.'"[18]

21. Some speak in a different way; they reason that it ought to be said that the Son of God is always born, because the preterite tense is called perfect, the present tense, imperfect.[19]

22. Hilary and others dare to say, "The Son is always begotten from the Father," and "the living one lives from the living," and "He is begotten from the unbegotten."

---

semper est verum, semper nascitur, natus et nascetur; heists in praeterito, so ists in futuro; heists in futuro, so ists in praeterito; heists in praeterito, so ists in praesenti, semper idem est. Hic non est tempus."

[16]Of course, for Luther, just because philosophy cannot allow for the incarnation does not mean that it did not happen. What is impossible from a philosophical standpoint is nonetheless possible for God. While the divine property of omnipotence does not allow the philosophical proposition that the infinite is finite, the infinite is nonetheless finite. Furthermore, for Luther, the jarring nature of the claim of the two natures of Christ cannot be comprehended philosophically.

[17]Philosophical dialect (which is the woman) must be silent in church; that is, it must be silent in the realm of theology.

[18]In this and all theses up to and including thesis 28, Luther discusses the semantics of eternity. Luther assumes the traditional notion of God's having timeless eternity. This means that God does not live through time, but all of time is eternally present in God. God is not "everlasting" in the sense of living through successive moments without termination, but is "eternal" in the sense of each and every possible moment of time already existing timelessly within God.

[19]Luther uses *semper* with *natum* to refer to all modes of time.

23. But I suppose that this has more to do with grammar or philosophy, by which the flesh or reason is moved, than with theological argument.

24. Although it is certain in divinity, since he is eternity itself, there is no place in grammar or philosophy where past, present and future is the same.[20]

25. Whence it is the same to say of the Son that He was begotten in the past time, is begotten in the present, and will be begotten in the future.[21]

26. Because the same Son is from eternity, was born, is born, and will be born in eternity, that is, eternal God from God.

27. Just as it is said rightly to us concerning God, "God remained, remains, and will remain" since nothing other is signified than that God always is, or is eternal.

28. His own past always is, his own future always has been, his own present always has been and will be, that is, eternal.

29. This is that name Jehovah, which the Jews call the sacred and ineffable tetragrammaton, even if they do not understand what they say.

30. Aristotle also perceives that eternity or infinity, in however many of its modes, is not known and is incomprehensible.

31. Moreover, he affirms that infinity or eternity, in however many of its modes, cannot exist, and he appears to speak rightly according to reason.[22]

---

[20]While Luther seems to think that philosophy cannot grasp timeless eternity, it is not clear why he should think this. There is nothing conceptually incoherent about the notion of timeless eternity.

[21]Luther realized that arguing about which tense of verbs to use when speaking of the divine was misguided. In this revealing passage from his 1509/1510 notes on Lombard's *Sentences* (WA 9, 61:21–31) he writes, "Respondetur, quod in deum non cadit praeteritum vel futurum, omnia praesenter ei sunt. Ergo quandocunque de deo differentiae temporum dicuntur singulariter, non excluditur aliqua de eis, quantum est de se, nisi quantum relucet in effectu. Ita praedicta authoritas non solum de praeterio intelligi debet, sed de omni [Tabelle] ratione scriptura tam sepe differentias temporum permiscet loquens de praeterito, quando vult intelligi de futuro et econtra."

[22]Aristotle distinguishes the actual and potential infinite. The actual infinite, as a collection to which no members can be added, cannot exist. There is no such set. A potential infinite, on the other hand, is one in which a whole can be infinitely divided, or one in which members can be infinitely added. Luther argues that since reason must judge the actual infinite not to exist, and since God has the property of actual infinity, then God cannot exist either.

32. But he does not see the consequence, or rather does not wish to see it, namely, that it follows from reason that God neither is, nor can He be.[23]

33. For that reason, he disputes so coldly about religion, and is completely Epicurus in the skin.

34. He concedes nevertheless that that infinite power both exists and can be known, even if again the eternity of the world confounds him.[24]

35. St. Paul says rightly in Romans I: "The knowledge of God is manifest to all people, that is, his eternal power and divinity."

36. But this knowledge is obscure and partial (although the knowledge of faith is also in its own way partial), as a line touches the whole sphere but at a point, and thus does not comprehend the whole thing.[25]

37. Whoever in searching wishes not to err, nor to be crushed by the glory of his majesty, let him by faith touch and lay hold of the Son of God manifest in the flesh.

38. For here the splendor of paternal glory touches the object, and it becomes the reflected ray illuminating every man coming into the world.

The *Promotionsdisputation* of Georg Major and Johannes Faber (December 12, 1544)

Luther wrote these forty-eight theses for a doctoral disputation that took place on December 12, 1544. The set of theses for Georg Major deals with trinitarian issues, while those assigned to Johannes Faber are concerned with justification and Christology. The first six theses for Major deal with truth and the necessity of defending it from enemies. Thesis 5 clearly states the trinitarian claim: "The truth is indisputable that God is one and threefold, and the sole creator of all things outside Him."[26] The unity here is so profound that Luther declares, "This unity of the Trinity (as we say it) is a greater oneness

---

[23]The reasoning is impeccable: if God is infinite "in whatever mode," and if the infinite "in whatever mode" does not exist, then God does not exist.

[24]While the potential infinite can exist, for Aristotle, Luther declares that infinity "in all its modes" does not exist, and this includes the potential infinite.

[25]This is a nice expression of the hiddenness of God. If one can only know God as a line intersects a circle at a point, then just as a point has no extension, so too is there "no extension" of human reason into divine affairs. Yet, of course, there is a "real intersection" of the human and divine in the incarnation.

[26]WA 39 II, 287:13–14.

than that of any other creature, or even of mathematical unity."[27] Moreover, the entire divinity is present in each person. Yet there is a real distinction of persons. Luther warns in thesis 11: "This distinction of persons is so strong that only the person of the Son assumed human being."[28]

Luther continues by pointing to some of the common trinitarian errors: thesis 12 defends against those who would claim an identity between the Father and Son; thesis 13 denies that mathematics can be used in thinking the Trinity; and, finally, thesis 14 attacks Scotus's formal distinction. The remainder of the theses attack Lombard's claim that the essence neither generates nor is generated. Over and against the author of *The Sentences*, Luther argues, with Joachim of Flora, that it is completely appropriate to say "the essence generates"—at least when "essence" is understood "relatively" and not "absolutely."

The theses assigned to Faber pertain to familiar themes on law, Christ, and justification. Sin cannot be satisfied through the law of righteousness of the law. Though the law is holy and must be kept, the human heart is "filth" (*stercus*) and cannot keep it. Fortunately, the dignity of the victim outweighs our filth and unworthiness. Through faith given by the Holy Spirit, we apprehend that our own true righteousness is the Son of God. Yet the righteousness of the law continues to show we are "filth," even though it is not imputed.

The Theses

GEORG MAJOR DEFENDED THESE THESES

1. God the Father wished to put to rest all disputations over articles of faith when He said concerning God His own Son: "Listen to this one!" [Matt. 17:5]

2. But all do not equally hear this teacher, and there are always some weak ones, whom Satan enlists.

3. This is therefore the perpetual work in the church through the ministry of the word by means of which the sick are cured and the adversary resisted.

4. Thus the Lord Christ Himself, though He did not need disputation, for the sake of the weak debated the Pharisees frequently.

---

[27]Ibid., 287:17–18.
[28]Ibid., 287:24.

5. The truth is indisputable that God is one and threefold, and the sole creator of all things outside Him.

6. And even if something here has been said improperly, nevertheless the matter itself should be defended through the Scriptures and against the devil.[29]

7. This unity of the Trinity (as we say it) is a greater oneness than that of any other creature, or even of mathematical unity.[30]

8. Nevertheless at the same time this unity is a trinity, or a divine threeness of distinct persons.

9. So that whichever of these persons you please is itself the whole divinity, even if no other one is there.[31]

10. And nevertheless it is true, no person alone is the divinity, as if the others were not.[32]

---

[29]Luther uses the term "improperly" (*improprie*) when referring to the new semantic situation arising in the use of theological language. In order to guarantee the right *meaning* of terms, they must apply to bearers in nonstandard ways; simply put, they are *used* in ways different from how they are employed in everyday (philosophical) discourse.

[30]White points out that Luther seems to suggest that numbers belong to the realm of created entities, and that is why mathematics is unfit to think the divine (White, *Luther as Nominalist*, 389). In a response in this disputation, we encounter the claim that the "unity of the Father and Son is greater than that of a [mathematical] point." See WA 39 II, 299:5–10.

[31]It is important to understand the difference between *solus* and *totus* used categorematically and syncategorematically. While categorematic subject and predicate terms signify and supposit completely, syncategorematic terms do not. The latter must be used with categorematic terms in order to fix the supposition (what the term stands for) of those terms. Thus, they ultimately affect the truth-value of the statements in which they appear. While the standard logical operator terms *conjunction*, *disjunction*, and *conditional* are syncategorematic terms, this term *syncategorematic* has a wider usage, including, for example, adverbs and prepositional phrases. In addition, terms used in quantification are included, for example, "all" or "every" (*omnis*), "except" (*praeter*), "all" or "whole" (*totus*), and "only" or "alone" (*solus*). In this thesis, Luther writes, "Ut quaelibet persona sit ipsa tota divinitas." *Tota* here is used syncategorematically because it distributes *divinitas* to each and every person of the Trinity. Allowing "P" to be person and "D" to mean the property of divinity, one asserts "$(x)(Px \rightarrow Dx)$." If the term were to be used categorematically, however, then a particular person would be itself the entire divinity. On the categorematic construal, "*tota divinitas*" would mean the *entire* divinity, person + person + person, and thus "quaelibet persona sit ipsa tota divinitas" would claim that that which is supposited for by "*persona*" is that which is supposited for by the "*tota divinitas*." But this is clearly false, for a single person is itself not the Trinity. However, syncategorematically construed, the statement is true because that which is supposited for by "*persona*" is that which is supposited for by "*divinitas*," and this is surely true of all three persons.

[32]In this thesis claiming "nullam personam esse solam, quasi alia non sit, divinitatem," it turns that the truth-value of the statement is not altered regardless of

11. This distinction of persons is so strong that only the person of the Son assumed human being.

12. It is, in fact, an error either that the Father is the Son, or that the Father was made a human being.

13. Therefore mathematics as a whole is in error, and must itself be crucified whenever it inquires about God Himself.[33]

14. Easily and coldly Scotus and the Scholastics console us with their formal and real distinctions.[34]

15. Indeed, the Master of the *Sentences* taught, not rightly enough, that the divine essence neither generates nor is generated.[35]

---

whether it is categorematically or syncategorematically construed. Taking "*sola*" to function syncategorematically, and allowing "P" to be person and "G" to be God, the expression could be symbolized as follows: "~∃x{[Px & (y)(Py → x =y)] & Gx}," that is, "it is false that one and only one person alone is divinity." It would also be false if it were understood categorematically because it would state that no person who is solitary is divine.

[33]While theology deals with the incomprehensibilities of the uncreated divine order, mathematics is oriented toward the created, temporal realm. We see the same ideas expressed in the Alberus disputation (WA 39 II, 254:7–8) and the disputation *Verbum caro factum est* (WA 39 II, 5:15ff.).

[34]Scotus argues for three fundamental distinctions: a *real distinction* between separable things that can exist on their own apart from human cognition, a *conceptual distinction* or *intentional distinction* that reason can draw among aspects of a thing, and finally a *formal distinction* objectively holding among things inseparable in reality. An example of a real distinction is that between two primary substances. An example of an *intentional distinction* is that between the Morning Star and the Evening Star, though both are "really" Venus. Finally, an example of a formal distinction is that between a primary and a secondary substance. The primary substance Socrates is himself a man. The secondary substance man is "said of" the primary substance Socrates. This secondary substance was thought by Scotus to be formally distinct from Socrates, though not some real thing in addition to or somehow outside of Socrates. Ockham criticized Scotus's notion of the formal distinction, and Luther followed Ockham in denying it. Ockham's arguments make use of the notion of the indiscernibility of identicals. Two identical things are indiscernible. But Socrates and humanity are discernible; thus by *modus tollens*, they cannot be identical. But if they are not identical, then there is a real distinction between them. A rejoinder to this is, of course, that the discernibility of Socrates and humanity is a discernibility with respect to form itself, and not to substances. If form A and form B are discernible, then by *modus tollens* on the indiscernibility of identical, form A and form B are not identical.

[35]Luther here speaks of Peter Lombard, whose influential book *The Sentences* functioned as the textbook of medieval theology. Lombard uses a reductio in book 1, d. 5, arguing that the divine essence cannot generate essence, for if it did, the same reality would generate itself, which is impossible. Rather, the Father alone (*solus*) generates the Son. Luther responds to this at WA 39 II, 291:19—292:2: "Hoc argumentum est, quod movit Magistrum, ut negaret hanc propositionem, et non vult eiusdem esse formae: Essentia divina generat aut se aut aliam, cum ita deberet statuere, essentiam neque aliam gignere neque seipsam, sed non debebat negare,

16. But he was rightly faulted by abbot Joachim, because he asserted a quaternity in the deity.[36]

17. Neither did the canon *Firmiter de Trinitate* accomplish anything, approving the Master and condemning the Abbot.

18. Since, in fact, on the basis of Augustine, the Master could not deny that substance is generated from substance and wisdom from wisdom.

19. In no way could he deny that essence is generated from essence, as well as whatever can likewise be said to be "born from God" [*de Deo vero*].[37]

20. Especially since everything is suspect which this abomination standing in the holy place has claimed.[38]

21. It seems that the Master feared that if one essence were born from another, then two or three essences would be spoken of.

22. But similarly he would have to worry that if one god were generated from another, there would then be two or three gods.

23. We concede that there is an essence in the creature, not talking "relatively" (as Augustine uses the term), but solely "absolutely."[39]

---

essentiam relative generare personam, praecipue cum videret ex Augustino, Deum de Deo, lumen de lumine generari, quare hoc cum concessit, non erat, quare in simili forma de essentia id negaret."

[36]The reference is to Joachim of Flora, who held that "the essence generates the essence" is orthodox and proper. Joachim of Flora is famous both for his attack on Lombard and for his theory of the three stages of history. He was condemned by the Fourth Lateran Council in 1215. Because he believed that history passes successively through the age of the Father, the Son, and the Holy Spirit, he took strong exception to Lombard's position, which he interpreted as making the divine essence ontologically distinct from the three persons. Joachim thought this led to a quaternity. In order to avoid quaternity and Sabellianism, Joachim understood the three persons as ontologically distinct while yet being so similar as to be "one substance *similitudinarie.*" He called this assimilative and collective unity an "*idemptitas.*" See Edmund Fortman, *The Triune God: A Historical Study of the Doctrine of the Trinity* (Philadelphia: Westminster, 1972), 197–99.

[37]This seems to be an allusion to the Nicene Creed's "true God from true God" (*Deum verum de Deo vero*).

[38]Luther is clearly not being charitable to Lombard here.

[39]The distinction between taking a term "absolutely" and taking it "relatively" descends from Augustine. When one speaks of the divine essence absolutely, one speaks of it as common to all three persons. Speaking of it relatively, one intends that which is relative to each individual person. Clearly, taking "essence" absolutely, one cannot say "the essence generates," because that which is common to all three persons cannot change.

24. But it seems "substance," "wisdom," "nature" and the like in divine matters are taken "relatively" by Augustine and Hilary.[40]

25. There was no reason why he should deny that "essence" is spoken relatively, and on that account let one word cause such a commotion.

26. Thus also, and not without reason, this determination greatly displeased Cardinal Cambrai, the most learned among the Scholastics.

MASTER JOHANNES FABERIUS FROM MONECAN DEFENDED THESE THESES

27. Therefore, the person of the Son alone, the Word coeternal to the Father and the Holy Spirit, was made flesh.[41]

28. He was to redeem the lost human race from a difficulty so grave, that such an excellent victim was necessary for it.

---

[40]If one were to take "wisdom" absolutely, then it refers to the numerical unity of the divine essence having wisdom. Taken relatively, however, "wisdom" can supposit for each and every person, because each and every divine person has the property of wisdom. Luther admits, however, that locutions such as "light from light" push the boundaries of natural (philosophical) language, because from the "earthly" perspective, any light coming from light cannot be equal to the light from which it emerges. In theology, however, "light from light" is properly employed because the Son has no less light than the Father—though the locution's propriety depends in part on the metaphorical extension of language.

In a fascinating reply at WA 39 II, 296:13—297:3, Luther declares: "Similitudo etiam in natura non currit quatuor pedibus. Dantur autem ad declarandas res. Filius est lumen de lumine, deradiatio et character substantie. In praedicimento substantiae non docetur, radios claritatis esse de substantia solis, et tamen Spiritus sanctus ita loquitur. In divinis dicitur character et quidem substantiae, id est, ut etiam ingrediatur in substantiam Patris, ut, quod Pater est, sit et Filius. Talis modus loquendi in creaturis non est, nt non dicitur: Sol est splendor, sicut dicitur: Filius Dei est splendor gloriae, character vel imago, quae habet in se substantiam Patris. Non exprimit natura penitus hanc similitudinem. Nulla enim similitudo tollit secum rerum assimilata. Filius est imago huius invisibilis Dei, Das ist schon extra creaturas hinwegk. Si Filius est imago, est etiam Deus, et extra creaturas, est quaedam imago, quae ipsa est Deus, et tamen est imago. Est similis Deo, et tamen ipse Deus. Das heist esse imaginem extra creaturas, et tamen esse Deum." Apparently "image," a term signifying something less than that of which it is an image, gets a "new signification" in theology, because now it is used properly to pick out a supposition that is not ontologically less than that of which it is an image.

[41]Here the word is *solius*, an adverb meaning "solely," that is, "in a sole manner." The person of the Son is the one and only one Word coeternal to the Father and the Spirit, and this Word was made flesh. Allowing "W" to be Word, "F" to be the Father, "S" to be the Son, "H" to be the Holy Spirit, "M" to mean is made flesh, and "Cxy" to mean "x is coeternal to y," we have "$\exists x(\{[(Px \ \& \ Sx) \ \& \ Wx] \ \& \ \exists y \exists z(Fy \ \& \ \sim Wy) \ \& \ (Hz \ \& \ \sim Wz)\} \ \& \ \{[(\sim x = y \ \& \ \sim x = z \ \& \ \sim y = z) \ \& \ (Cxy \ \& \ Cxz)] \ \& \ Mx\})$."

29. Wherefore it was impossible through the law or the righteousness of the law for sin to be satisfied.

30. In fact, through the law sin was increased and the damnation of humankind all the way to the very depths of hell.

31. Nevertheless, the law is just, holy and good, and from a good, just and holy God.

32. He sets forth the righteousness of the law, both the ceremonial and even now the civil, and seriously commands it to be kept.

33. [Phil. 3:8] Even though He knows that the human heart itself is filth [*stercus*] and refuse, as the Apostle says.

34. [1 Cor. 1:29] Certainly no flesh may boast in his sight concerning the righteousness and wisdom of the law, that is, since it is damned within itself just as much as in its own filth.

35. More than three or four times filthier than that is the righteousness of human traditions, which is the very filth of the devil.

36. The righteousness of the law must therefore be known relatively, that is, as obedience to the law as well as to the magistrate.

37. For the sake of this temporal life, which is wholly death and misery, the law must be kept in order that we might have peace.

38. But, in the presence of God, let us recognize that our legal righteousness is filth, shame and confusion.

39. This is why our righteousness and glory before God is that victim alone, the Son of God, apprehended by pure faith.

40. After this faith, when one has received the Holy Spirit, the obedience of the law does not placate by its own dignity.

41. For much remains in it of filth and defeat, that is, the unworthiness of the old man.

42. But the dignity of the victim outweighs infinitely the unworthiness of our filthiness [*stercorariae*].

43. Moreover, even if by the righteousness of the law, and in view of the pride and vanity, one can judge himself as filth, even now this is not imputed.

44. For the merciful and just God raises up the poor man from the filth, so that he might place him among the leaders of his own people.

45. But one is not permitted to become haughty and stiff-necked and fierce with the pride of the righteousness or wisdom of the law or of works.

46. It regards itself alone to be holy, and therefore it alone is foolish, and is damned eternally.

47. And the strength of the victim is given into the hands of sinners, on account of whom he came into the world, in order that he might save them.

The *Promotionsdisputation* of Petrus Hegemon (July 3, 1545)

Peter Hegemon's examination gave Luther opportunity to write theses for his final disputation. The themes Luther treats are by now familiar. The first ten theses of the disputation deal with issues of absolute and relative predication. Absolutely considered, "wisdom" refers to a property of the divine essence; relatively considered, "wisdom" refers uniquely to the second person of the Trinity. "Wisdom comes from wisdom" is true when "wisdom" is construed relatively; it is false when understood absolutely.

The question of the distinction between theology and philosophy arises next, with Luther claiming that the term *relatio* differs in philosophical and theological contexts: "A relation pertaining to the divine ought to be understood in a far different way from any which is in the creature or in philosophy"[42] Luther gives Hegemon some very interesting theses to defend in this disputation. For instance, this poor student must defend the claim that "a relation does not here demonstrate a distinction of things, but three distinct things prove to be a relation,"[43] while at the same time defending the identity of the relation and the hypostasis: "In divine matters a relation is a thing, that is, a hypostasis and subsistence, truly, the same as divinity itself; there are three persons, three hypostases and three subsistences."[44]

The next section deals with issues of faith and reason, concluding that from the standpoint of reason, the highest things are nothing, but from the standpoint of faith all things are spoken and known rightly.[45] He then takes up the question of the incarnation, claiming that next to the Trinity, "it is the highest, for here the finite and the infinite was placed in proportion—which is impossible."[46] Because of sin, human beings cannot know the Creator, but they have some access to the Creator through the incarnation of Christ. After developing the

---

[42]WA 39 II, 339:26–27.
[43]Ibid., 339:6–7.
[44]Ibid., 340:3–5.
[45]Ibid., 340:12–13.
[46]Ibid., 340:14–15.

theme of human sin, Luther again takes up the issue of generation of the divine essence, claiming now that "personally" God can be said to generate God, but "essentially" God cannot be said to generate God.[47] The remainder of the disputation addresses issues of law, sin, justification, divine wrath and mercy, and misplaced power in the pope.

The Theses

1. With respect to divinity, the Word is called the wisdom of the Father, or as St. Paul says, the wisdom and the power of God (1 Cor. 1:24).

2. Not that the Father in His person is wise or wisdom only through the Word, and not also through Himself.[48]

3. In fact, whichever person you please is the wisdom, the power, and the goodness of God, just as he is the essence, the substance, and anything else that can be said of God.[49]

4. Faith does not allow that the person of the Father, through himself, is without wisdom, or that the person of the Son is without power or virtue [*potentia et virtute*], or that the Holy Spirit is without either.[50]

5. This would be to say, that the persons in themselves are without substance, essence, eternity, immensity, majesty; that is, without divinity, and, in short, are nothing.

6. Therefore, this rule is handed down from St. Augustine: Whatever is said absolutely, and not relatively, about the divine persons, ought to be said and known commonly.[51]

7. Even if sometimes common names, which are called attributes, were spoken about them to discern and manifest the persons.

8. So because in the Son, the wisdom and power of God were shown through the flesh, the wisdom and power of God are attributed to Him.

---

[47]Ibid., 370:8–14.

[48]Luther is denying that God would be wisdom because of the second person of the Trinity, and not because of a common essence of divinity. To say that God is wise because one of his persons (but not all) is wise is to tend toward modalism.

[49]Taken *relatively*, this is surely so. Each person is the wisdom, the power, and the goodness of God, because while these terms signify the divine essence, they can supposit for each person having that divine essence.

[50]By virtue of the divine essence being in each and every person, anything predicable of the Godhead is predicable of each person. Taken absolutely, wisdom does not generate; however, taken relatively, it surely is so.

[51]Luther had been thinking about this distinction for a very long time, as is witnessed in his work in 1509–1510 (WA 9, 20:22ff.).

9. So the virtue or power [*virtus seu potentia*] of the person of the Father is attributed from creation, since those things are common to all three, that is, to the one creator God.[52]

10. Thus goodness, as well as vivification, are attributed to the Holy Spirit, although the Father and the Son are not excluded from this common work of the Trinity.

11. Certainly, nevertheless, a relation pertaining to the divine ought to be understood in a far different way from those which pertain to creatures or in philosophy.[53]

12. A relation in things does not affect the thing; as they say, the relation is a minimal entity and does not subsist through itself; moreover, it is nothing according to the Moderns.[54]

13. In divine matters a relation is a thing, that is, a hypostasis and subsistence, truly, the same as divinity itself; there are three persons, three hypostases and three subsistences.[55]

14. A relation here does not demonstrate a distinction of things, but three distinct things prove to be a relation.[56]

---

[52]Since the properties of virtue and power are predicable of God Himself, these properties are true of the Father as well.

[53]A relation in the divine is a *relativum* that is identified with a person. This is a notion descending from Augustine, who holds that the persons cannot be *substances* (because then we would have tritheism) or *accidents* (because then we would have modalism).

[54]In Ockhamist-inspired thought, only particular objects exist, and relations must be defined externally among them. However, when considering the Trinity, a relation is identifiable with a hypostasis or subsistence. A relation within theology is not a "minimal entity" at all but individuates the very persons of God.

[55]Luther does claim that the "nature and relation makes the person" in one of his responses. He says at WA 39 II, 384a:9–20: "Persona constituitur ex relatione et essentia Patris, sic oportet nos loqui, quamvis non proprie sic loqui possumus, tamen ad res explicandas ita dicendum est: Natura et relatio faciunt personam, relatio est res, essentia est res, et sunt duae res constituentes unam personam. Das ist impropriissime geredt, aber wie soll man im thun, natura humana non potest aliter, es heist crede." The relation is a thing, the essence is another thing, and the two things constitute one person.

[56]This appears to give precedence to the processional account, for nonrelational, monadic properties distinguish the persons. Accordingly, relation R holds between f and s by virtue of the properties A and B respectively exhibited by f and s. Simply put: "$(Af \ \& \ Bs) \rightarrow Rab$." This is consistent with a very minimal view of relations. According to *reductive realism*, the relations are simply the nonrelational properties that each object supposedly related has. On this view, there is nothing more to the relation Rfs than Af and Bs. This view is *reductive* in that it states that the relation is reductively identical to its foundations.

15. This does not follow: 'The Father is wise in Himself, therefore the wisdom of the Father in Himself—since it is relative to Him—is a distinct thing from Him."[57]

16. Nevertheless, it is rightly said that the Son is relative to the Father; therefore He is another hypothesis from the Father, so too is this rightly said of the Holy Spirit.

17. In sum, through reason and philosophy nothing can be said or believed about these matters of the divine majesty, but through faith they can properly be said and believed.[58]

18. After the article of the Trinity, that concerning the incarnation of the Son of God is the highest, where the concrete relation (*proportio*) of the finite and the infinite (which was impossible) was accomplished.[59]

19. This person, simultaneously finite and infinite, was made a servant of sinners and the last and weakest of all things; this is not believable [*incredibile*], but is most pleasing to believers (*credentibus*).

20. It is as if you should say, "That man, who is alone, and who alone made all things from nothing, he alone was made nothing and put underneath all things."[60]

21. Nevertheless, the article concerning the creation of things from nothing is more difficult to believe than the article concerning the resurrection.

22. And Christ through His own incarnation leads us into the knowledge of the creator (Eph. 3:10; I Pet. 2:12), by which knowledge the angels are blessed.

23. This could not have been done except that He, who in His own person is the image of God, took sin (which is the reign and victory of death) from us.

---

[57]WA 39 II, 340:8–10: "Non sequitur: Pater est sapiens in se ipso, ergo sapientia Patris in se ipso, cum sit relativa ad eum, est distincta res ab eo." This claims one cannot move from "f = w" to "(Wf ≠ f)."

[58]Luther often refers to the "incomprehensible majesty" of the things of faith. See WA 39 II, 4:32–33: "Non quidem vitio formae syllogisticae, sed virtute et maiestate materiae, quae in angustias rationis seu syllogismorum includi non potest."

[59]Luther believes that it is more incomprehensible to think the "three-in-oneness" of the Trinity than to think the paradox that some being is both infinite and finite at the same time.

[60]Luther employs the traditional distinction between *abstract* and *concrete* in using "man," "divine," and so forth. Abstractly considered, "this man created the world" is false because no human can do that, but "man" supposits for the second person of the Trinity in christological predication, and hence it picks out that which can, indeed, create the world.

24. Sin, in fact, had blinded human nature, so that human beings no longer recognized the creator, even if the work of His special governance was sniffed out from afar.

25. In fact, human beings ignored sin itself, and reckoned their own blindness to be the highest wisdom.

26. It is truly a terrible thing that the anger of God is against the entire human race, corrupted, lost, and damned by the one sin of one human being.

27. But the greatness of His mercy far overcomes the magnitude of His anger, and by this great person the Son was made a victim for the lost human race.

28. Reason that ignores God seems justly to murmur against God, e.g, iniquity, and the most severe tyranny.

29. Many sought comfort here by reconciling the righteousness of God with the mercy of God, but apart from faith in the incarnate God reason is nothing, and there is no comfort.

30. They miss the mark equally who, with an insult to the creator, suppose that fault and sin inhere in nature because it is made from nothing, since such is not in the angels, the sun, stars, and the entire heavens.

31. Those who thought that the soul comes from transmission [ex traduce], do not seem inwardly to have known that this notion is foreign to Scripture.

32. Moreover, they will more readily defend the propagation of original sin, than they who think differently since, according to the author Augustine, original sin is also impiety.

33. Augustine confesses that he is ignorant about whether that opinion is truer and more certain and, nor was he, up to that time, the one who determined the question.

34. Others follow Jerome from Psalm 33 [32], "he formed their hearts individually," but nothing here suffices to settle the matter.

35. Truly, we have most righteous cause for the extermination or execration of the Pope and his synagogue.

36. For he has neither the right nor the faculty of determining anything either in the doctrine of the faith or in the church of God.

37. He does not have the right, because he has been called neither by God nor by men, but by his own temerity intrudes himself as an idol and an abomination.

38. He does not have the faculty, for that unlearned beast and deaf belly is to holy Scripture as an ass is to the lyre.

39. Nor should that Pythagorianism be brought into the church: for the man himself, in whose place alone the pope ought to rule, said that to the contrary, the one who speaks the words of God, just as Peter says, he ought to be heard.

40. Therefore, the pope is nothing, and all the things he says and does are nothing by his right, as the law and nature testify together with the word.

41. It is better in this matter that reason should resolve what the poet says: "The offspring follows the Father."

42. It is well known that the character of the offspring is shaped not by some general rule, but instead reflects the customs and qualities of the parents.

43. So that it comes to nothing what is said, "The intellectual soul is infused by being created, and is created by being infused."

44. Whoever approved this, or whoever will prohibit it, can every other soul be spoken of similarly?

45. And they will fashion an even more difficult question: How would God not be iniquitous, who joins the pure soul to the flesh and defiles from the outside?

46. Wherefore any Christian may ignore this matter without danger, as does St. Augustine and the whole church.

47. Nevertheless, one should avoid that overconfidence which verges on insult to the Creator.

48. Since it be certain that God also created the angels, who have succeeded to eternal life without suffering corruption, from nothing.

49. What difficulty remains for God who once brought forth the intellectual soul from nothing, now to do so from corrupt seed?

50. Just as he brings forth a head of grain vitiated by blight from a single vitiated seed, so also many other vices come forth from vices.[61]

---

[61]This is difficult to render. Luther ends the disputation with these words (WA 39 II, 398:9–22): "Deus Pater exsistit a se ipso ab aeterno, Filius exsistit a se ipso ab aeterno, Spiritus sanctus exsistit a se ipso ab aeterno, non habent principium neque finem, ut Micheae 5 dicitur: Egressus eius ab initio, ante dies mundi. Sic progressus est Spiritus sanctus ab aeternitate, et illa processio est generatio aeterna. Loquitur autem quoad nos seu quoad extra. Sed quod ad intra, alia res est. Intra divinitatem Filius habet sapientiam aeternam Patris." The last phrase is telling.

INDEX